LLOYD-JONES
MESSENGER OF GRACE

Books by Iain H. Murray

The Forgotten Spurgeon

The Puritan Hope: Revival and the Interpretation of Prophecy

The Life of Arthur W. Pink

D. Martyn Lloyd-Jones: The First Forty Years

D. Martyn Lloyd-Jones: The Fight of Faith

    (The Two Volume Authorised Biography)

Jonathan Edwards: A New Biography

The Life of John Murray

Australian Christian Life

Revival and Revivalism:

    The Making and Marring of American Evangelicalism 1750–1858

Spurgeon v. Hyper-Calvinsim: The Battle for Gospel Preaching

Pentecost – Today? The Biblical Basis for Understanding Revival

Evangelicalism Divided:

    A Record of Crucial Change in the Years 1950 to 2000

Wesley and Men Who Followed

The Old Evangelicalism: Old Truths for a New Awakening

A Scottish Christian Heritage

LLOYD-JONES

MESSENGER OF GRACE

. . . affectionate in look,
And tender in address, as well becomes
A messenger of grace to guilty men.

WILLIAM COWPER: *THE TASK*

IAIN H. MURRAY

THE BANNER OF TRUTH TRUST

THE BANNER OF TRUTH TRUST
3 Murrayfield Road, Edinburgh EH12 6EL, UK
P.O. Box 621, Carlisle, PA 17013, USA

*

© Iain H. Murray 2008

ISBN–13: 978 0 85151 975 3

*

Typeset in 11/15 pt Baskerville MT at
The Banner of Truth Trust, Edinburgh
Printed in the USA by
Versa Press, Inc.,
East Peoria, IL

To
John Richard and Jane de Witt
With thankfulness for so much of our lives
shared through forty years.

CONTENTS

PART 2

ILLUSTRATIONS

End-Papers: The congregation at Westminster Chapel in the late 1950s, drawn from a newspaper photograph

Frontispiece: Lloyd-Jones, a portrait photograph, by Desmond Groves, late 1970s

PREFACE

I write this Preface on the 50th anniversary of the first Banner of Truth Trust books being sold at Westminster Chapel, London, in January 1958. But an anniversary is no part of the reason for this book. My chief reason has been to restate some of the main lessons of the ministry of Dr Martyn Lloyd-Jones, beginning with the preaching of the word of God. Preaching is a gift from heaven. Revelation is necessary to understand the vital importance of preaching, and why its absence is a disaster worse than the lack of bread and water. The advance of the church is ever preceded by a recovery of preaching, and in that recovery the memory of those who have spoken 'with the Holy Spirit sent down from heaven' (*1 Pet.* 1:12) has often played an important part. Eminent examples give light to later centuries.

Much has been said and written on Lloyd-Jones in more recent years. That some misconceptions would arise was inevitable. Not least among them is the idea that when you have said he was a 'preacher' there is little else to say. But that one word description is insufficient. He said of Paul: 'He was an evangelist and preacher . . . theologian and teacher, and at the same time a tender-hearted and sympathetic pastor.' It was such an all-round ministry that he sought to follow. While these pages are not biography, I hope they will show that what he said at the end of his life was true, 'I did not live for preaching.' To be a Christian was the greatest thing he knew.

Some have spoken inadvisably of Dr Lloyd-Jones as though he was an all-sufficient model for others to follow. God does not build his kingdom by repetitions. It is true that the men whose ministry shaped their times bear real similarities, and in their common features they may all be safely followed. Yet there is also an individuality that rules out imitation. None was a mere echo of another. They were all different, and all, in measure, imperfect too. To arrive at the fullness of the stature of Christ is not for this world. The command of Christ, 'Call no man Teacher', relates even to the most eminent of his servants. In the belief that it is helpful not to consider just one leader, I have compared Lloyd-Jones to Spurgeon in one chapter. While both men held the same essential beliefs, there were real differences. Both are only among the many from whom we are to learn.

Only part of one chapter in this book has previously appeared in book form.[1] Much of the other material concentrates on aspects of his ministry that appear of particular importance to me. This has to include the on-going criticism of the difference occasioned by the Evangelical Alliance National Assembly of 1966. For speaking and acting as he did at that time, Lloyd-Jones has been repeatedly accused of 'dividing' evangelicals. One of the latest writers on that theme describes him as holding a position of 'obdurate exclusivity', and of 'charting a course into the separatist wilderness of an extreme and exclusive Reformed isolationism.'[2] I seek to show how such a view confuses the real issue. Let the reader listen to the recording of the Evangelical Alliance meeting in 1957, when Lloyd-Jones spoke harmoniously alongside an Anglican, and ask why there was no division then.[3] The answer is that in the ten years that followed 1957 a new policy was adopted and promoted by

---

[1] Much of chapter 3 first appeared as an Introduction in *D. M. Lloyd-Jones, Old Testament Evangelistic Sermons* (Edinburgh: Banner of Truth, 1995).

[2] Rob Warner, *Reinventing English Evangelicalism 1966-2001* (Milton Keynes; Paternoster, 2007), p. 215.

[3] This CD, number 5714, can be obtained from the Martyn Lloyd-Jones Recordings Trust; see p. 234 for contact details.

Anglican evangelicals that brought on division. Just how relevant this remains at the present time can be seen in such movements as 'Evangelicals and Catholics Together' and the threatening disruption of the Church of England over the homosexual issue.

Of first importance to Lloyd-Jones were not church issues but the recovery of true spiritual power amid the decline of Christianity in Britain. The current weakness was directly connected, he believed, to the lack of a stronger assurance of salvation among Christians. That need lay at the heart of his concern for the churches. On the way such assurance is received he disagreed in one respect with the Puritan school to which he belonged, and differed still more with the burgeoning charismatic movement. He feared adherents to the former gave too little place to the experimental, while the latter too readily confused experience of the Holy Spirit with emotionalism. Further serious thought on this subject is surely a contemporary need. The reader will see that I do not agree with my friend in all he says on this subject; but I do repudiate the idea, falsely attributed to him, of disengagement from present endeavour in order to wait for a future revival. It is true he believed the decline in the churches was so serious that nothing but a fresh outpouring of the Holy Spirit would arrest it; but he also believed that Christians have warrant to rejoice in Christ every day they live, for God is never thwarted in his great redemptive purposes. He saw no conflict between expectancy and a believing thankfulness for present victory. Whatever the times, he exemplified the Pauline call 'Be always abounding in the work of the Lord'.

It remains for me to express my gratitude to Lady Catherwood and Mrs Ann Beatt, the daughters of Dr and Mrs Lloyd-Jones, for their kind permission to use material in these pages and for permission to use the evangelistic sermon that is attached to this book. It is one of the most memorable of such sermons that I ever heard and I am thankful it can now be heard by so many more for heard and I am thankful it can now be heard by so many more for the first time since it was preached. Many other such sermons can now be obtained through the ministry of the Martyn Lloyd-Jones Recordings Trust for whose work we are all thankful. As this Preface was being written, a letter from Australia reported the importance of the circulation of the Lloyd-Jones sermons by cassettes and CDs in that nation.

Finally, I would like to thank my colleagues in the Banner of Truth Trust for all their help. As ever, I am indebted to my wife for her close and necessary attention to the text at proof stage.

Iain H. Murray
Colinton,
Edinburgh,
28 January 2008

PART 1

1

THE LLOYD-JONES LEGACIES

C. H. Spurgeon, who died in 1892, said 'I shall live and speak long after I am dead.'[1] While Martyn Lloyd-Jones did not use the words, he also bequeathed much to future generations. The legacies he left are real, and the way they differ from bequests of monetary value only make them the more important. Legacies of the latter kind only benefit those specifically named in a will; the spiritual legacies of the kingdom of God are inherited by a great many and in a different manner. The Lloyd-Jones legacies are today in the hands of millions whom he never knew, and they have spread spiritual wealth across the earth.

Before I turn to the legacies, the main facts of his life need to be summarized. David Martyn Lloyd-Jones, or ML-J, as I shall frequently call him, was born in Cardiff, South Wales, on December 20, 1899 – seven years after the death of Spurgeon, and two days before that of D. L. Moody. He lived with his parents and two brothers in Wales until financial hardship drove them to London in 1914. There, at the beginning of World War I, he completed his education, and with such ability that by the age of twenty-

---

[1] 'I beseech you', he also said to students, 'to live not only for this age but for the next also.'

one he had graduated in medicine at St Bartholomew's Hospital, which was probably the foremost teaching hospital in the world at that date. By that age he had already caught the attention of Sir Thomas Horder, the King's physician, who practised in London's famous Harley Street. When Lloyd-Jones became Horder's assistant in 1921 the way was open for a spectacular career in medicine. Sir James Paterson Ross, President of the Royal College of Surgeons, would later say that the young Welshman was 'one of the finest clinicians I ever encountered'. Then in 1926, to the astonishment of his friends, the successful physician announced that he was leaving medicine to become the preacher in Sandfields Mission Hall at Aberavon, Port Talbot, South Wales. ML-J remained there until 1938, when he agreed to assist Dr Campbell Morgan for a short period at Westminster Chapel, London. In fact he was to stay for thirty years, until 1968. After that date he continued to preach in many parts of the country until his eightieth year. He died on March 1, 1981.

Legacy 1

An Example of What a Christian Minister Ought to Be

In the twentieth century there was a great change in the way the Christian ministry was regarded. In the year 1900, and earlier, the Christian minister in Britain was commonly regarded with respect; his word carried weight, and his church was well attended Sunday by Sunday. But the century that followed saw the status and influence of the ministry in striking decline. From a position of eminence the office became one of minor consequence and significance. Long before the end of the twentieth century the preacher was a popular subject for amusement in the entertainment media.

Why did this alteration in the way the Christian ministry was viewed occur? It will not do to blame the change on social conditions, or on a failing public interest in Christianity itself. The explanation is rather within the church herself, for it was there that the biblical view of the ministry was first lost. Instead of a divine calling, it became another career: men did three years at university, perhaps three at a theological college, and then, in many instances, they went into churches, not to live and teach the Word of God, but to talk as men who had lost faith in Scripture. So the history of the Old Testament was repeated. It was to a worldly priesthood in the time of Samuel that God said, 'Them that honour me I will honour, and they that despise me shall be lightly esteemed' (*1 Sam.* 2:30). Again, in Malachi, God said to those who should have been his messengers, 'The priests' lips should keep knowledge, and they should seek the law at his mouth: for he is the messenger of the LORD of hosts. But ye are departed out of the way; ye have caused many to stumble at the law . . . Therefore have I also made you contemptible and base before all the people, according as ye have not kept my ways' (*Mal.* 2:7-9). Where the Word of God is despised judgments are sure to follow.

But when the true idea of the minister is lost, God has often restored it by calling individuals to the office in unlikely ways. Amos was called from being a farmer; John Knox from his post as a church lawyer; and Lloyd-Jones from the hospital and the consulting room. He had none of the credentials of a theological college training. His entrance into the ministry could scarcely have been more unlike what had become the accepted routine. As a training school for preachers of the Bible, St Bartholomew's Hospital was about the last place imaginable. It was more a temple to scientific rationalism than to creation. Nothing he learned there could explain Lloyd-Jones's message; or why, in 1927, he turned his back on Harley Street – the Mecca of medicine – for a stipend of £225 a year, and a small house in a working-class district of South Wales. Plainly he had not gone to a mission hall for a more lucrative salary. There was no reason, unless it was that God does call men to preach.

To answer this call of God was not easy for ML-J. He loved medicine; he also loved his fiancée, Bethan Phillips, and in 1925 she doubted whether he should change direction in the manner he was considering. For a year-and-a-half he struggled with the decision. It became a burden that cost him both loss of sleep and weight. Yet his response to God's call was not with a spirit of self-sacrifice, but rather with the conviction that he was being given an immense privilege and responsibility. In later years, when his readiness to give up so much was praised, he rejected the suggestion with the words, 'I gave up nothing, I received everything. I count it the highest honour God can confer on any man to call him to be a herald of the gospel.'

If Lloyd-Jones differed in the manner of his calling to the gospel ministry, the contrast was no less between the current religious scene and his preaching. He spoke with certainty and authority. When he told his hearers that the soul was more important than the body, they knew he believed it. And those who came to know him in Aberavon were convicted by his life as well as his message. What he said was in harmony with what he was. There was nothing of self-importance about him. God had humbled him and shown him what an empty thing it is to live for the approval of men. The desire for fame and reputation that had once possessed him was mortified.

The result of this was that ML-J gave a new meaning to the Christian ministry. He never saw himself as a model for anyone, but his high view of the gospel ministry introduced that vision to many others. As one example of this I mention the life of Argos Zodhiates. After ministering effectively in Katerini, Zodhiates was driven by persecution to leave his native Greece for North America. En route through London, Zodhiates and his wife were in Westminster Chapel on Sunday morning, October 21, 1957, when ML-J 'happened' to be preaching on Ephesians 4:11, 'And he gave some apostles, some prophets; some evangelists; and some pastors and teachers.' Such was his treatment of the pastoral office that the visitors determined at once to return to Katerini, convinced that God had spoken to them. They were still in Greece when visited by the preacher four years later.[1]

When the executive committee of the Christian Medical Fellowship wrote to thank ML-J for what his ministry had meant to them, on his retirement from Westminster Chapel in 1968, they said: 'We would like first to refer to your personal example, which has emphasised in so unique a manner the importance and dignity of the Christian ministry.'

LEGACY 2

THE TRUTH THAT CHRISTIANITY IS GOD-CENTRED RELIGION

God-centred Christianity does not mark churches in decline and it was rare in twentieth-century Britain. In the Welsh chapel life of ML-J's own background, the pulpit ethos was mainly sentimental, moralistic, and anecdotal. It was worse in the many churches where liberal theology held sway; the message was akin to saying that a God of love exists for man's comfort and happiness. Even in evangelical circles the message of the gospel was too often reduced to the forgiveness to be gained by responding to Jesus Christ.

---

[1] For his two sermons on these verses see D. M. Lloyd-Jones, *Christian Unity: Ephesians 4:1–16* (Edinburgh: Banner of Truth, 1980), pp. 181-208.

For Lloyd-Jones the whole approach was different. Preaching needs to start from where the Bible starts: 'In the beginning God' – God the Almighty, the Eternal, the Ruler and Judge of all.

> The Bible is the record of the activity of God. God is the actor. God is the centre. Everything is of God and comes from God, and turns to God. It is God who speaks. It is God who acts. It is God who intervenes. It is God who originates, who plans every-thing everywhere.[1]

Without the Bible's revelation of the majesty and holiness of God, man has no conception of the glory from which he has fallen, or of his present predicament. His need is for a reconciliation that will change both his status and nature as a sinner. It is a need that cannot be met without divine action. When Christianity ceases to be God-centred, a superficial understanding of sin will always follow; sin is treated as mere unhappiness or dissatisfaction instead of rebellion against God. Consequently the wrath of God passes out of sight, and with it, the necessity of the substitutionary death of Christ.[2] Men reject the penal sufferings of Christ 'because they do not see the problem'.

In the same way, low views of God and light views of sin bring superficial ideas of what is involved in regeneration, when sinners are brought from death to life and created anew in the image of God. God alone can achieve such a change: 'With men it is impos-sible, but not with God' (*Mark* 10:27). All is 'to the praise of the glory of his grace' (*Eph.* 1:6). 'For of him, and through him, and to him, are all things: to whom be glory for ever. Amen' (*Rom.* 11:36).

---

[1] *Westminster Record*, September 1943, p. 68. Reprinted in D. M. Lloyd-Jones, *The Christian in an Age of Terror*, Michael Eaton, ed. (Chichester: New Wine Press, 2007), p. 65.

[2] Precisely such low views of the demerit of sin led the false prophets in the Old Testament to say, 'Peace, peace, when there is no peace' (*Jer.* 6:14; 8:11).

Fundamental to Lloyd-Jones's thinking was the conviction that where Christianity is presented in man-centred terms its distinctive nature is lost:

> If I were asked to state the main difference between religion and Christianity, I would say that religion always puts its emphasis on what man does in his attempt to worship and please God . . . Christianity on the other hand is primarily a listening to God. God is speaking! Religion is man searching for God; Christianity is God seeking man, manifesting Himself to him.[1]

The outbreak of World War II so soon after Lloyd-Jones's settlement in London was the backdrop to a message startlingly different. He saw the world was facing the War 'solely and entirely in terms of man; God is not mentioned at all'. In that context he preached that God controls history, and that war is his judgment upon sin. God is not indifferent or impotent:

> Had we a right to peace? Do we deserve peace? Were we justified in asking God to preserve peace and grant peace? What if war has come because we were not fit for peace; because we by our disobedience and godlessness and sinfulness had so utterly abused the blessings of peace?[2]

This theme ran through the sermons, preached in the autumn of 1939, which made his first book, *Why Does God Allow War?* The subject of his second book – addresses given in March 1941 – was man in relation to God, taken from Romans chapter 1. It was prophetic preaching:

> God has decided and ordered and arranged that a life of forgetfulness of Him, and of antagonism to Him, shall not

[1] D. M. Lloyd-Jones, *The Puritans: Their Origins and Successors* (Edinburgh: Banner of Truth, 1987), p. 380.
[2] D. M. Lloyd-Jones, *Why Does God Allow War? A General Justification of the Ways of God* (London: Hodder and Stoughton, 1939), p. 92.

be successful and happy. Cursing falls on such a life. Mankind has refused to recognise this – indeed, has ridiculed it. It has been confident it could succeed without God. But what of the results? Constant failure. God cannot be thwarted. The facts of life, the story of history, proclaim the wrath of God against all ungodliness and unrighteousness. That is our first problem. We have sinned against God. We are in a wrong relationship to Him. His wrath is upon us. We have made it impossible for Him to bless us. His holy nature demands that He must punish us and our transgressions.[1]

It is no wonder that ML-J was out of step with contemporary spokesmen for Christianity. The point was made succinctly on one occasion by a man who had gone to hear the three men judged to be the leading preachers in London in the 1950s: Donald Soper, Leslie Weatherhead, and Lloyd-Jones. His verdict was: 'Soper preaches love; Weatherhead preaches Jesus; the minister of Westminster Chapel preaches God.'[2]

Where did Lloyd-Jones learn this emphasis? His answer would be that he did not learn it, and that man cannot learn it of himself. He was taught it. As he came to adulthood, and then set out in medicine, things happened to him over which he had no control. The early death of one of his two brothers, and then of his father in 1922, raised disturbing questions. God was interrupting his smooth and successful career. Problems appeared that he could not resolve, despite his nominal Christianity and his regular churchgoing: a conviction of the pride and vanity of his heart took away any inward peace, and new questions forced themselves

---

[1] D. M. Lloyd-Jones, *The Plight of Man and the Power of God* (London: Hodder and Stoughton, 1942), pp. 88-9.

[2] It has to be said that neither the 'love', nor the 'Jesus', so preached by these liberals were scriptural.

on him.[1] In this condition he now began to notice features in the lives of his seniors whom he had so much admired. These were brilliant men, with the highest reputations in the medical world, distinguished by their abilities to diagnose and treat all manner of physical conditions. But there was something for which they had no remedy: they could not deal with the greed, selfishness, lust, and pride, which marred their lives as those of other men.

Lloyd-Jones's background was that of the Welsh Calvinistic Methodists. In the Bible classes of his youth he had often debated such things as Calvinism, but only now, for the first time, did he begin to realise what it meant. It means that because all that is of man is marked ultimately by failure; all is hopeless unless God has planned and purposed what we cannot do for ourselves. God is supreme, and all hope lies in his love set on the unworthy, and his life implanted in the moral ruins of human nature. Faith and repentance spring from the soil of broken and contrite hearts, and assurance follows – not that I love God but that he loves me; he has made me new in Christ, and will keep me to the day when we shall be like him and sin no more.

Lloyd-Jones was not interested in reviving the term 'Calvinism'. On one of the rare occasions when he mentioned the word in a sermon he said:

> A good friend once told me that he was somewhat disappointed, because in my exposition of the second chapter in this Epistle to the Ephesians I had not once mentioned Calvinism as I worked through the chapter. My simple reply to him was, The text does

---

[1] What he preached in general terms was true in his own experience: 'The Spirit of God often deals with us for some time before we come to a realisation of what is happening. All we know is that we are being caused to ask certain questions which we have never asked before. All we know is that we suddenly become dissatisfied with ourselves and with our lives.' D. M. Lloyd-Jones, *God's Way of Reconciliation: Ephesians 2* (Edinburgh: Banner of Truth, 1979), p. 467.

not mention that term. My friend was so much in the grip of a party-spirit that he was becoming doubtful of my position!'[1]

But at the same time he believed the truth often designated by that term is of 'very great importance'.[2]

I will mention two reasons why he so thought.

1. Understanding what this truth means will change a person's whole viewpoint.

By nature man thinks it is what he does that is of chief importance. When that idea is carried into the pulpit the preacher aims to be popular in order to gain an acceptance for his message. The right response, he thinks, will depend on his hearers not being offended. The Bible presents the truth very differently. It announces what God has done; and describes men without God as 'fools', 'ignorant', and deservedly under wrath – 'none righteous, no, not one' (*Rom.* 3:10). 'The heart is deceitful above all things, and desperately wicked' (*Jer.* 17:9). But it came to be thought that the church would only lose people if they addressed men in such a fashion. The idea came directly from a wrong standpoint; and it was not modern, for the very same thinking was in Simon Peter when he advised Christ that his speaking of the corruption of man was offending hearers (*Matt.* 15:12).

Deliverance from that viewpoint comes from a true vision of God. It is God who is to be feared, not man. Only with this knowledge is the preacher released from being governed by what people think of his message. Speaking of man's dependence on the grace of God, ML-J said, 'All of us dislike this truth because we feel it is insulting to us. The natural man hates this truth more than

---

[1] *Christian Unity*, p. 251.
[2] D. M. Lloyd-Jones, *God's Ultimate Purpose: Ephesians 1* (Edinburgh: Banner of Truth, 1978), p. 92.

any other.'[1] But that did not deter him. He believed that human arrogance has to be challenged: 'Some of us would be much more popular in the Church, as well as in the world, if we did not say certain things. If a preacher wants to be popular he must never offend.'[2] He knew that the power to change men belongs to God. Lloyd-Jones saw the twentieth-century attempt to make the Christian message more acceptable to people as an utter failure. 'The more the Church has accommodated her message to suit the palate of the people the greater has been the decline in attendance at places of worship.' God-centred Christianity is vital to the presentation of the gospel. It sees God at the head of things, and puts courage in his servants; it 'gives iron to the soul', as he was to say in recommending the reprinting of Calvin's *Institutes*. The nature of his preaching, and its continuance in the face of opposition, is only to be explained as this is understood. Both in Wales and England he stood against the popular tide. He did offend, especially the academic world.[3] To a real extent it could be said of him, as William Cowper said of Whitefield, he 'bore the pelting scorn of half an age.' He once said to me with feeling, 'If I had depended on men for encouragement I should have been dead long ago.' The consolation was

> Men heed thee, love thee, praise thee not;
> The Master praises: what are men?[4]

---

[1] Ibid., p. 89.

[2] D. M. Lloyd-Jones, *The Unsearchable Riches of Christ: Ephesians 3* (Edinburgh: Banner of Truth, 1979), p. 22.

[3] Evidence for this is in my biography of Dr Lloyd-Jones and elsewhere. 'When a man sees this truth [the truth of God] he has no choice. He does not force himself to stand alone. He does not even want to do so; but he can do no other.' D. M. Lloyd-Jones, *The Christian Warfare, Ephesians 6:6-10* (Edinburgh: Banner of Truth, 1976), p. 119. A main focus of criticism was his 'unwillingness to consider other views'.

[4] From a verse of Horatius Bonar's hymn, 'Go, Labour On'.

2. Lloyd-Jones also regarded what is called 'Calvinism' as essential to his spiritual peace.

'There is no doctrine which is as comforting as this.' He knew he was not where he was by his own choice, and that the outcome did not depend upon him. 'He has chosen to save a certain number of people; the fullness of the Gentiles and the fullness of Israel have got to come in.'[1] This kept him both humble and thankful. It restored him when he was cast down, as happened once in St Andrew's Hall, Glasgow when he was on a visit to war-time Scotland. A difficult train journey, no time for a meal, a headache, a long public meeting (at which two professors of divinity and a professor of medicine spoke before him), left him feeling utterly unfit for preaching. But as he rose to his feet the words of 1 Corinthians 15:10 came to him with force, and, bypassing the compliments of the chairman, he began by telling the people, 'I can say positively that "I am what I am by the grace of God."' The sermon that followed was long to be remembered.[2]

This same peace was with him in his last months when dying of cancer. One afternoon when I saw him, he had been reading reviews of the biographies of two non-Christians, G. M. Trevelyan, Master of Trinity College, Cambridge, and the same University's eminent physicist, J. D. Bernal. With much feeling he said,

> These reviews turned out to be a tremendous blessing to me. Here in Trevelyan is human nature at its best, and it came to me with such force: Why did God ever choose to look upon me? Why me in contrast with these men and the despair in which they died?[3]

[1] D. M. Lloyd-Jones, *Sanctified Through the Truth* (Eastbourne: Kingsway, 1989), p. 146.

[2] Iain H. Murray, *D. Martyn Lloyd-Jones, The Fight of Faith 1939-1981* (Edinburgh: Banner of Truth, 1990), p. 68.

[3] *Fight of Faith*, p. 737. For a fuller personal statement on what these truths meant to him, see *God's Ultimate Purpose*, p. 92.

There was good reason why he saw the recovery of God-centred Christianity as the greatest need of the churches.

Legacy 3

The Local Church Is Always the Primary Means of Evangelism

This statement may appear an obvious truth, but it was not obvious in the mid-twentieth century. Many supposed that the best hope for penetrating society lay in para-church agencies and movements. Local churches were too small to command public attention in the way that a 'big event' can do, especially if supported by celebrities. High expectations thus tended to be connected with the large crowds that were sought for campaign and crusade meetings. The idea was widespread that most people are likely to be converted apart from the local church.

Lloyd-Jones challenged this thinking. He was, of course, sympathetic to every evangelistic endeavour that did not compromise any biblical truth; but he believed that the gospel preached in a worshipping church, and in a local setting, has an advantage over other situations. Here the preacher is not just one man addressing a crowd: he is part of a community of believers who are not onlookers; they are involved; they too are witnesses in whom the Holy Spirit is present. When this is a reality, the incomer is confronted by something that has no counterpart in the world – 'thus are the secrets of his heart made manifest; and so falling down on his face, he will worship God, and report that God is in you of a truth' (*1 Cor.* 14:25). Something of eternity may be felt on such an occasion: 'Our coming together in public worship should be a foretaste of heaven.'[1]

That this is not always the case is not an argument for giving priority to other forms of evangelism. Rather it demonstrates the need for the life of the church to be raised: 'To evangelise successfully the church must become a spiritual church. Then she will challenge the world; but not until then.'[2] For Lloyd-Jones it was the power of the Spirit in the lives of Christians which is the essential witness to the message. When he first preached in the mission hall at Aberavon, E. T. Rees, the enthusiastic church secretary, had a large poster put up outside the church advertising the important preacher. To his surprise Rees was at once told, 'I don't like that, don't do it again.' Rees could not understand it at the time, but what subsequently happened in the congregation opened his eyes. As the inner life of the church was changed, the attention of the district was awakened in a way nothing else could do. It was seen for example in the conversion of a well-known spiritist medium, whose living had depended on her part in séances. Her later testimony of what had happened to her was this: 'The moment I entered your chapel and sat down on a seat amongst the people, I was conscious of a supernatural power. I was conscious of the same sort of supernatural power as I was accustomed to in our spiritist meetings, but there was one big difference; I had a feeling that the power in your chapel was a *clean* power.'[3]

---

[1] *God's Ultimate Purpose*, p. 308. When the church suits her services to the taste of the world, however well-intentioned the endeavour, the ultimate result will never be biblical Christianity. Merle d'Aubigné, visiting such 'progressive' churches in Germany in the 1840s, noted: 'In their meetings we see nothing of the holy gravity of the apostles and reformers; but in their stead we find enlivening music, numerous banquets, and noisy toasts.' *Germany, England and Scotland*, J. H. Merle d'Aubigné (London: Simpkin, Marshall, 1848), p. 60.

[2] *The Christian Warfare*, p. 272.

[3] Iain H. Murray, *D. Martyn Lloyd Jones, The First Forty Years 1899-1939* (Edin-

From New Testament times onwards, a vibrant, praying, witnessing church has always been the strongest authentication of the gospel. For ML-J mass evangelism without a recovery within the churches was no solution. The biblical order is, 'God shall bless us; and all the ends of the earth shall fear him' (*Psa.* 67:7). Or to quote the words of one of the foremost preachers of the nineteenth century: 'I have reached the conclusion that the best way to reach the unregenerate is to show him what Christianity is able to do for the believer.'[1] And on the same subject another said: 'If all Christians were as happy as it is their duty to be, there would be no resisting the spread of a faith so visibly rich in power and blessing.'[2] These were precisely ML-J's convictions.

LEGACY 4

TRUE PREACHING OF THE WORD HAS LIFE-CHANGING POWER

Examples could be multiplied of the consequences that often followed ML-J's preaching of the Word of God. They were to be seen in South Wales in the 1930s, among the unemployed, and where shoeless children went to school without breakfast. A professor of law at Liverpool University once observed that two men kept South Wales from Communism in that period. One was the Socialist, Aneurin Bevan; the other the preacher at Aberavon. But it was by no means only one section of society that was thus

---

burgh: Banner of Truth, 1982), p. 221. The story of what happened among the people of the Mission is best told by an eye witness, Bethan Lloyd-Jones, in *Memories of Sandfields* (Edinburgh: Banner of Truth, 1983).

[1] T. C. Johnson, *The Life and Letters of Benjamin Morgan Palmer* (repr. Edinburgh: Banner of Truth, 1987), p. 425.

[2] C. R. Vaughan, *The Gifts of the Holy Spirit* (repr. Edinburgh: Banner of Truth, 1975), p. 228.

influenced. C. Stacey Woods (1909-1983), leader of Inter-Varsity in North America and in the work of the International Fellowship of Evangelical Students (IFES), heard him preach in the Scots Church in Paris and wrote, 'Never have I witnessed or experienced such preaching.' Paul Tucker went to listen to him addressing members of the medical fraternity, who were expecting him to speak along medical lines. Instead he preached on the parable of the rich fool (*Luke* 12:13-21), with its conclusion, 'Thou fool, this night thy soul shall be required of thee.' It was 'the power of compassion' in that message that stayed with Tucker and others.

One of the most demanding situations ML-J ever faced in the pulpit was at Aberfan, Wales, on November 15, 1967. The occasion marked the anniversary of a disaster the previous year when 116 children and 28 adults died as a great heap of coal slurry slipped from a hillside and engulfed the village school. The close-knit community was plunged into an abyss of sorrow from which it seemed it would never recover. But on that November anniversary comfort came from God in the words of Romans 8:18-23. One eye-witness, a local minister, described what followed that sermon: 'I saw mothers who had lost little ones, and fathers also, smile with renewed hope in their faces. I know they will face the future now with more confidence.'

I give another example of the way ML-J's preaching was used that is recorded in a recent publication, the biography of Stacey Woods. Woods came from an evangelical background of Arminian persuasion, and some of his early meetings with Calvinists in the United States had not impressed him. He probably shared the view of his friend Charles Troutman who complained, 'They are ready to die for the "Reformed Faith", but are quite pleased to curse everyone else.' 'It would be hard to over-estimate the influence that Martyn Lloyd-Jones had on Stacey Woods', his bio-

grapher writes. When ML-J chaired the first general committee meeting of IFES in Boston in 1947, his preaching led to a life-
long friendship with the Australian. We are told:

> The evening addresses by Lloyd-Jones were all memorable, but
> the final Sunday-morning message was never forgotten by those
> present. The text from Psalm 90 he chose as a parting injunction
> stayed with many of those present for the rest of their lives, and
> set the tone of the IFES for a generation: 'Let thy work appear
> unto thy servants, and thy glory unto their children' (*Psa.* 90:16
> KJV). The group were deeply stirred.[1]

These records do not explain, however, how Lloyd-Jones's
preaching remains anything more than a memory today. In what
sense can it be a legacy?

Part of the answer lies in the medium which earlier generations
never knew. From the early 1950s, much of ML-J's preaching was
recorded, and through the work of the Martyn Lloyd-Jones Recordings Trust, and other agencies, his voice is heard on both sides of
the Atlantic today, sometimes by large numbers on radio (as I have
heard it in the United States). As is well known, he was not enthusiastic about the circulation of his tape-recorded sermons. One reason was an apprehension over their possible misuse; for the human
voice, delivering the message, is very secondary to the presence of
Christ in a service of worship and no human means can reproduce
that presence. Sermons should be heard in the context of worship,
not listened to casually as one might listen to anything else. Nonetheless, the survival of his spoken word is a very considerable aid to
the understanding of what preaching ought to be.

---

[1] A. Donald Macleod, *C. Stacey Woods and the Evangelical Rediscovery of the University* (Downers Grove, IL: IVP, 2007), p. 104. After this meeting Archbishop
Mowll's suggestion that ML-J be 'a roving ambassador for IFES' was enthusiast-
ically endorsed by the general committee. He did not accept. Among other things
that ML-J did for Stacey Woods was to introduce him to the Puritans.

More important for him than tapes was the written word, and his own books are the most enduring legacy of his preaching. They are read today in many langauges all over the world. Since books had much influence in his own life, it is surprising that he had comparatively little published until he was fifty-nine years of age; and it was not until he was turned seventy that his volumes on Ephesians and Romans began to appear. This was because he saw preaching, not writing, as his calling. But why could his preaching not be reproduced in print earlier? A main part of the answer was that the printing of sermons had been done on a considerable scale by the previous generation and religious publishers had come to the conclusion that there was no market for such books.[1] Much discussion, as well as editing, thus preceded the publication of his two volumes, *Studies in the Sermon on the Mount* by Inter-Varsity in 1959 and 1960. There was still hesitation on his part when, almost by way of trial, a single volume on Romans appeared in 1970. There was no assurance at that point that the whole series on Romans or Ephesians would be printed.[2]

---

[1] In an address in 1967 that analysed what had harmed true preaching, he included 'the publication of sermons'. When his hearers laughed, he went on: 'You laugh at this, but I mean it very seriously. I think that the printing of sermons in the last century was one of the most harmful influences upon preaching . . . If you prepare a sermon for publication, you are not going to be a good preacher when you preach that sermon.' Spurgeon's sermons, as his own, were not prepared for publication until after the event. 'There is all the difference in the world between these two things.' D. M. Lloyd-Jones, *Knowing the Times* (Edinburgh: Banner of Truth, 1989), p. 272. See also his important comments in his Preface to *Studies in the Sermon on the Mount*, vol. 1, where he writes: 'A sermon is not an essay and is not meant, primarily, for publication, but to be heard and to have an immediate impact upon the listeners . . . I have a suspicion that what accounts for the dearth of preaching at the present time is the fact that the majority of printed books of sermons have clearly been prepared for a reading rather than a listening public.'

[2] This is why the first volume to appear on Romans started with chapter 3, and the first on Ephesians with chapter 2. Ultimately there would be 14 volumes on Romans and 8 volumes on Ephesians.

It was the demand for his printed volumes of sermons that changed everything. During the 1970s the books came to be read in more than fifty countries by more than a million people. No exact figures exist. A minister in the Hebrides had one of the Lloyd-Jones books 'sent to every fishing boat in Scalpay'. A missionary in Papua New Guinea reported, 'All round New Guinea are friends of ours reading Dr Lloyd-Jones.' The books were seen in shops in Korea, read on buses in Singapore, and found in prisons – from Wormwood Scrubs in London to penitentiaries in New Zealand. An American holiday-maker, on a cruise in the Baltic, discovered *Studies in the Sermon on the Mount* in the ship's library, and went home to buy fourteen copies for every elder in his church. 'The outcome in our church has been remarkable', he later reported. A woman in South Africa, driven by loneliness and unhappiness 'into the pit', was loaned a ML-J volume. 'It brought me', she said, 'to understand how someone with absolutely nothing could be reconciled to God. For the first time in my life I wept for joy.'

These books all belonged to the category that had so recently been regarded as virtually unsaleable. They were sermons; and, what is more, sermons not in the current evangelical mould – no humour, no stories or anecdotes, and very rarely any personal reference. 'They were a very big pill to swallow', a minister wrote to him from South Africa; 'for yours was very much a small voice crying in the wilderness – against the tide of much evangelical thinking.'[1] But what made the books so influential and compelling was that they carried into print what was so distinctive about his preaching. It is true that unction cannot be put on the printed page, but the sermons showed what theology and doctrine should do in the exposition of Scripture. The Pauline method, ML-J

---

[1] *Fight of Faith*, p. 653. In the chapter from which this is taken there is much more on the effect of his sermons on those who read them.

believed, in addressing Christians was 'to open out doctrines, to teach them, to instruct them, to establish them, to ground them . . . The spiritual butterflies are the people who do not know doctrine. It is not entertainment we need. It is truth. It is knowledge.' The preacher should see that his people 'have delved into doctrines; they are taking hold of something. To watch this happening is a great privilege.'[1]

The tragedy in the twentieth century was that 'doctrine and theology' were supposed to be things for the academic and the student. Lloyd-Jones's belief that 'Preaching is theology coming through a man that is on fire' – truth explained and applied, directly, personally, lucidly, to every hearer – was a new kind of preaching. It challenged the contemporary church scene as nothing else had done for a long time. And it was not classroom theory, it was in the church where there was the evidence of life-changing power. This lesson about the true nature of preaching is not unique to the Lloyd-Jones legacy, but the way he led in recovering and exemplifying what was needed will remain an enduring legacy.

LEGACY 5

THE KEY TO THE TIMES IS THE STATE OF THE CHURCH

Lloyd-Jones's times are no longer our own, yet in the way he interpreted the scene in England and Wales in his own lifetime there is guidance for us. He was an itinerant as well as a local pastor. From about 1930 he was accustomed to travel in all parts of Britain. At many times of the year, he made it a practice mid-week

---

[1] D. M. Lloyd-Jones, *Romans: Exposition of Chapter 1, The Gospel of God* (Edinburgh: Banner of Truth, 1985), pp. 227-228, 240.

to visit towns and villages far and wide, preaching in churches of almost all Protestant denominations. Accordingly he came to know the contemporary spiritual situation as few could have known it. The conclusion to which he came was that the country was in the midst of a great religious decline – a decline in church membership, in attendance, and in faith. The popular solutions to this condition were not his. For some the solution was 'more evangelism'. For others it was to subject the churches to a radical programme of modernisation in order to close the supposed 'communication' gap between the church and the world. Not so Lloyd-Jones. Any idea that the churches confronted a problem unique to the twentieth century and to 'modern man', he regarded as a serious mistake:

> Man himself has not changed at all. All the changes about which men boast so much are external. They are not changes in man himself, but merely in his mode of activity, in his environment.[1]

The fundamental answer for the church always lies in Scripture, and what the contemporary church needed to address was a change in her own life: the call had to be for faith, repentance, discipline and revival within. 'The first question with regard to the problem of evangelisation is not the state of the world outside, it is the condition of the Church.' I have referred to this point already but there is more that needs to be said.

Looking at the national scene, Lloyd-Jones came to the firm conclusion that, given the confusion and the apostasy in the major

---

[1] D. M. Lloyd-Jones, *Truth Unchanged Unchanging*, (London: James Clarke, 1951), p. 110. 'All the sins that are being committed in the modern world you find mentioned in the Old Testament . . . Man as man does not change at all. He still remains the same contradictory person he has been ever since the fall' (p. 112). This proposition is a key to ML-J's outlook and explains his refusal to accept current fashions of thought in the world as constituting a new problem for the church.

denominations, the priority should be strong evangelical congreg-ations, and for closer relationships between them. He was not looking for any formal structure; he knew that real Christians are already one in Christ. But the contemporary situation was too serious to allow traditional differences over secondary issues to hinder fuller co-operation and mutual support. In a darkening scene, the need for strengthening evangelical unity was a priority in his thinking in the 1960s.

The leaders of the denominations read the situation very dif-ferently. Granted the churches were losing ground and Christian belief declining, the best way to turn things round would be in the reunion of the denominations. What they could not do apart, they could do together; united they could impress the world afresh. Such was the thinking that gave the ecumenical movement its great impetus. Suddenly enthusiasm for a united church was wide-spread and even dates were set for a reunion of denominations. Simultaneously, an olive branch was held out to evangelicals. Hitherto, it was said, they lacked influence and positions in their denominations because of their tendency to stand apart. Let them join with the majority; stop being 'negative'; and they would find their voice would be much more significant and welcome.

While numbers of evangelicals wavered in the face of this appeal, ML-J was unmoved. He argued that it is the gospel that makes unity, yet the ecumenical movement in their anxiety for unity looked for no prior agreement on what the gospel is: such questions as, 'How is anyone united to Christ?', 'What is a Christian?', were not to be allowed to hinder their purpose. It was as though they were too minor for discussion. Lloyd-Jones seized on the fundamental issue: Is evangelical belief a view to be allowed alongside others, or is it unique? Is their witness to *a* gospel or to the *only* gospel? If evangelicals can profess to be united with those who do not believe

24

the gospel of faith alone, by grace alone, is that not the same as saying the gospel is unnecessary for Christian unity?

For evangelicals to leave these questions unanswered in order to share in the ecumenical movement would inevitably weaken their own testimony. They would be forced to be neutral or silent, instead of maintaining the primary New Testament duty of contending for the faith. According to the Bible, error and unbelief are not trivial things; they 'eat like a cancer', and destroy churches.

For so speaking, Lloyd-Jones brought on a major disagreement. Many argued that sharing with non-evangelicals in the ecumenical movement could be worthwhile and beneficial; it could give evangelicals the opportunity and influence they had been waiting for. He replied that the comprehensiveness condoned by ecumenism was contrary to the gospel. The unity it advocated put believer and unbeliever side by side; and with no insistence on the biblical definitions once common in Protestantism, there was nothing to prevent the ultimate inclusion of Roman Catholicism.

Today the scene is somewhat changed. With the denominations still dwindling, and little done in the way of actual reunion, ecumenical interest has waned. But the latitudinarian spirit that ecumenism engendered has only gained in strength;and what ML-J foresaw with regard to openness to Roman Catholicism can no longer be dismissed as 'scare-mongering'.[1]

The root failure of evangelicals in understanding the times was, ML-J believed, in their weak theology, in their allowing others to set the agenda, and a readiness to think of influence and success in terms of numbers.[2] He did not deny that some

---

[1] See below, p. 257, *Is the Reformation Over?* A Review.

[2] 'We must not be ashamed of being a remnant, weak and small. We must cease to think in terms of numbers, we must think in terms of the purpose of God and the purity of the witness and testimony. God will preserve this seed. He will carry it on in spite of everything.' D. M. Lloyd-Jones, *Romans: Exposition of Chap-*

evangelicals were supporting ecumenism in the hope of seeing truth advanced and denominations turned round, but he was certain that the policy was the opposite of what was needed for a true evangelical awakening. He denied that circumstances could ever justify any movement from first principles. The unregenerate world is essentially always the same. The real problem does not lie in any contemporary school of thought; it is man's plight as an enemy of God. The principles by which he assessed the scene in his own day are abiding.

LEGACY 6

THE GROWTH OF THE CHURCH DEPENDS ON THE PRESENCE AND POWER OF THE HOLY SPIRIT

Ecumenism was not the only proposed solution for the decline of the churches. Other remedies included a renewal of 'scholarship' in order to gain for evangelicals more recognition and respectability. For ML-J, giving emphasis to such solutions was due to an underestimation of the real problem, namely, fallen human nature. If it is true that man is 'dead in trespasses and sins', and ruled by the 'prince of the power of the air, the spirit that now works in the children of disobedience', then the need is beyond all human efforts and abilities. Certainly he did not despise the need for learning, but he knew that alone would do nothing. Even correct doctrine was far from being enough. His concern for a recovery of biblical truth was that it taught that lesson: 'Calvinism of necessity leads to an emphasis on the action and activity of God the Holy Spirit. The whole emphasis is on what God does to us.'[1]

---

ter 9, God's Sovereign Purpose (Edinburgh: Banner of Truth,1991), p. 326.
[1] *The Puritans,* p. 210.

The Spirit alone can change situations. The church's faith in man had to be abandoned, and the meaning of speaking 'in demonstration of the Spirit and of power' learned afresh (*1 Cor.* 2:4).

ML-J saw a real parallel between what members of the church at Corinth were ignoring and what was missing in the twentieth century. Paul warned them with the words, 'I will come to you shortly, if the Lord will, and will know, not the speech of them that are puffed up, but the power' (*1 Cor.* 4:19). In ML-J's paraphrase: 'I am coming to see you, and I am going to test you. And let me make it clear to you – I am not interested in your words. It is one thing to talk, but "the kingdom of God is not in word, but in power." Any fool can get up and speak. The question is, Is there power in the man's speech? What does it accomplish? What does it lead to?'[1]

Lloyd-Jones was saying this before the charismatic movement ever came into being. The emphasis, for instance, is in his address on the authority of the Holy Spirit in 1957, where he spoke of the neglect of the Holy Spirit as 'the main source of weakness in modern Evangelicalism'.[2] The later peculiarities of charismatic teaching, such as belief in the recovery of apostles, the presence of tongues, and the 'claiming' of healing, he never believed. But in praying for the Spirit, and for fuller baptisms of the Spirit he did believe; and in so doing he stood in the long line of preachers most used of God to keep the faith alive, and to pass it on to succeeding generations. In a sentence, it could be said, the message of his ministry was, 'Cease from man', and the corresponding conclusion:

---

[1] *Romans: The Gospel of God (1:1-32)*, p. 222.

[2] D. M. Lloyd-Jones, *Authority* (1958; repr. Edinburgh: Banner of Truth, 1984), p. 64. On the place of scholarship he said: 'I believe that apologetics has its rightful place, but I am certain we are attaching far too much importance to it, and far too many of our books are defending the faith in this way. We are trying to reason, to show our knowledge, and to make accommodations. But it does not seem to avail much. We do not seem to be making much of an impression on our opponents' (pp. 79-80).

27

Not unto us, O LORD, not unto us, but unto thy name give glory,
for thy mercy, and for thy truth's sake (*Psa.* 115:1).

2

PREACHING AND
THE HOLY SPIRIT

One Sunday during the Second World War, a Scottish member of the armed forces found himself in London and, in the hope of gaining the spiritual help he knew he needed, went to Westminster Chapel. His first disappointment was to find the building closed, damaged by bombing. But a notice indicated that there would be a service in a hall not far away. When he got there, he later recorded:

> There was a thin congregation. A small man in a collar and tie walked almost apologetically to the platform and called the people to worship. I remember thinking that Lloyd-Jones must be ill and that his place was being taken by one of his office-bearers. This illusion was not dispelled during the first part of the service, though I was impressed by the quiet reverence of the man's prayers and his reading of the Bible.
>
> Ultimately he announced his text and began his sermon in the same quiet voice. Then a curious thing happened. For the next forty minutes I became completely unconscious of everything except the word that this man was speaking – not his words, mark you, but someone behind them and in them and through

them. I didn't realise it then, but I had been in the presence of the mystery of preaching, when a man is lost in the message he proclaims.[1]

Tom Allan, who himself became a preacher, here puts his finger on the word which Dr Lloyd-Jones was often to use in the same connection: 'To me preaching is a great mystery; it is one of the most mysterious things of all, and that is why I find it eludes any kind of analysis.'

Looking only at the surface of things, the reference to 'mystery' may seem exaggerated. It is customary to explain effective speaking in terms of natural abilities, including those of mind, voice and eloquence. But this is not the biblical definition; rather the New Testament uses words that take preaching to a different level. The Lord Jesus Christ (of whom it is witnessed, 'Never man spoke like this man') is repeatedly described as speaking with 'authority' and 'power'. 'He taught them as one having authority, and not as the scribes' (*Matt.* 7:29). 'They were all amazed and spoke among themselves, saying, What a word is this! for with authority and power he commands the unclean spirits, and they come out of him' (*Luke* 4:36). These same descriptive terms reappear in the preaching of the apostolic age, along with the parallel word 'boldness'. In the Acts of the Apostles Christians are described as speaking with 'great power', and as being 'full of faith and power'. Titus is told to 'speak and exhort with all authority'. In the original language, we can probably best understand 'authority' as the right or warrant to command, and 'power' as the ability to do so.

Certainly these terms show that preaching is more than effective speaking. It does not belong to the realm of expressing opinion or sharing experience. Yet authority, power and boldness, are not the final explanation; we have to ask where these elements come

[1] Tom Allan, *Evening Citizen*, Glasgow, November 18, 1961.

from. The answer of the New Testament is that their author is God, the Holy Spirit. Jesus, returning from the wilderness 'in the power of the Spirit', began his ministry with the words, 'The Spirit of the Lord is upon me because he has anointed me to preach' (*Luke* 4:14, 18). It is the same with the first disciples: 'Peter filled with the Holy Spirit said to them'; 'they were all filled with the Holy Spirit and spoke the word of God with boldness' (*Acts* 4:8, 31). The same pattern runs through the proclamation of the gospel that followed, beginning in Jerusalem. The gospel message came to Thessalonica 'in power and in the Holy Spirit'. Paul gives the same explanation of the gospel's entrance at Corinth, and tells us that in Asia Minor his experience was to preach 'according to his working, which works in me mightily' (*Col.* 2:29).

So this much ought to be plain. True preaching does not belong to the sphere of natural gifts. It is not a thing to be obtained through teaching or training. It is the result of the presence of the Spirit of God, and that is exactly where the mystery enters. God is above all our studying: 'Can you by searching find out God?' If the Israelites were mystified by manna falling from heaven, it is no wonder that man should be reduced to silence when he recognises the presence of the Holy Spirit. The actions of the Holy Spirit in creating new life in an individual, and in inspiring men to write inerrant truth, are asserted in Scripture but not explained. So it is with regard to preaching. The subject is higher than our present comprehension. But if there is one word best suited to describe the phenomenon we are discussing it is the word 'unction'. No-one is self-anointed. All Christians are anointed by the Holy Spirit (*1 John* 2:20); that is basic and must be reflected in the life of the church. At the same time it is clear in Scripture, and basic to ML-J's understanding, that there are anointings of the Spirit connected with preaching in a special way and it is in that narrower use of the term that the word 'unction' is applied to preaching. It

31

is better felt and experienced than analysed, yet some things can be said with profit.

Unction can be considered from two standpoints, namely the pulpit and the pew. For as Daniel Kidder once wrote, unction is 'the joint product of the Spirit's influence in the heart of the speaker, and of his sanctified efforts on the hearts of the hearers.'[1] I will take the second of these first.

UNCTION AND THE PEW

Lloyd-Jones did not draw attention to himself by illustrating the effects of preaching from his own ministry. But numbers who heard him have left testimonies that are to the glory of God, as already quoted in these pages. What they witnessed of the effects of unction and authority under his ministry is in full harmony with the records of powerful preaching throughout church history. The following are some of the marks of such preaching.

1. Preaching under the anointing of the Holy Spirit is preaching which brings with it a consciousness of God.

It produces an impression upon the hearer that is altogether stronger than anything belonging to the circumstances of the occasion. Visible things fall into the background; the surroundings, the fellow worshippers, even the speaker himself, all become secondary to an awareness of God himself. Instead of witnessing a public gathering, the hearer receives the conviction that he is being addressed personally, and with an authority greater than that of the human messenger. This is what the spiritist medium,

---

[1] Daniel P. Kidder, *A Treatise on Homiletics* (New York: Methodist Book Concern, 1894), p. 262.

already quoted, felt at Aberavon, and a still larger number knew the same at Westminster Chapel. In the words of Jim Packer, 'I never heard another preacher with so much of God about him.'[1]

Among examples of this which could be cited, I recall one of the most memorable in my own experience. It happened at Westminster Chapel on Friday night, April 22, 1955. The next day I was to be married. It was his usual Friday night 'lecture' (so called) and the subject was unfulfilled prophecy. On that theme ML-J had reached the last judgment, the final overthrow of the ungodly at the coming of Christ. His text was Revelation chapter 18 and especially the words of verse 21: 'A mighty angel took up a stone like a great millstone and cast it into the sea, saying, Thus with violence shall that great city Babylon be thrown down, and shall be found no more at all.' The truth was overpowering. The end of all things was not an idea but an absolute certainty. Transitory events vanished before the magnitude of eternity and there was no possibility of attention straying to weddings or to anything else.

The subject on that occasion was intensely serious yet the same impact could accompany any part of Scripture he was treating. Sometimes superficial hearers of Lloyd-Jones criticised him for telling them that every subject was 'most important'; implying that he used exaggerated language to gain attention. The truth is that in handling the word of God that is how he commonly felt, and he believed others should feel the same. How can any true preaching be less than important? ML-J knew what Andrew Bonar meant when he wrote: 'It is one thing to bring truth from the Bible, and another thing to bring it from God himself through the Bible.' As another writer says, unction appears in that 'affecting, penetrating, interesting manner flowing from a strong sensibility of heart in the preacher to the importance of those truths which he delivers,

---

[1] Quoted in Clyde E. Fant Jr and W. M. Pinson Jr, *Twenty Centuries of Great Preaching*, vol. 11 (Waco, Texas: Word Books, 1971), p. 269.

and an earnest desire that they may make a full impression on the hearts of his hearers.'[1]

2. Where there is power in preaching there is little wandering of attention in the pew.

There is an obvious reason why preaching too often lacks the ability to hold the interest of those who listen. It is because the word spoken has no more than a fleeting access to the hearer's mind. A statement is briefly heard only to be crowded out by the individual's own thoughts, which he may well find more interesting and pleasant. Thus the twenty or forty minutes of a sermon may pass, with a person in the pose of a listener, yet actually paying attention to very little. In contrast, powerful preaching takes hold of the whole person. It gets within a man. It first arrests the mind and then speaks to the heart, the conscience, and the will. Where this element is present inattention becomes a near impossibility. Skilful oratory and carefully crafted speech can go some way to hold the hearers but it does not command attention in this manner. Powerful preaching penetrates more than the surface of the mind; it does more than merely present teaching; it is capable of causing a moral and emotional earthquake – 'not simply with words, but also with power, with the Holy Spirit, and with deep conviction' (*1 Thess.* 1:4).

An eighteenth-century church-goer who was also a shipbuilder confessed that he had often built a ship from stem to stern during a sermon, but when he heard George Whitefield he found himself unable to lay a single plank. The reason for this was noted by another of the evangelist's hearers: 'Whitefield preached like a lion, he spoke as one conscious of his high credentials, with authority

---

[1] Quoted in Kidder, *Homiletics*, pp. 262-263.

and power.' So it was with Lloyd-Jones. His message often carried the conviction that it was more important than any other possible consideration.

Some of my own clearest memories of the attention-gaining power of his preaching were in situations where he was away from his own congregation and among people who scarcely knew him. A country chapel, near Cambridge, for instance, with a mid-week afternoon congregation in which the hubbub of talk before the service began left me wondering how serious a hearing he would receive. I need not have wondered. Another time, in the old parish church at Melton Mowbray, he was preaching on the eve of a General Election that was distracting and exciting the nation. Politics and the future of the country were on every mind and in almost all conversation. To change such a mood would be akin to changing the course of a river, but it happened before his sermon finished that night.

3. Where there is unction in preaching children also may listen and benefit.

It was Lloyd-Jones's conviction that churches make a great mistake when they do not expect children to be present during a sermon. The mistake is due, he believed, to a wrong idea of preaching. Certainly there is a type of preaching which is unlikely to profit children: a sermon which is intended for the intellectual benefit of adults does not readily suit the capacities of children. But where preaching is more than intellectual – where it engages the heart, where the word of God speaks to the conscience – then the age of the listener becomes far less significant. Children are as capable of being conscious of the presence of God as adults, and under such preaching they can gain impressions which will be life-long. The infant listener to Whitefield who said that 'he made God look big' had gained something not to be forgotten. The same was true at

35

Westminster Chapel. From the published sermons of Dr Lloyd-Jones it might seem very improbable that such material could hold the attention of the younger age group. Yet it did. From before the age of five, infants were present throughout the service. When he was ill on one occasion, a girl of twelve wrote to him on behalf of herself and her brother to say she hoped he would soon be back because he was the only preacher she could understand. She was not unique. We have every reason to believe that children bene-fitted under the powerful preaching of New Testament times and so it should be today.[1]

4. Powerful preaching is preaching which results in a change in those who listen.

The nature of the change will be varied: it may be repentance; restitution made for wrongs done; it may bring the end of long-standing antagonisms between individuals; it may be new strength given for difficult duties, or comfort and joy for the grieving; it may be a restraint laid upon evildoers. Alternatively, instead of any apparently beneficial result, the effect of such preaching may be indignation, anger and hostility on the part of nominal Christians and unbelievers. Certainly powerful preaching does not necess-arily lead to conversion. Men may know 'the powers of the world to come' and yet resist the Holy Spirit. Listening to Paul, Felix trembled, yet as far as we know he did not come to faith.

The one thing sure is that where there is unction in preaching there will be a breaking down of indifference and apathy. Some-times the change in hearers at Westminster Chapel was far from hopeful at first. Hearers were known to leave the building vowing

---

[1] An exception to this in ML-J's ministry would be his *Romans* series, which he considered as 'lectures'; these were delivered on Friday nights when children (and families) were seldom present.

that they would never attend again; yet it could be the first stage in a conviction they could not shake off and their vow would be broken as they were seen there again.

UNCTION AND THE PREACHER

1. As anointed preaching is the work of the Holy Spirit, the preacher knows this is a gift that is not under human control.

In the Church of England, as directed by the Book of Common Prayer, a bishop may say, 'Receive the Holy Ghost for the Office and Work of a priest', but God cannot be so imparted. In all denominations the office of the ministry may exist without the Spirit and so may the pulpit. For Lloyd-Jones no small part of the problem in the twentieth-century church was that there were too many preachers without God-given authority. 'What is needed in the pulpit is authority, great authority.'[1] It is the absence of this element that tempts preachers and churches to employ all kinds of expedients to fill the void.

'We are not in control of the situation; this is of God.'[2] It follows that where the Holy Spirit is at work in preaching what happens is unpredictable. The preacher himself cannot anticipate it:

Sometimes God has been gracious on a Sunday and I have been conscious of exceptional liberty, and I have been foolish enough to listen to the devil when he says: 'Now then, you wait until next Sunday, it is going to be marvellous, there will be an even larger congregation.' And I go into the pulpit the next Sunday and I see a smaller congregation. But then on another occasion I stand

[1] D. M. Lloyd-Jones, *Preaching and Preachers* (Hodder and Stoughton: London, 1971), p. 158.
[2] Ibid., p. 300.

in this pulpit labouring, as it were left to myself, preaching badly
and utterly weak, and the devil has come and said: 'There will be
nobody there at all next Sunday.' But, thank God, I have found
on the following Sunday a larger congregation. That is God's
method of accountancy. He is always giving us surprises. You
never know what he is going to do.[1]

For this same reason, he urged, the preacher should not be
confined to saying only what he has previously prepared. Vital as
previous preparation has to be, the message ultimately delivered
may well be more than what was prepared:

> I have often found when I have gone into the pulpit with a pre-
> pared sermon, that while I have been preaching, my first point
> alone has developed into a whole sermon . . . What one had never
> thought of, or even imagined, suddenly happens in the pulpit
> while one is actually preaching.[2]

Given this possibility, it was impossible for ML-J to plan and
announce a series of sermons, to be begun and concluded on certain
dates. In the Preface to the second volume of the *Sermon on the Mount*
he thought it important to explain that although the sermons in
the two volumes numbered sixty in all, that was

> quite accidental and not planned nor contrived. It has never been
> my custom to divide up a portion of Scripture into a number
> of parts and then issue a syllabus announcing what will be done
> each week. That seems to me to limit the freedom of preaching,
> quite apart from the fact that in actual practice I sometimes find
> that I succeed in doing only about half of what I had planned
> and purposed.

---

[1] D. M. Lloyd-Jones, *Spiritual Depression: Its Causes and Cure* (London: Pickering
and Inglis, 1965), p. 131.
[2] *Preaching and Preachers*, p. 299.

He believed that the type of preaching that commits the preacher
to repeat only what he has written before him, or memorised before-
hand, is very unlikely to be preaching with unction. On this point there
has been some disagreement among teachers of homiletics. William
Arthur, for instance, was criticised by the Presbyterian divine, Patrick
Fairbairn, for writing the following words:

> The feeling of every man standing up in the Lord's name ought
> to be, 'I am not here to acquit myself well, nor to deliver a good
> discourse; but after having made my best efforts to study and digest
> the truth, I am here to say just what God may enable me to say, to
> be enlarged or straitened, according as He may be pleased to give
> me utterance or not' . . . He is *trusting* for utterance to help from
> above, and not *insuring* it by natural means, – either a manuscript or
> memory.[1]

Fairbairn regarded this statement as tending to 'fanaticism' – con-
fusing 'the Spirit's ordinary influence with a supernatural afflatus' –
and he described Arthur's book, *The Tongue of Fire*, as representing 'the
Methodist point of view'.[2] In which case, Lloyd-Jones was unashamedly 'Methodist'. But it would be misleading to understand the difference in denominational terms (the term 'Methodist' once applied to
Whitefield as much as to the Wesleys). Presbyterians who were familiar
with revival would be more sympathetic to Lloyd-Jones's position than
to Fairbairn's. They saw a relation between the Spirit's aid in the act of
preaching and the way in which the sermon was delivered.[3]

[1] W. Arthur, *The Tongue of Fire, or The True Power of Christianity* (London: Mullan,
1877), p. 322.
[2] P. Fairbairn, *Pastoral Theology* (Edinburgh: Clark, 1875), pp. 227-30. He argued that Arthur's same principle of trusting the Spirit for freedom in preaching
could be used to argue for no preparation at all. It is true, some have made that
deduction with very unhappy consequences, but because a truth can be misused
it is no argument that it must be wrong. Fairbairn, nonetheless, remains a valuable author.
[3] For instance, J. W. Alexander, and his father, Archibald Alexander, believed
that the Holy Spirit was not being given the prominence he receives in the New

2. The more a preacher knows of unction, the less will he think of himself and his own work.

The greater the preacher's concept of speaking in the name of God, and of the responsibility involved, the more he will understand why Paul said, 'I was with you in weakness, and in fear, and in much trembling' (*1 Cor.* 2:3). It was no mere concern over circumstances in Corinth that gave the apostle his fear. Rather as Luther once said to Philip Melancthon, 'I have never troubled myself with fears about not preaching well, but I have often been troubled and terrified, that I must stand in God's presence and speak of His great majesty and glorious nature.'[1] 'I wonder', ML-J says, 'whether a man has a right to be in a pulpit at all and even to attempt preaching unless he knows something about this fear and trembling . . . Any man who has had some glimpse of what it is to preach will inevitably feel he has never preached. But he will go on trying.'[2] 'I can say quite honestly that I would not cross the road to listen to myself preaching.'[3] This latter sentiment ML-J expressed with a quotation from one of the greatest preachers of the nineteenth century, James Henley Thornwell:

Testament. The latter quotes a hearer of William Tennent, leader in the Great Awakening, who later changed his manner of preaching: 'Mr Tennent was never worth anything after he came to Philadelphia; for he took to reading his sermons, and lost his animation.' A. Alexander, *The Log College* (repr. London: Banner of Truth, 1968), p. 52.

[1] Quoted in John Ker, *Lectures on the History of Preaching* (London: Hodder & Stoughton, 1888), p. 156. Ker also speaks of the seraphic Scots preacher, John Welsh, who preached before the famous University of Saumur as though he were only in a country village. When a friend commented on this, Welsh 'replied that he was so filled with the dread of God that he had learned to have no apprehension of man at all.' 'This', Ker wisely adds, 'is misapplied by some forward preachers, who neither fear God nor regard man.'

[2] *Knowing the Times*, p. 261.

[3] *Preaching and Preachers*, p. 3.

It is a great matter to understand what it is to be a preacher, and how preaching should be done. Effective sermons are the offspring of study, of discipline, of prayer, and especially of the unction of the Holy Ghost . . . My own performances in this way fill me with disgust. I have never made, much less preached, a sermon in my life, and I begin to despair of ever being able to do so.[1]

Distrust in oneself must mark the preacher. The most-used preachers in the churches have always been those who say, 'No-one knows how to preach.' A self-confident preacher ought to be a contradiction in terms. Equally the pulpit is no place for light-heartedness. For a preacher to launch his sermon with humour was, for ML-J, a strange contradiction of his message.

Preparation for Preaching

While the Holy Spirit is sovereign, ML-J believed there are several things present in those whom he aids.

1. Sermons will be formed from truth which the Holy Spirit can honour.

In no other way may preaching with divine authority and unction be expected. This means that in the preacher's life and thought the word of God must take precedence over everything else. His work is to explain, illustrate, and apply divine revelation. Sometimes this is too readily assumed by evangelicals, as though it may be taken for granted that we preach the Bible. The danger of such thinking is that the delivery and reception of the sermon can be more important to us than the content. Then, if the sermon

---

[1] Ibid., p. 99. See also *Knowing the Times*, p. 263.

produces some interest and feeling, we may be satisfied.[1] But for Lloyd-Jones where biblical truth becomes in any way secondary great preaching is destroyed. The preacher's first and supreme concern has to be that his words are an expression of the mind of God in Scripture. 'If any man speaks, let him speak as the oracles of God' (*1 Pet.* 4:11). The preacher is nothing unless he is an interpreter and exegete of revelation. Apart from that he has no right to command the attention of his fellow men. To expect the Holy Spirit to give his aid to what are merely our ideas is to desecrate the pulpit.

The subjective condition of the preacher is important, but it is a fatal mistake for the authority of Scripture not to be put first. Spiritual power does not lie in human thought any more than it lies in human energy. When faith in the Bible is lost, preaching is lost. 'The pulpit and the Bible go together. If the one sinks, it carries down the other: if one drops out of the popular faith, the other dies. Neither is ever resuscitated alone.'[2]

Throughout Lloyd-Jones's ministry he protested against preaching that was weak in biblical, doctrinal content. The certainty of his message was based on the authority of Scripture. It was inevitable that those who did not see all Scripture as divine revelation would complain about his 'dogmatism'. 'A Puritan Pope', one Nonconformist leader called him. Even evangelicals sometimes said that the thoroughness of his appeal to Scripture made needless demands on his hearers. 'According to the modern ideas and theories', he once said, 'I am too much of a teacher, and there is too much reason and argumentation in my sermons.'[3] He was

---

[1] 'The day was when the churches were much more concerned than we, about the truths conveyed, and much less about the garb of the truths. Doctrine, rather than speaking, was what drew the audience.' J. W. Alexander, *Thoughts on Preaching*, (repr., Edinburgh: Banner of Truth, 1975), p. 32.

[2] Austin Phelps, *The Theory of Preaching* (New York: Scribner's, 1882), p. 13.

[3] *Preaching and Preachers*, p. 127.

far from thinking his sermons were above criticism, but *this* criticism, he believed, represented a failure to understand what preaching is about. The preacher should be a man absorbed with 'the glory and greatness of the truth'. That means his mind has ever to be engaged with Scripture. He must live in the word of God, and read it constantly in private: 'the very minimum of the preacher's Bible reading' ought to be going 'right through the Scriptures every year omitting nothing.'[1] This was his own practice. He followed Robert Murray M'Cheyne's scheme of daily readings, covering the whole Bible in a year, and did this 'for at least 53 or 54 years'.[2] Nor should the minister's reading end with Scripture. Among other types of reading, he says:

> The first is theology. There is no greater mistake than to think you finish with theology when you leave a seminary. The preacher should continue to read theology as long as he is alive. The more he reads the better.'[3]

The Lloyd-Jones definition of preaching has often been quoted, 'Preaching is theology coming through a man who is on fire.' But the position which he gave to *theology* in that sentence is too often overlooked. Preaching, then, has to begin with the objective, with divine revelation. It would be an entire mistake to think that Lloyd-Jones was primarily interested in the subjective or the emotional. At the same time it was patently clear to him that something more than a possession of the truth is essential to preaching.

---

[1] Ibid., p. 172.
[2] The words are those of his daughter, Elizabeth Catherwood, quoting her mother. *Martyn Lloyd-Jones: the Man and his Books* (London: Evangelical Library, 1982), p. 35. For M'Cheyne's Calender of Daily Readings, see Andrew A. Bonar, ed., *The Memoir and Remains of Robert Murray M'Cheyne* (London: Banner of Truth, 1966, repr. often), pp. 618-628.
[3] *Preaching and Preachers*, p. 177.

2. The life of the preacher will be part of the sermon.

To say that the man himself is a part of the message is a paradox. For the less of self there is in preaching the better; 'We preach not ourselves', says Paul. Yet, at the same time, the work of the Holy Spirit in preaching is not *apart* from the preacher, but in him and through him. As has been said, 'A preacher is in some degree a reproduction of the truth in personal form.' To expect preaching to be effective irrespective of the spiritual condition of the one who speaks, is to fly in the face of Scripture. It is patently clear in the book of Acts that there is something distinctive about the disciples which compelled attention to their message. God does not simply give truth that can be delivered by any kind of means; he prepares and sends men. As James Stalker has written: 'The effect of a sermon depends, first of all, on what is said, and next, on how it is said; but hardly less, on who says it.'[1] On the same point, Spurgeon says, 'Extremely pointed addresses may be delivered by men whose hearts are out of order with the Lord, but their results are small . . . God connects special success with special states of heart, and if these are lacking he will not do mighty works.'[2]

While maintaining the unpredictability that attends preaching, Lloyd-Jones knew it is what happens in the preacher's life and thought before he ever enters the pulpit that most commonly affects the outcome. 'I know I can preach to myself', he told his future wife in 1925, when she had never heard him preach, and doubted if the pulpit was his true vocation. In the power with which the truth came to his own heart he knew it could come to others, and this remained his lifelong conviction. He was to say to theological students in 1969:

---

[1] J. Stalker, *The Preacher and His Models* (London: Hodder and Stoughton, 1892), pp. 166-7.

[2] *Lectures to My Students*, (repr., Edinburgh: Banner of Truth, 2008), p. 423.

When you yourself are gripped and moved in preparation you will generally find that the same happens in the preaching. I emphasise that it is when you are gripped and moved, not when you have composed well. It is when you have been stirred in this way, when the message you are preparing comes with power to you, that it is likely to do the same to the people.[1]

Such private experiences were by no means necessarily joyful to the preacher. On one occasion, when preaching on the life of the unconverted from Ephesians 2, particularly on the words, 'fulfilling the desires of the flesh and of the mind', he described a number of those desires, and then interjected:

> I do not know how you feel as I go through this sorry and terrible list, but as I was preparing this sermon it filled me with loathing and a hatred of myself. I look back and I think of the hours I have wasted in mere talk and argumentation. And it was all with one end only, simply to gain my point and to show how clever I was.[2]

The principle involved here is that the preacher cannot rightly handle truth impersonally. His feelings need to be in harmony with the words he has to speak. Cotton Mather has written that when the Holy Spirit inspired men to write the Scriptures he produced in their hearts affections which 'were agreeable and answerable to the matter then flowing from their pens'. Mather rightly argued that there is a parallel to this when it comes to authority in preaching, as the example of Paul makes clear. Some subjects demand distress of spirit, even tears; others call for joy.[3] The old saying is true, 'The heart makes the best oratory.' If the preacher is not affected by what he says there is little likelihood that his hearers

---

[1] *Preaching and Preachers*, p. 299.
[2] *Ephesians: God's Way of Reconciliation*, p. 65.
[3] See *2 Cor.* 2:4; 5:11; *Phil.* 2:17; 3:18.

will be.[1] This conception of a preacher's duty is well stated by a one time professor at the Sorbonne:

> He should blot himself out in the presence of the truth and make it alone appear. This will happen naturally, spontaneously, whenever he is profoundly impressed by it and identifies himself with it, heart and mind. Then he grows like it, great, mighty and dazzling. It is no longer he who lives, it is the truth which in him lives and acts. The man vanishes in the virtue of the Almighty, and this is the preacher's noblest, his true glory . . . Oh, ye who have taken the Lord for your inheritance and who glow with the desire to announce to men the Word of God, ask urgently of Him the grace to forget yourself and to think of Him – of Him only![2]

Parallel with the above words and equally valuable are the words of the veteran American preacher Theodore L. Cuyler:

> When truth gets full possession of a man's conscience; when his sensibilities are aroused and his sympathies in full play; when the soul becomes luminous, until the interior light and glow blaze out through every nook and crevice; when, from head to foot, the whole man becomes the beaming, burning impersonation of truth, – then is he honestly, naturally, irresistibly eloquent. To this a great head is not always essential: a great heart is, and must be.[3]

---

[1] Bunyan could say, 'I preached what I felt, what I smartingly did feel.' *Works of John Bunyan*, vol. 1 (Edinburgh: Banner of Truth, 1991), p. 42. One of his hearers said that his sermons were 'full of love of God', and 'so New Testament like that he made me admire, and weep for joy.' John Brown, *John Bunyan* (revised ed., London: Hulbert, 1928), p. 369.

[2] The words are those of Bautain, quoted by David R. Breed, *Preparing to Preach* (New York: Hodder and Stoughton, 1911), p. xvi. Like John the Baptist, says Breed, the preacher is to be only a 'Voice' – 'the voice of something other than himself, intangible, mysterious, and mighty.'

[3] Theodore L. Cuyler, *Thoughts on Heart and Life* (London: Hodder and Stoughton, 1890), part 3, pp. 102-103.

I have already drawn attention to Dr Lloyd-Jones's dissatisfaction with his own preaching, and some have expressed surprise at his words. Part of the explanation lies in what has just been said. He knew that his own spirit fell far short of the magnitude and wonder of the message he had to deliver. He preached and exhorted with feeling, but in his eyes the feeling was feeble compared with what it ought to be. In other words, perhaps the most difficult part of preaching is to get one's own spirit in full harmony with the subject.[1] The man who does not know this difficulty is not qualified to be a preacher.

3. There will be dependence on the Holy Spirit for his present aid.

Dr Lloyd-Jones believed that neglect of the work of the Spirit in relation to preaching was often connected with mistaken belief. Some held that the indwelling of the Spirit in all Christians leaves no need for believers to seek his presence; others seemed to believe that the Spirit rests equally on all orthodox ministry. ML-J regarded this as contrary to Scripture. Why the commands to be 'filled with the Spirit' if his indwelling which takes place at regeneration is sufficient? What sense could there be in the apostolic direction to appoint men 'full of the Holy Spirit and wisdom' if his fullness marks all Christians? While there is mystery in the mode of the Spirit's presence, it is surely clear that his work is not static but ongoing and repeated. Thus what happened to the disciples in Acts chapter 2, verse 4 is found again in chapter 4, verse 31.

Unless this is understood, he held, there can be no true understanding of revival. Revival is a larger effusion and giving of the Holy

---

[1] This has been the common testimony of all men much used of God. John Livingston for example, wrote: 'I found that much studying did not so much help me in preaching, as the getting my heart brought to a spiritual disposition.' *Select Biographies*, W. K. Tweedie (Edinburgh: Wodrow Soc., 1845), p. 194. See John Owen on the same subject in his *Works*, ed. W. H. Goold, vol. 9 (Edinburgh: Banner of Truth, 1968). p. 455.

Spirit to many at one time – the churches baptised with fresh endue-
ments of life and power. As is well known, that was an emphasis in his
ministry. But he also knew that there is the on-going giving of the Spirit
to individuals in the daily life of the church. Because there is no 'revival'
it does not mean there can be no present expectation and receiving.
The promise of the Spirit's aid is not restricted to select periods of
history, rather it is certain that God 'shall give the Holy Spirit to them
that ask him' (*Luke* 11:13). So ML-J challenged would-be preachers:

> Do you always look for and seek this unction, this anointing before
> preaching? Has this been your greatest concern? . . . Seek Him!
> Seek Him always. But go beyond seeking Him; expect Him. Do you
> expect anything to happen when you get up in a pulpit?[1]

Certainly more is involved here than a preacher simply seeking
special aid when he is about to preach. To pray for the Spirit, without
living and 'walking' in the Spirit, is to treat being a preacher as more
important than being a Christian. If prayer is communion with God
then it belongs to everyday life. An 'anointing' that exists only for times
in the pulpit is most likely to be artificial. Where it is genuine the home
will be sacred as well as the pulpit. The gravity that comes from being
with God, and that marked ML-J's life, is no periodic thing. When
asked if he was not disappointed that he could not preach during the
illness at the close of his life, Lloyd-Jones replied, 'I did not live for
preaching.' In this respect, as in some others, he resembled Thomas
Chalmers, a leading Scots preacher of the nineteenth century, whose
power as a preacher, said James Buchanan, was often misunderstood:
'It lay more in his deep convictions and heart-felt experience as a converted man, than in his natural gifts as a man of genius.'

For Lloyd-Jones 'the greatest thing we ever do is to pray.'[2] While
he drew a veil over his own life of prayer, he encouraged Christians to

---

[1] *Preaching and Preachers*, pp. 305, 325.
[2] 'Praying in the Spirit', *God's Way of Reconciliation*, p. 338.

study the lives of others in this regard. He would have agreed with the judgment of his fellow-countryman, William Williams of Wern, who 'believed there was no real power attainable by any one in the pulpit but through prayer. He considered it the chief thing in all the work of the Church here on earth.'[1]

But he would have added to the last quotation that it is a Person, not power, we are to seek. The way to become a better preacher is to follow Paul in seeking closer fellowship with Christ himself (*Phil.* 3:7-14).

That ML-J regulated his life with priority given to prayer is beyond doubt. Bethan Lloyd-Jones could assert: 'No-one will understand my husband unless they recognise that he was first an evangelist and a man of prayer.' If we knew more of his private praying I do not doubt that there would be found within it something akin to the testimony of another of his contemporaries. Dr C. John Miller of Philadelphia advised fellow preachers: 'We should stay on our knees until we have the assurance that God's love for the "perishing" includes us. Then we can go to the congregation and preach Christ by faith, going as repentant sinners who love God and His people more than we love human approval.'[2]

It is a strange fact, and probably not without a divine reason, that almost nothing has survived of perhaps the most important part of the church services at Aberavon and Westminster in Lloyd-Jones's time. I refer to his leading in public prayer. What an old writer says is very relevant:

> Preaching is only the means of religion; prayer is part of religion
> itself . . . When the devotions of the sanctuary have their proper

---

[1] Owen Jones, *Some of the Great Preachers of Wales* (London: Passmore and Alabaster, 1885), p. 342. The whole book underlines this truth. Henry Rees said: 'We are not aware of the thousandth part of the power praying has upon preaching' (p. 397).

[2] C. John Miller, *Outgrowing the Ingrown Church* (Grand Rapids: Zondervan, 1986), p. 129.

effect, they prepare the hearers to listen with deep and solemn interest to the instructions delivered from the pulpit. Just as far as the prayer, in which they have joined, has brought them to feel the impression of a present God, their minds are divested of listlessness and prejudice.[1]

In public prayer it was hard for those present to resist the conviction that ML-J was speaking to God, and speaking for them. It was not his practice to quote hymns while praying, but one verse, urged familiarly with God as his Father, was often repeated:

> When all things seem against us
> To drive us to despair,
> We know one gate is open,
> One ear will hear our prayer.[2]

For the troubled, the anxious, the doubting, and the guilty, the assurance of being in the presence of God was as profound an experience as they would ever have under preaching.

4. There should be an awareness that Christianity is both a body of truth and doctrine, and a life to be experienced.

If balance is lost between these two things, either in direction of the over-intellectual or the over-experimental, a departure from the New Testament will follow. Lloyd-Jones was addressing this subject at a time when it seemed to be of interest to few others. He adjusted his emphasis in different periods of his ministry according to changes taking place within evangelicalism. Throughout he held to the principle that the subjective and experimental

---

[1] Ebenezer Porter, *Lectures on Homiletics and Preaching* (London: Ward, 1834), p. 99. Porter was president at Andover, America's first theological seminary. His valuable *Letters on Revival* are in print (Edinburgh: Banner of Truth, 2004).

[2] Oswald Allen's hymn, 'Today Thy Mercy Calls Us'.

must never be put first. Mysticism, he warned, does that. It can produce emotional experiences, but 'I must distrust any emotion that I may have within me with respect to God unless it is based solidly upon the Lord Jesus Christ.'[1]

When widespread attention was given to the Holy Spirit in the 1960s ML-J was at first hopeful, as some of his sermons preached in 1963 show.[2] But he saw the danger of putting such emphasis on the Holy Spirit that there follows a greater interest in subjective experience than in the objective truths of the gospel. To his regret the charismatic movement became characterised by its focus on experiences of the Spirit and the gifts of the Spirit. He feared this was repeating 'the tragedy of the Quaker movement', which 'tended to put its exclusive emphasis upon the Spirit and has been ignoring and forgetting the doctrine concerning our Lord and Saviour Jesus Christ.'[3] A pre-occupation with the subjective is not to be regarded as evidence of advanced spirituality.[4] By 1971 he could describe the charismatic movement, and the teaching that 'nothing matters except "the baptism of the Spirit"', as something that 'threatens our whole position as evangelicals.'[5]

The biblical check to aberrations must always be present. What that check is he repeatedly stated in sermons on 1 John: 'We must start always by realising the doctrine, always start with the truth . . . The way the people John wrote to experienced the love of

---

[1] D. M. Lloyd-Jones, *The Love of God: Studies in 1 John*, vol. 4 (Wheaton: Crossway, 1994), p. 145. All 1 John in 1 volume as *Life in Christ* (2002).

[2] See below, pp. 132-133.

[3] *God's Way of Reconciliation*, p. 328.

[4] Occasionally some of his hearers would comment to him on the point in the sermon when they thought he began to know the Spirit's aid. He did not value any such assessments; they were often wrong. Two ministers were once about to begin a service when one of them said to the other, 'The Holy Spirit is not here tonight.' His wiser colleague replied, 'Don't be foolish. You have eaten too much dinner!'

[5] Because 'it undermines the importance of arriving at definitions and descriptions of the faith.' See 'What is an Evangelical?' in *Knowing the Times*, pp. 312-314.

God was in terms of sin, condemnation and loss, and what God has done about it. It is there they found love, and especially in the statements about our Lord's death on the cross.' ML-J believed that, both to unbelievers and believers, the preaching of the love of God in the atonement has to be the most prominent truth in any biblical ministry.[1] At the same time he insisted that belief, which does not lead to experience, is not true Christianity.

5. Chief attention will be given to Christ himself.

The Holy Spirit is given to turn attention to Christ. He glorifies Jesus by empowering faith to see the greatness of the Saviour's person and work. By the Spirit, Christ's indwelling presence is made a conscious reality to faith. And where this happens something more is bound to follow; there will be the deepening awareness of 'the love of Christ that passes knowledge'. This is the sequence that Scripture states in Ephesians 3:16-19 and elsewhere. 'God is love; and he that dwells in love dwells in God, and God in him' (*1 John* 4:16).

The anointing of the Spirit gives assurance of God's love and then makes that love overflow through the messenger. The more there is of such anointing the more the preacher himself will recede into the background and forget himself. The human instrumentality remains, but the 'glory of God in the face of Jesus Christ' is made known through 'earthen vessels, that the excellency of the power may be of God, and not of us' (*2 Cor.* 4:6-7). Where there is unction, it is Christ who is being made known. For the Spirit's

---

[1] In this connection his preaching dealt with the error that Duncan Matheson tells us he fell into as a young Christian: 'My eyes were fixed within myself, and my comfort was drawn from my frames [spiritual moods]. The Spirit's work in me was the ground of my peace and hope, rather than the work of Christ in our room.' John MacPherson, *Life and Labours of Duncan Matheson* (Kilmarnock: Ritchie, n.d.), p. 35.

ministry is to fashion a people who will be like Christ and the preacher's ambition and yearning will harmonise with that purpose: 'Christ in you, the hope of glory: whom we preach, warning every man, and teaching every man in all wisdom; that we may present every man perfect in Christ Jesus' (*Col.* 1:27-28).

Powerful preaching, then, is both Christ-centred and Christ-like preaching. It may at times be with the severity of fire, but its supreme characteristic will be the tenderness and compassion of divine love. The preacher is given a love for people which is Christ's love for them, and he is to be taken up in its reality. Thus preaching, in one sense a 'burden', is overtaken by 'indescribable joy'. Something can happen which fills the preacher with amazement and gratitude, 'longing for the next Sunday to come and looking forward to it eagerly'.

Just as it distorts the ministry of Jonathan Edwards to represent it as chiefly in terms of justice and judgment, so it would falsify Lloyd-Jones's preaching to represent it only as serious and awesome. Certainly he preached with what might be called a 'terrible earnestness' yet the only time I remember seeing tears at Westminster they were tears of joy. That was because 'Love is the greatest thing in religion and if that is forgotten nothing can take its place.'[1] In his own words, 'The hallmark of the saints is their great, increasing concern about the element of love in their lives.'[2]

Lloyd-Jones deplored any discussion of preaching that treated it as an end in itself. The aim of preaching is to help people, and to show them the amazing love of God. And the final test of what is of the Holy Spirit in any ministry is how far there is evidence of the presence of Christ himself. For the God-given purpose of preach-

---

[1] *The Puritans*, p. 187. The words are those of the Calvinistic Methodist hymn writer, William Williams.

[2] *The Love of God*, p. 172.

ing is not preaching about Christ, but that men may so speak in the power of the Holy Spirit that men and women hear his voice and meet with him. This is the transforming difference between preaching with or without unction.

I have referred above to preaching in the 'Methodist' tradition. Another preacher in that tradition was Thomas Cook and an incident in his life well illustrates this mystery of preaching. Cook was an itinerant Methodist preacher who was much used of God in Britain and overseas. On one occasion he was to make a week-end visit to a church, and the Christian home where he was to be given hospitality was full of expectation. There was a maid servant in that house, however, who was not a Christian. She could not understand the fuss in preparation for the preacher, and on going to the butcher's shop to collect the meat on the Saturday morning before his arrival, she declared to the butcher, 'You would think that Jesus Christ was coming.' That Sunday something happened to her under the preaching of this man. When she was in the shop again the next Tuesday, the butcher remembered her irreverence and asked light-heartedly if Jesus Christ had come. With great earnestness the girl replied, 'Yes. He came.'[1]

Let the churches pray for preachers 'full of the Holy Spirit and of faith', and again it will be said:

> How beautiful upon the mountains are the feet of him who
> brings good news, who proclaims peace, who brings good tidings
> of good things, who proclaims salvation, who says to Zion,
> 'Your God reigns!'

---

[1] Quoted in W. E. Sangster, *The Approach to Preaching* (London: Epworth Press, 1951), p. 17. It is regrettable there is no worthy life of Cook. Perhaps the best impression of the man can be found in his book, *Days of God's Right Hand: Our Mission Tour in Australasia and Ceylon* (London: Kelly, 1896).

3

THE EVANGELISTIC USE OF
THE OLD TESTAMENT

It is worthy of thought why, if Bethan Lloyd-Jones regarded her husband as an evangelist, a different impression of him should be more
common. Certainly that description is not usually prominent in any
assessment of his ministry. His memory is associated with expository
preaching or opposition to ecumenism, but hardly with evangelistic
preaching. Yet we think it can be shown that Mrs Lloyd-Jones was
right.

One reason for the common misapprehension is that Lloyd-
Jones's published works have been taken as an accurate represent-
ation of the balance of his ministry. That is not the case, but the
impression has some justification. The demand for evangelistic
sermons for non-Christians is small, compared with material intended
to help believers. Publishers therefore recognised that those who
would seek Lloyd-Jones's sermons in book form would be mostly
Christians and decisions were made accordingly.[1] So, while more
than half his preaching was directly evangelistic,[2] the proportion
that appeared in print has been a great deal smaller. Part, then, of

---

[1] Publishers, however, did not control publication of his work. Until his death
in 1981 ML-J was himself the prime mover over what was published, and thereafter the family took the leading part.

[2] See below, p. 231.

the reason for the misapprehension rests on the bulk of what has been chosen for publication.

But there is another reason. Dr Lloyd-Jones's known opposition to features of modern evangelism led those who wanted to defend those features, and who were uncomfortable under his strictures, to allege that he was 'a teacher, not an evangelist'. In other words, he was not qualified to speak about evangelism. This was an assessment of him which gained some popularity and ML-J has referred to it: 'I have heard that certain people never take their newly converted friends to listen to me, or advise anyone who seems to be under conviction to listen to me. They say it would be too much for them, that they would not be able to follow and so on. Later on, yes, but not at this stage.'[1] During a discussion on evangelism, a critic of his position once challenged him with the question, 'When did you last have a campaign at Westminster Chapel?' The answer, 'I have one every Sunday', was not intended to be humorous. He was referring to his Sunday night service which always had this purpose; a practice he continued from the beginning of his ministry in 1927 until he concluded his pastoral oversight in 1968.[2] Many people became Christians at Westminster Chapel. Like Whitefield's Tabernacle of an earlier day, the place could have been called a 'soul trap'.

The idea that ML-J was not an evangelist no doubt gained some credence from his unwillingness to make any announcement of numbers converted. Indeed, he deliberately avoided any attempt to ascertain that number for himself. It was one of his most deeply held convictions that no public action should be required as a part

[1] *Preaching and Preachers*, p. 127.
[2] 'I urge that there should always be one evangelistic service in connection with each church once a week. I would make this an absolute rule without any hesitation whatsoever.' Ibid., p. 151. As his itinerant preaching was also predominantly evangelistic, as I said above, such preaching constituted at least half of his ministry, and very probably more than half.

of coming to faith in Christ. Converts were never asked to identify themselves publicly. Years might pass before he heard of particular cases and there were many, I am sure, of which he never heard. I was reminded of this a few years ago when I met an old friend of Westminster Chapel days in a country village in Suffolk. Although I was myself close to the work at Westminster in the period of which we began to speak (which was more than thirty years before), it did not surprise me that I had heard nothing of two conversions of which my friend now told me for the first time.

The first concerned his aunt, a worldly woman, twice divorced, who had no time for spiritual things. One Sunday, when my informant was having lunch with her, she asked about his movements for the rest of the day. Hearing that he was going to a chapel, she surprised him by saying that she would come as well. The sermon that night proved to be far from 'appealing' to a non-Christian and about her only comment afterwards was the exclamation, 'I love darkness!' But, unknown to her nephew, she returned alone in succeeding weeks, slipping in at the back of the building, and before long she was brought to hate forever what once she loved so much.

The second case was that of a younger woman who had, in those days, recently arrived from the Continent to study architecture in London. My friend was one of her instructors and, noticing how she was struggling with her English, he took the opportunity to advise her that her language problem would be eased if she could hear more of the best-spoken English, as it might be heard, for example, at Westminster Chapel! She took the advice, though at first with results which were sometimes humorous. It was noted that her vocabulary was being enlarged by the word 'abomination' and other terms equally improbable in modern London! Before long this foreign student came to rejoice in something far more important than better English. Had these and other such testimonies been gathered together years ago they would have made a large book, but it would never have gained the approval of the minister of Westminster Chapel. He assured all who sat under the preaching of the gospel that he would be more than willing to talk privately with any troubled soul. Other than that, he left all in the hands of God.

WHY EVANGELISTIC PREACHING?

ML-J believed that evangelistic preaching ought to exist *as a special category of preaching.* For him, as already said, direct gospel preaching was a main part of preaching and the priority which he gave to it can be seen by the fact that it was his Sunday night evangelistic sermon which he generally wrote in full while he was at Aberavon. Today there is a need to re-establish the recognition that the type of sermon most likely to be used to aid the non-Christian is not the same as one intended for those who already believe. Of course, all true preaching has common elements to it. Preaching is the orderly presentation of the word of God; it must therefore always contain instruction; and it should bring men into the presence of God. But it is a serious mistake to think that, provided the content of a sermon is biblical, the preacher need not be concerned whether his text is likely to be used of God to help the converted or the unconverted. There is too much preaching today which suggests that the preacher has no definite conviction about the persons to whom his text and sermon are primarily intended. Spurgeon warns against this in an address to his students on 'Sermons Likely to Win Souls':

> God the Holy Spirit can convert a soul by any text of Scripture apart from your exposition; but there are certain Scripture pass-

ages, as you know, that are the best to bring before the minds of sinners, and if this is true about your texts, much more is it so in your discourses to your hearers.'[1]

Lloyd-Jones believed, as all evangelists have believed, that there ought to be a distinct difference in the approach of the preacher when he is speaking to the unconverted. For one thing, when a sermon is directed to Christians the existence of some measure of interest can be assumed. But to awaken and hold the attention of the non-Christian is a different matter. Here nothing can be assumed. There may be no real interest at all. Some may be present without any intention of actually listening – mere casual onlookers; and some may mean to listen only to be silent critics. It is no use preparing to address non-Christians as though they were all waiting to hear the word of God. Their real interests presently lie in an altogether different direction, and evangelistic preaching has to break into the world where they are. This was one reason why ML-J regarded the preparation of a true evangelistic sermon as making more demands upon the preacher than any other type of preaching.

But, more important, the evangelistic sermon is a sermon much narrower in its intention than one addressed to Christians. Preaching directed to Christians has to deal with their many and varied needs – it may be of more faith and love, more strength and patience, or whatever. Christians need a wide range of help and instruction. But the non-Christian needs only one thing: he needs to be convicted, to be humbled, to be brought to an end of himself. All preaching ought to be *more* than teaching, but in the case of evangelistic preaching it is imperative. It *must* reach the heart and the conscience or it will fail. It has got to be per-

[1] C. H. Spurgeon, *The Soul-Winner* (London Passmore and Alabaster, 1895), p. 92. See also his chapter 'On Conversion as our Aim' in *Lectures to My Students*, p. 412.

sonal and pointed, and awakening. It may well need something
alarming about it. Men have to be made to face the fact of their
spiritual condition.

Theodore Cuyler, a well-known nineteenth-century preacher
in Brooklyn, on one of his visits to London, was struck by the
question Spurgeon put to him: 'How far do your ablest American ministers aim mainly at the conversion of souls?'[1] We are
not told the answer but we know what it was both in the case of
Spurgeon and of Lloyd-Jones. It may be surprising to note the
large use which Lloyd-Jones made of the Old Testament in the
course of his ministry, and that it was very often an evangelistic
use. In his first pastorate in Aberavon approximately a third of
his texts were taken from the Old Testament. At Westminster
Chapel the percentage was only slightly lower, with around 430
Old Testament texts. These texts were drawn from all over the
Old Testament. When Wilbur M. Smith heard him one Sunday
night in 1955 he tells us that the preacher's text was one that he
had never noticed before. It was Jeremiah 17:14-15 ('Heal me,
O LORD, and I shall be healed; save me, and I shall be saved . . .')
and, as usual on a Sunday night, the sermon was evangelistic.
Smith wrote:

> You cannot hear him preach for three minutes without realising
> that he believes God is speaking in His Word, that the Word is
> infallible, and that what we do with the Word of God will deter-
> mine our eternal destiny . . . I have not heard such preaching for

---

[1] Theodore Cuyler, *The Young Preacher* (London, 1893), p. 76. Alexander Mac-
Rae, commenting on this same subject as it affected Scotland, quotes Lord Over-
ton who, when laying the foundation stone of the Free Church of Scotland at
Fearn, said: 'It is one thing for the Church to be evangelical, and another to be
evangelistic. The Church might be evangelical, and hold sound doctrines, but,
if the Church was not living in Christ, and leading many souls to Him, it might
hold these evangelical truths in vain.' *Revivals in the Highlands and Islands in the 19th
Century* (London, n.d.), p. 16.

years. One thing I determined in my own soul. I would never be satisfied again, as long as I live, with preaching but the very best that I have in deadly earnestness and, pray God, in the power of the Holy Spirit.[1]

It has also to be remembered that as well as the work of his settled ministry, ML-J was constantly preaching in many other places, and here also his use of the Old Testament was striking. When he took a mission at Oxford University in 1943 his main addresses were from Jeremiah 6:14-16. Invited to speak at the International Congress for Reformed Faith and Action in France in 1953, his text was 1 Samuel 5:1-4, with its subject, Dagon, fallen on his face in the temple of the Philistines. One of the most solemn evangelistic sermons he ever preached was at a civic service in Cardiff in 1957. The text was Isaiah 22:8-14, with the words, 'In that day did the Lord GOD of hosts call to weeping, and to mourning, and to baldness, and to girding with sackcloth.'[2] Again, on his very last tours in Scotland and mid-Wales the year before his death, his preaching was supremely evangelistic and was based on the words of Psalm 2. These references are enough to illustrate the extent of his use of the Old Testament but the question is, why did he attach this degree of importance to it? Let me offer two reasons:

1. Because he saw the neglect and near disappearance of the Old Testament as exercising a detrimental influence on contemporary Christianity.

Here was one of the great contrasts between historic Christianity and the ministry of the twentieth century. In the writings of the Reformers or of the Puritans one of the first things which tends

---

[1] Quoted in *Fight of Faith*, p. 330.
[2] These two sermons will be found in D. M. Lloyd-Jones, *Old Testament Evangelistic Sermons* (Edinburgh: Banner of Truth, 1995).

to surprise us is the extent to which they employed the whole Bible. The same is true of such nineteenth-century preachers as Spurgeon. An index exists of all the texts from which Spurgeon preached and it shows that about half of all his texts were from the Old Testament.[1]

A very different position obtained when Dr Lloyd-Jones began his ministry. And today any Old Testament preaching, let alone of an evangelistic nature, is often hard to find. Those of us who preach are probably conscious of our deficiency in this regard. But why should it be? One reason is that we have been living in the after-shock of the assault which was made on the Old Testament by an unbelieving scholarship towards the end of the nineteenth century. At the beginning of the twentieth century the Scottish Presbyterian minister and higher-critic, Professor George Adam Smith, gave eight lectures at Yale which were subsequently published as *Modern Criticism and the Preaching of the Old Testament.* Smith's case was that higher criticism had provided a new understanding of what was dependable in the pages of the Old Testament. Ministers would therefore now be able to discriminate and deal with the Old with more confidence. The result, Smith assured his hearers, could only be beneficial to their preaching. There could not have been a greater delusion. N. L. Walker, reviewing Smith's Yale lectures, said:

> The book is fitted to do a great deal of mischief . . . Written apparently for the purpose of relieving the perplexities of such preachers as have been disturbed by the higher critics, it has unquestionably failed in that aim. Many preachers will continue to have as many difficulties as before. Professor Smith fails to meet the situation. He has done

---

[1] See C. H. Spurgeon, *Commenting & Commentaries* (London: Banner of Truth, 1969), pp. 201-212, lists O.T. texts, and pp. 212-224 those from the N.T.

worse than that. He has awakened doubts where none previously existed and seriously hindered the evangelistic work of the Church.[1]

Walker was more right than he knew. Higher criticism almost silenced the evangelistic use of the Old Testament. Even evangelicals became so conscious of the general disregard for Old Testament Scripture in the modern world that they were to be, in measure at least, inhibited from using it as truth for unbelievers. They were tempted to think that they could hardly speak of Adam and Eve, or of such events as the flood and the parting of the Red Sea, without being a little defensive, if not apologetic.

Perhaps, however, it was chiefly for other reasons that the decline in the use of the Old Testament affected evangelicals. They were so subjected to the cry for the contemporary and the relevant, so pressured by the insistence that modern life, with all its problems, is uniquely different from anything that has gone before, that the fear entered that even the mention of the Old Testament began to sound remote and archaic.[2] And if that fear were not enough to deter, evangelicalism was assailed from within by those who claimed that, in any case, the Old Testament has little to do with Christians: 'The Old Testament was for the Jewish dispensation'; 'There is no grace in the Old Testament', etc.; so we can manage well enough without it. In reflecting on

---

[1] 'The Case of Prof. George Adam Smith' in *The Presbyterian and Reformed Review* (Philadelphia, October 1902), p. 596. I have written further on this in 'The Tragedy of the Free Church of Scotland' in *A Scottish Christian Heritage* (Edinburgh: Banner of Truth, 2006).

[2] A. W. Tozer wrote: 'One of the most popular current errors, and the one out of which springs most of the noisy, blustering religious activity in evangelical circles, is the notion that as times change the church must change with them. That mentality which mistakes Hollywood for the Holy City is too gravely astray to be explained otherwise than as a judicial madness visited upon professing Christians for affronts committed against the Spirit of God.' A. W. Tozer, *Renewed Day by Day: A Daily Devotional* (Camp Hill, PA: Christian Publications, 1980), February 7.

this situation, ML-J once gave an address on 'How Evangelicals unconsciously deny the Word of God.' One of his headings was, 'Too much separation of the O.T. and the N.T.' He spoke of the feeling that the Old Testament has nothing to do with us now, of the failure to see that there is but one over-all covenant of grace, and of how this attitude leads to the ignoring of the Old Testament except as devotional literature.[1]

2. Dr Lloyd-Jones viewed the disuse of the Old Testament as serious because, being an essential part of divine revelation, such neglect is bound to have far-reaching practical consequences.

The Bible is contained in two parts, the first covering the millennia between the creation and c. 400 B.C., the second, the redemptive history of the first century A.D. But these two parts form one whole. In a typical comment on this point, ML-J said:

> This book is one. We call them Old Testament and New Testament, but it is only one book, you know. Some people say this is a library of books; that is a terrible fallacy. This is not a library, this is one book, sixty-six sections in it, but only one book as there is only one theme, one message.[2]

The difference, he would say, lies only in the form in which the message is presented.

So strong was his conviction about this that he says in another place, 'I have never been happy about the practice of printing the two Testaments apart; it leads some people to read only the New Testament.'[3]

---

[1] *Fight of Faith*, p. 388.
[2] On *2 Kings* 5:8–16; February 21, 1950.
[3] D. M. Lloyd-Jones, *Romans: Exposition of Chapters 3:20-4:25, Atonement and Justification* (London: Banner of Truth, 1970), p. 157.

But to understand the practical consequence of the disuse of the Old Testament we have to ask: What is the special purpose of the Old Testament? Why was the revelation before Christ spread through such a long preparatory period? Why did God permit such a delay between the fall of man and the coming of his Son into this world for the work of redemption? Is not the answer that the Old demonstrates at length and in detail that man is in a condition from which only a divine Saviour can deliver him? The Old is a voice crying in a wilderness of sin, 'Prepare ye the way of the LORD' (*Isa.* 40:3). Its purpose is, 'that every mouth may be stopped, and all the world may become guilty before God' (*Rom.* 3:19).

If that is so then we may surely deduce an obvious lesson: to suppose that we can expect to find people ready to take up Christianity, although ignorant of the message of the Old Testament, is to make ourselves wiser than God. Men need to know that it is the Creator of the universe, the Lord of the nations, the God of Abraham and Isaac and Jacob – this God and no other, who so loved the world that he gave his only-begotten Son. B. B. Warfield once wrote an article on 'How to Get Rid of Christianity'.[1] The way it is done, he argued, is this: Evaporate the facts out of the Bible; set aside and ignore the historicity of the narratives; and the result will be that men will see no need for Christianity. They will be left unconcerned and indifferent.

Early in the nineteenth century there were some earnest but poorly instructed missionaries who went to Tahiti in the South Pacific with the thought that the natives were waiting in childlike simplicity for the gospel. They had a terrible shock. But the same error is to be found today where the idea exists that all we need to do is to tell people about Christ and salvation and they will want to

---

[1] John E. Meeter, ed., *Selected Shorter Writings of B. B. Warfield* (Nutley, N.J., 1970), vol. 1, pp. 51-60.

accept him. Were that true there would have been no need of any Old Testament revelation at all. To by-pass the Old Testament is to ignore the fact that men must be awakened to the sinfulness of sin. Where its testimony is unknown we should not be surprised that men remain indifferent, apathetic and unconcerned.

It was inevitable that a mighty change should take place in the Christian world when the Old Testament was no longer faithfully preached. The inevitable consequence was a loss of the sense of sin and of reverence for God. Sometimes witness to this loss was to be heard in unexpected quarters. R. W. Dale was the successor to John Angell James in Birmingham, and to one of the great evangelical pulpits of the nineteenth century. But sadly, Dale was one of the many who abandoned the historic Christian view of the Old Testament. He lived to see the result and before the end of his life he confessed one day to a friend, 'Ah, Rogers, no one fears God now.'[1]

When Dale's confession is taken in conjunction with a statement by W. G. T. Shedd it cannot but be related to what is missing in contemporary Christianity. In a sermon on 'The Use of Fear in Religion', Shedd wrote: 'All the great religious awakenings begin in the dawning of the august and terrible aspects of the Deity upon the popular mind, and they reach their height and happy consummation, in that love and faith for which the antecedent fear has been the preparation.'[2] On the same subject Lloyd-Jones

---

[1] Quoted by G. H. Morrison, *Flood-Tide* (London, Hodder and Stoughton, n.d.), p. 108. Seeking to counter the tide of popular opinion, Morrison spoke of the Old Testament as 'preserved to counteract a natural tendency of man. For God in the Gospel comes so near us, and the love of God shown in the love of Jesus is so brotherlike, that only to realise it is to run the danger of forgetting reverence and growing very familiar with God . . . O living Spirit, open our eyes and give us back again something of the fear of God! For we shall never learn to love or serve Thee well till we have learned to reverence Thee more!'

[2] W. G. T. Shedd, *Sermons to the Natural Man* (1876; Banner of Truth, 1977), p. 331.

noted, 'The importance of keeping your eye on the Old Testament emerges here in the whole question of evangelism and revivals.'[1]

HOW DR LLOYD-JONES CAME TO HIS USE OF THE OLD TESTAMENT IN PREACHING

If neglect of the Old Testament had become common early in the twentieth century, how did it come about that Dr Lloyd-Jones made such major use of the Old Testament in his preaching from the very outset of his ministry? Where did he learn this? Had he observed, perhaps, models of this type of preaching in his childhood which he now began to follow? The answer, very definitely, is, no. In the denomination in which he grew up, and in which he early became a communicant, all were encouraged to regard themselves as Christians. 'It was not', he writes,

> a true assessment of my condition. What I needed was preaching that would convict me of sin and make me see my need, and bring me to true repentance and tell me something about regeneration. But I never heard it. The preaching we had was always based on the assumption that we were all Christians.[2]

Such preaching as he did hear in his youth from the Old Testament was sentimental and moralistic. His own preaching was to be entirely different.

Can it be, then, that he acquired his insight into the evangelistic use of the Old Testament from Christian literature, old or modern? In 1925, the very year when ML-J was struggling over the call of God to the work of the ministry, two articles appeared from the pen of O. T. Allis in the *Princeton Theological Review* entitled

[1] *Romans: The Gospel of God (1:1-32)*, p. 95.
[2] *Preaching and Preachers*, p. 146.

'Old Testament Emphases and Modern Thought'. Speaking of these emphases, Allis wrote:

> The most striking thing about them is the extent to which they are ignored or denied, even by those who call themselves Christians. This fact makes it only the more evident how necessary it is that the minister of the Word should set himself in all earnestness to restore these lost emphases to their rightful place in the faith and life of 'modern' man who needs them no whit less than did the men of yesterday and of years and centuries that are gone.[1]

Can it be that ML-J saw these two fine articles by Allis and was influenced by them? Again, the answer has to be no. It is certain he read and knew nothing of the Princeton theologians in 1925. Nor did he read anything else on the subject which was formative in his thinking. While books were to be a major aid in his future ministry, I believe they played little or no part as far as this issue was concerned. The conclusion has to be that ML-J learned the application of the Old Testament to the unconverted from an entirely different source, and what that source was is patently clear: he saw the history of the Old Testament being repeated in the London of the early 1920s! In those years, as already mentioned, he was on the threshold of what would have been a very eminent career in medicine. He was rubbing shoulders with the successful and the great, with some of the most brilliant medical minds of his day. And through his chief, Sir Thomas Horder, he had access to medical notes and personal observations on kings and prime ministers. What did this experience and information reveal? Why, here was human nature precisely as depicted in the word of God – arrogant, proud, unhappy, covetous, lustful, and dissatisfied. More than that, the testimony of Old Testament Scripture had come powerfully alive in his own conscience. His own heart was 'deceitful above all

[1] *Princeton Theological Review* (Princeton, N. J.), July and October, 1925.

things, and desperately wicked'. He was the fool who thought he could live without God. He was the restless unbeliever, depicted in Psalm 107 who 'wandered in the wilderness in the solitary way' who 'found no city to dwell in'. Then, when like the Psalmist he at last cried unto God in his trouble, God intervened and brought him from darkness into the kingdom of his dear Son.

We know little of the details of Lloyd-Jones's conversion but we know that his new life and his call to the ministry were close to each other. He saw the need of others as soon as he saw his own, and when he went straight from medicine to a mission pulpit it was supremely clear to him that nothing had changed in human nature since the Old Testament was written. Its characters under different names were all alive in Port Talbot. Let the Bible, therefore, be held up like a mirror and, in God's mercy, men would come to see themselves and discover their need of a Saviour. The certainty and authority with which he preached this was born straight out of his own experience.

It was typical of ML-J's view of preaching that in the pulpit he generally said nothing about himself. Yet it is certain he saw himself in the text before he applied it to anyone else, and just occasionally indications of this slip into a sermon. For example, in a sermon preached during 1960 his subject was Naaman, captain of the army of the king of Syria. As described in 2 Kings 5, 'Naaman was a great man . . . a mighty man in valour, but he was a leper.'

Perhaps it can be anticipated how ML-J would handle this. He began by proving that there is always a 'but' in human experience, some trouble, some disappointment, some running sore. No life is whole, unspoiled and complete in happiness and peace. Sin is the universal problem, affecting even the greatest and the most successful; and it is a problem beyond all human remedy. Here are two kings, of Syria and of Israel, and both utterly incapable of finding a solution to Naaman's disease. The problem is too deep for them, 'the disease is too foul for them' and the medicaments are inadequate. But in the midst of human helplessness there came the report of an Israelite kitchen girl who declared that there was a prophet of the living God in Samaria named Elisha. She knew that through him God could recover even the leper. So at length the great Naaman goes to Elisha only to be enraged by the way the prophet treats him. Naaman thinks he is being humiliated and insulted. He will not have a cure on the humbling terms which the prophet proposes.

It is at this point, in a second sermon on the subject, that ML-J becomes most experimental and blazing. Naaman was offended because he received no special treatment, and, said the preacher, 'There are many in this congregation who are in that precise position at this moment.' They dislike the way the gospel treats all alike and gives special attention or respect to none. Naaman was only a leper like any other leper; why should he have special treatment? Because the prophet's message hurts his pride he will not have the cure that is offered:

> Look at this man Naaman. Here he is, a leper, he cannot cure himself, the physicians, wise men and astrologers cannot cure him, his king cannot cure him, the king of Israel cannot cure him and yet, look at the fool, what else can you call him; though he is helpless and hopeless as a leper and everybody can do nothing for him, he is fool enough to criticise what Elisha does and to argue and to put up his objections and protestations. What can you say of the man but that he is a fool and a lunatic?

The preacher is then fairly carried away as he applies the point further both to Naaman and to his unbelieving listeners. All men, he says, are miserable failures yet they have the folly to criticise the salvation which has been sent into the world by God.

But then, after more such words, ML-J allowed a brief and certainly unpremeditated personal reference which speaks volumes: 'You know I am sounding harsh about this man Naaman, I am really very sorry for him because I understand him so well. *I have been in Naaman's position,* like everyone else you see.'[1]

In those words we have the key to his evangelistic preaching from the Old Testament: it came out of his own experience. As with John Bunyan, he preached what he 'smartingly did feel'.

THE CHIEF EMPHASES OF THE OLD TESTAMENT

1. Scripture reveals sin in its true nature.

Lloyd-Jones believed that the difference between moralising preaching on the Old Testament and true evangelistic preaching is that moralising deals only with sin in terms of its symptoms and secondary features. The essence of sin, the true seriousness of sin, can only begin to be understood when it is seen in terms of a wrong relationship and attitude to God himself. Sin is revolt and rebellion against God. It is man asserting his will against God's will. It means defying God, fighting against God, refusing to live for the glory of God. Scripture speaks of man being in a state of 'wrath' against the true God. Preaching on 'Surely the wrath of man shall praise thee' (*Psa.* 76:10), ML-J said:

> Man has turned his back upon God and has enmity in his heart towards God and is trying to live his life in this world without God and apart from God, and he regards God as one who interferes and upsets everything . . . That is what our author means

[1] *Old Testament Evangelistic Sermons*, p. 137.

by referring to the 'wrath of man'. And of course you find this great story unfolded in the pages of the Bible and it is the whole key to the understanding of secular history, man fighting God, man refusing to humble himself before God, and arrogantly and proudly doing the exact opposite, so that what you have in the Bible is an account of the conflict between this glorious God and man in sin.

Unless men are brought to know that, because of the fall their entire relationship to God is wrong, they cannot begin to understand how their problem is to be dealt with. As a point of contact with unconverted hearers, ML-J often introduced sermons by speaking of the various problems of life and of the world. He used them to show that there was something profoundly wrong, but the tragedy of man is that he continues to be blind to the real nature of his problem. He can recognise something of his troubles but he cannot see that his fundamental problem has to do with God himself.

In 1947, at a time when the whole western world was agog with the issue of the atom bomb and the possibility of atomic warfare, ML-J preached two sermons on the conversion of Jacob at Penuel.[1] Here is Jacob, returning to Canaan after his long absence and afraid of the anger of Esau which he deserved. He sees his problem as the threat of Esau and Esau's four hundred men, and so makes his various arrangements to deal, as he hoped, with the danger. But Jacob had to be shown something far more fundamental. He had to be brought to forget all about Esau:

> Jacob discovered there at Penuel that his real problem, if I may put it with reverence, was not Esau, but God. You see this man's primary error was, 'How can I appease Esau?' but what God said was, 'My dear Jacob, what you need is not to be recon-

---

[1] *Old Testament Evangelistic Sermons*, pp. 11-32.

ciled to Esau, but to be reconciled to me', and that, I say, is the essence of the modern difficulty and the modern problem . . . Man was made by God, in the image of God – man was meant for companionship with God . . . The gospel comes to us and makes us see that by living a life apart from God, and apart from Christ, we are living a life which is a travesty of human nature and we are doing something that is utterly insulting to God . . . There is the danger of the atomic bomb – I am not here to say that there is not a danger but, my dear friends, infinitely greater and more important than the danger of being killed perhaps in a few years with an atomic bomb, is this danger that my everlasting and eternal soul may go to hell and spend itself there in misery and torment because I am wrong with God – that is my danger! Esau isn't the problem, the atomic bomb isn't the problem – No, no, you yourself are the problem ultimately, not Esau but God, not Esau but myself, not being what I am meant to be; not land and possessions and goods but the loss of my immortal soul.

This was Dr Lloyd-Jones's starting point and he held it to be the only sound starting point for true evangelism. By one historic fall the whole human race stands alienated from God. This emphasis ran right through his entire ministry. He was constantly bringing his hearers to such questions as these:

Have you ever faced the question of your attitude to God? Are you a rebel against God? Are you a hater of God? Do you feel you know better than God? If so, well, I tell you what you are suffering now is nothing to what you will have to suffer. That is the root cause of all ills and troubles, it is the cause of all suffering, all pain, all confusion. The only hope is to acknowledge it, to face it, to go to God in utter contrition and repentance.[1]

There are two deductions which he constantly made from this starting point:

(i) Sin must never be preached as though it were primarily a matter of actions. Sinfulness is a graver problem than sins. 'The carnal mind is enmity against God' (*Rom.* 8:7). A 'religious' church member who remains self-centred will be as surely lost as the most profligate.

(ii) Until a person comes to know the truth about himself he can never approach the gospel in the right spirit. Without self-knowledge he may investigate, discuss and reason but it will do him no good at all. Because the real need is for a personal meeting with God and until we come to him in submission we cannot come at all. A typical example of the way ML-J insisted on this can be read in his sermon on Moses at the burning bush.[2]

2. Scripture reveals the absolute futility of life without God.

It was Lloyd-Jones's conviction that the gospel itself is not necessarily the main subject in true evangelistic teaching, rather the main subject must often be truth which brings home to men and women their need of the gospel. That was exactly how he saw much of the purpose of Old Testament history. Here is a record of people as individuals and as nations. With one voice they tell us that all human existence is the story of weakness, failure, and death. Man is a feeble, ruined creature whose inner longings can never be satisfied apart from God. Man aims to restore himself and

[1] Sermon on Isaiah 1:1-2; February 3, 1963. See *God's Way Not Ours*, (Edinburgh: Banner of Truth, 1998), which contains a series of nine sermons on Isaiah 1:1-18.
[2] *Old Testament Evangelistic Sermons*, p. 33.

others to paradise but he will never succeed. His hopes of ultimate peace can never be fulfilled. This is what the Holy Spirit proves in Scripture and ML-J saw it as the preacher's calling to prove it too. He never had a problem in moving from an Old Testament character to his own day. It is characteristic of his thinking that when, for instance, he is preaching on Adonijah from 1 Kings 1:41, he asserts, 'What explains the story of Adonijah is precisely the same thing as explains the lives of hundreds of people living at this present time.'

Sometimes he took the history of nations in the Old Testament as declaring the same lesson. Man cannot deal with his problems. The power of Egypt, of the Canaanites, of Babylon, of all the great empires is transitory and soon gone for ever. These great civilisations came up one after another, but they all failed.[1] And the history of Israel itself, far from showing that the chosen people possessed some natural religious genius, as liberals claimed, reveals how men, even when highly privileged, constantly depart from God.

On this subject his preaching in his early days in South Wales shows only one difference from his later preaching in London. In his later ministry he made more direct use of the supporting testimony of modern non-Christians to show the emptiness of all human expectations.

So far was ML-J from being intimidated by the popular idea that the Old Testament was too far behind modern times to speak to us, that he would often meet that argument head-on. He did so memorably in a sermon in 1961, at a time when the world was agog with the news of the Russian cosmonaut, Major Yuri Gagarin, and his first manned flight in space. The text for that sermon was Job chapter 28, verses 12, 28: 'But where shall wisdom

---

[1] *Romans: The Gospel of God (1:1-32)*, p. 84.

be found? and where is the place of understanding? . . . And unto man he said, Behold, the fear of the Lord, that is wisdom; and to depart from evil is understanding.' In the course of developing the interest of his hearers, he conceded that mankind across the centuries had accumulated much information and, alluding to the Russian exploit, confessed that Job had never heard of Major Gagarin. Never heard of him! But then he proceeded to demonstrate that wisdom was a very different thing from mere knowledge or information. What had the modern man really got, what was all his knowledge producing? What is the use of being able to travel from London to New York in five hours if man does not know how to live when he gets there? The modern view of man is that he is just an animal who is in the world to eat or drink or to indulge in sex. It is the part of wisdom to ask, What is life? Where is it leading? How can I put my head down on the pillow and rest in peace, and not be afraid that I am going to die suddenly? How can I look into an unknown eternity? Then the preacher proceeded to prove man's ignorance of God until, at the end of a long sermon, he shut his hearers up to the sure conclusion:

> "The fear of the Lord, that is wisdom." What does this mean? My dear friend, it is as simple as this, you have to submit yourself utterly, entirely, and absolutely to God and his way. There is no wisdom apart from God. Money cannot buy it. You can have it for nothing. It is the free gift of God!

3. Above all else, the Old Testament is a book about God.

Nowhere was his thinking more contrary to the modern view of the Old Testament than at this point. According to the modern view the Old Testament is the story of man's religious development, a record of the Jews' progress of discovery. To say that, ML-J believed, was sure proof of blindness. The Bible is revelation. Its answer to the question, 'Canst thou by searching find out God?' (*Job* 11:7) is an emphatic, No! 'Behold, God is great, and we know him not' (*Job* 36:26). God has come to us and made himself and his will known in Scripture which is his word:

> When men come to the Bible, and find all this history about kings and people, they say, What is the meaning of it all? This is the meaning of it all, it is just to manifest the sovereignty and glory and the might and majesty and the dominion of God. The assertion of the Bible is that God is over all and, whether we like it or not, God will remain over all. The man who does not submit and recognise and accept it joyfully, and glorify God, is the man who sooner or later will be forced to do so.[1]

The purpose of preaching is to confront men with this vision of God, not the gods which the nations have conjectured – 'the gods of the people of the earth, which were the work of the hands of men' (*2 Chron.* 32:19) – but the living God, almighty, infinite and eternal. Our maker, who knows us individually and yet who upholds all things by his power; our sovereign ruler, who has our breath in his hand; our holy judge, whose image we have lost, and to whom we must all soon give an account. Jonathan Sacks, the British Chief Rabbi, wrote that 'God has been exiled by much of our culture. But He exists where we let Him in.'[2] Such words represent a view of God alien to the Bible. Rather, God speaks to us as one altogether above our actions and decisions, and whose will can never fail. Christ charges his disciples to fear God on the grounds that he 'is able to destroy both soul and body in hell' (*Matt.* 10:28). Modern religious man affects to despise a message which comes to us with words of warning and threat but that is precisely how God

---

[1] Psalm 70:10; March 25, 1951.
[2] 'Credo: God exists where we let Him in', *The Times*, May 8, 1993.

addresses us. He spoke in that way before the flood. He spoke in that way before fire fell on Sodom and Gomorrah. He spoke in that way at Sinai and so he continues to speak: 'For the wrath of God is revealed from heaven against all ungodliness and unright-eousness of men' (*Rom.* 1:18). We have wilfully withheld from God the glory which is his due and we all stand deserving of hell.

Lloyd-Jones believed that there can be no true evangelistic preaching where the wrath of God is not being made known. Any such preaching has to be unscriptural. 'In the Old Testament alone more than twenty words are used to describe the wrath of God, and these words in various forms are used 580 times in the Old Testament . . . If you take out of the Bible this idea of the wrath of God against sin there is very little Bible left.'[1]

To hide this truth from men is to hide biblical proof that our present relationship to God is wrong and that it must be changed if we are not to perish. False views of God's character inevitably cause men to misread what Scripture reveals. Thus men turn the Old Testament into a code of ethics, a book calling for our moral effort and endeavour. But to do this is to be blind – as the unbe-lieving Jews were blind – to its greatest and most glorious theme, namely, the acts of God. The Old Testament is divine testimony to redemptive history. So ML-J, preaching from it, can say:

> If we fail to realise that the gospel and all it professes is primarily an activity on the part of God and not on the part of man, we have entirely failed to understand it. Of course, man has something and indeed much to do in the scheme of salvation, but all that is second-ary. Man only begins to act after God has first acted and has rendered man capable of action. What is the Bible after all but an account of God's activity and action in the matter of human salvation.[2]

---

[1] *Romans: Atonement and Justification (3:20-4:25)*, pp. 74, 79.
[2] Port Talbot sermon on Jeremiah 30:18-19.

The preaching of the gospel is not meant to be an appeal to men and women to do something that will make them Christian – it is an announcement, a proclamation to them about something that God has done and that will make them Christian.[1]

For ML-J the rejection of the note of judgment in the Old Testament led inevitably to the suppression of the true glory of redemptive love. From Genesis 3 onwards there is the disclosure of salvation from judgment by the wonderful provision of God: there is a promised substitute; propitiatory sacrifice and 'the blood of sprinkling' – these are the means whereby sinners are to be restored to God at amazing cost. The way of Isaac's deliverance is the only way for us all: 'My son, God will provide himself a lamb for a burnt offering' (*Gen.* 22:8). On this subject a certain Professor Lofthouse wrote earlier in the last century: 'At the present day it must be confessed that to large numbers sacrificial teaching has no appeal at all . . . The evangelical "plan of salvation" strikes them as cumbrous and artificial.'[2] Of course! ML-J would have replied. Men unconvinced of sin will remain disinterested in the gospel. 'They that be whole need not a physician, but they that are sick' (*Matt.* 9:12). The whole position changes when an individual recognises his true condition in the sight of God, when he learns that he cannot save himself, and feels, with Naaman, the leprosy that is destroying him. Let these things be understood and the knowledge of how God can both be just and 'delight in mercy' is life eternal.

For ML-J all the essential elements of the gospel are present in Old Testament revelation. He regarded any idea that the new birth only belongs to the New Testament era as 'thoroughly unscriptural'. Foremost among these elements, and foremost in

[1] Genesis 32:24; April 27, 1947.
[2] Quoted by O. T. Allis in *Princeton Theological Review*, October 1925, p. 600.

his preaching, was that because salvation is the work of God it is something large and vast, something 'which completely and entirely changes us', and something, therefore, which leads men to wonder and amazement. A 'gospel' which merely exhorts men to live a better life, to be good and kind, has no such effect: 'it ceases to be something which breaks in upon us and overwhelms us with its majesty and graciousness. But such is always the effect of the gospel which announces God's action. He amazed Abraham and Jacob and David and the prophets and all the New Testament saints.'

I quote these words from the introduction to one of his most memorable sermons of the 1930s. The text was the words of Jeremiah 30:18-19: 'Thus saith the LORD; Behold, I will bring again the captivity of Jacob's tents, and have mercy on his dwelling places; and the city shall be builded upon her own heap . . .' His divisions of his subject were as follows:

'1. The task with which the gospel is faced.'

Man in ruins, just as Jerusalem was a ruined heap in the time of Jeremiah. All that man was meant to be has been ruined and demolished.

'2. A task with which only the gospel can deal.'

The children of Israel with their city destroyed were captives in Babylon, powerless to help themselves. So too all men are failures, unable to deal with their past, and defeated in the present. They are no more able to renew their own souls than were the Israelites able to rebuild Jerusalem.

'3. The task to which the gospel alone is equal.'

The words of the text were actually fulfilled; God brought the people back, and on the very site and ruins of the old city the new city was built: 'God offers to do the impossible. And he does the impossible. He comes to us and speaks to us in our deepest trouble and woe. He comes to us when we are defeated and helpless and miserable, realising what we have done and our desperate plight. He comes to us and announces what he purposes to do. It is his moment, his action, his initiative. He announces that he is going to work a miracle upon us – "the city shall be builded upon her own heap." He promises us life and joy. Just when we are most unhappy and forlorn the wondrous word comes. How does it come? In and through Jesus Christ, the Son of God.'[1]

To the critic there was an inconsistency in ML-J's gospel preaching. He preached man's inability and absolute dependence upon God but then he speaks of the arms of divine mercy thrown open to all, of the love of God in Christ as ready to embrace all, of an atonement freely offered as a gift for all. But this 'inconsistency' belongs in Scripture itself. Certainly there is a universal love revealed in Scripture and its wonder is not to be belittled. But the love that saves is the love made known to those who, having heard of their lost condition and entire undeservedness, are ready to be saved by grace alone. One type of emphasis in preaching is needed by men unhumbled in their natural pride and another by those who have come to an end of themselves. When it comes to addressing the latter the preacher has to be as unfettered as Scripture is unfettered in the proclamation of salvation to all.

The theorist may analyse such preaching but it was supremely wonderful to those who passed from death to life under its message. This writer will never forget a man sharing the same pew with him at Westminster Chapel one evening and weeping tears of joy at the sense of God's love he had just received. As though to apologise for his emotion, he explained to me that he came from an area where such preaching was not to be heard. True gospel preaching will always leave some saying,

---

[1] For the whole, see *Old Testament Evangelistic Sermons*, pp. 242-254.

How Thou couldst love a wretch like me,

And be the God Thou art,

Is darkness to my intellect

But sunshine to my heart.

From the time Thomas Charles heard Daniel Rowland preach, he tells us, 'I have lived in a new heaven and a new earth . . . my mind was overwhelmed and overpowered with amazement. The truths exhibited to my view appeared too wonderfully gracious to be believed.'[1] Such a God-given experience was known to numbers at Aberavon and Westminster Chapel. Preachers are only as the kitchen maid in Naaman's house who had the answer that others did not know. Lloyd-Jones believed that modern preaching was weak because of a failure in handling 'the sword of the Spirit, which is the word of God' (*Eph.* 6:17); Scripture was not being 'rightly divided', and often because men thought evangelism would be more effective if it did not start where Scripture starts. 'The tragedy is that we do not believe in the power of the Holy Ghost as Paul did. Paul did not ask "will the Romans like this doctrine? I wonder whether, when they see that this is my message, they will stay away!" Paul knew that it all depended upon the power of the Holy Spirit.'[2]

The solution to the present predicament of the churches does not lie simply in a new understanding of preaching. There must be men filled with new faith in the word of God. Lloyd-Jones would have concurred with the words of John H. Leith:

> The recovery of great preaching involves the renewal of faith.
> The origin of preaching is in the heart, not in the head, nor
> in reasoned argument but in the passionate conviction of the

---

[1] D. E. Jenkins, *The Life of Thomas Charles of Bala* (Denbigh, 1910), vol. 1, p. 35.

[2] *Romans, The Gospel of God (1:1-32)*, p. 330.

human heart. Hence preaching is the gift of the Holy Spirit for which we must hope and pray.[1]

[1] J. H. Leith, *From Generation to Generation: The Renewal of the Church According to Its Own Theology and Practice* (Louisville: John Knox Press, 1990), p. 113.

The first of three sides of pulpit notes for ML-J's first 'lecture' in the series on Romans, October 7, 1955.

4

SKELETONS IN THE CUPBOARD

'**B**e sure you tell everything', and 'Leave out nothing', were counsels I sometimes received while working on the concluding volume of the biography of Dr Lloyd-Jones. That work completed, I now reflect on the various areas in which I have fallen short and one thing especially occurs to me. The reader of the biography may too easily miss the skeletons which lay behind his ministry. That they existed I do point out in the biography, but their number—not only in cupboards but in desk drawers and in his pockets—and the way they affected his entire pulpit ministry is all-too-little explained. In the case of preachers (and lest there be any mistake, it is their kind of 'skeletons' to which I here refer) this omission could well be a real loss.

A dictionary gives the following as one of the ordinary meanings of skeleton: 'The supporting framework of anything; the principal parts which support anything, but without the appendages.' Transferring this to the world of preaching, a skeleton is the initial plan or outline of what is to be the finished sermon. 'The sermoniser should uniformly have a plan before beginning to compose', writes W. G. T. Shedd; 'skeletonising is to sermonising what drawing is to painting', and he proceeds to illustrate that from the work of Michelangelo. All the great works of art, Shedd argues, began with simple outline sketches.[1]

There are special reasons why the skeletons in Dr Lloyd-Jones's cupboard are likely to be ignored. Firstly, Shedd's words are not taken very seriously these days. Interest in skeletons is out of fashion. They conjure up impressions of dry, old things which we can do without. But more than that, it is possible for some to make the mistake of thinking that ML-J himself was no patron of skeletons on the grounds that they were not obvious in the sermons and addresses which he delivered. Such a supposition is based on a fallacy. It is only a *bad* skeleton, of the type which sets the congregation wondering how long it will be till the preacher announces his last 'head', which is obvious. The choice is not between bad skeletons or no skeletons. Dr Lloyd-Jones's skeletons were certainly not obvious yet they were there, and they controlled the shape and structure of every message. As in the preaching of Archibald Alexander, it could be said of him that in his sermons there were 'the steel links of reasoning red with the ardours of burning love'.

Perhaps Dr Lloyd-Jones himself contributed to a mistake about preaching. While balance was the key-note of most of his thinking, when it came to preaching it has to be admitted that he was inclined to speak to fellow ministers as though virtually nothing mattered in preaching save the anointing of the Holy Spirit upon the message. That was his supreme concern. He spoke much more of preparing *men* than he did of preparing sermons. He abominated the idea of preachers as professional communicators and books with such titles as *The Craft of Sermon Construction* did not have his sympathy.

I do not mean that he ignored speaking of the practical side of sermon preparation in his counsel to others. He did not. He

[1] W. G. T. Shedd, *Homiletics and Pastoral Theology*, (London: Banner of Truth, 1965), pp. 185-186.

could say, and the words ought to be marked, 'The Spirit generally uses a man's best preparation.'[1] And in his very valuable address on 'What is Preaching?' he speaks of the importance of the *form* of the sermon.[2] Yet his overall emphasis was so strongly on the *spirit* of the preaching that one could too easily fail to realise the immense amount of sheer work that went into his own preparation of sermons. Basic to that hard work were his skeletons and for him they represented the most creative part of all his work.

To clarify this subject further it must be said at once that a skeleton is not necessarily the same as the sermon notes which most preachers take with them into the pulpit. They were not the same in ML-J's case. Through the last thirty or more years of his life he usually had some four sides of notes with him in the pulpit. These notes came far short of being a full manuscript of the sermon to be preached, but they were usually an enlargement of his skeleton. The skeleton had come first. The pulpit notes were the second stage. The skeleton was often in pencil and on all kinds of scraps of paper. The notes, at least from the early 1950s, were commonly in ink and standardised on sheets of paper some 8 inches by 5 when folded. Once he had the skeleton, the hardest part, in his view, of the preparation was done. Further meditation and writing would fill out the main thoughts but the real substance of what he meant to say, and what his hearers would carry away, was all on that initial scrap of paper.

Some of his surviving skeletons were probably never used as they stood in their first draft. On Judges 2:10 he has no less than

---

[1] D. M. Lloyd-Jones, T*he Christian Soldier: Ephesians 6:10-20*, (Edinburgh: Banner of Truth, 1977), p. 135. 'The men whom God has used signally have been those who have studied most, known their Scriptures best, and given time to preparation.'

[2] *Knowing the Times*, 1989, p. 270. Perhaps I should not assume that all ministers reading these lines will have studied *Preaching and Preachers* (1971), possibly his greatest work. Note his words on skeletons on p. 173 of that volume.

four outlines. The text reads: 'And also all that generation were gathered unto their fathers: and there arose another generation after them, which knew not the LORD, nor yet the works which he had done for Israel.' Parts of his first outline on this text are illegible but these were his main heads:

Why things are as they are
Explanation
   1. Cannot live on tradition or history
   2. Knowing about these things . . . They are of value . . .
      but only as we use them correctly
   3. The real trouble is the lack of knowledge of God
            His greatness and glory
            His judgment and power
            His great and glorious salvation

A second outline on the same text shows a good deal of change:

   1. Without knowledge of God history and tradition soon die
      Cannot live on tradition . . . Why? . . .
   2. Value of history
   3. Great lesson of history – Knowledge of God alone matters
      God's character – in greatness and glory. Living God. Acting.
      God's plan and purpose . . . plan of salvation . . .
      God's power and certainty of fulfillment of plan
      God's holiness and justice and anger
      God's pity and mercy and compassion
   4. Conclusion
      God still the same
      Humbling and repentance
      Utter submission to Him and His Word
      Crying out unto Him for deliverance and looking to Him expectantly

One can see the same process of development in many of his surviving papers. A first rough draft on the Tower of Babel (*Gen.* 11) reads:

Man in confusion today. Why? Bible alone gives the
  explanation.
Man's ultimate trouble is pride. This is cause of his original Fall.
  Same ever since.
1. Man in sin always believes he can be equal with God and
  replace God.
2. Also believes he can achieve safety, happiness and security
  by his own effort.
3. This always leads to disaster and confusion.
Lessons
The tragic folly of this:
    Not realising greatness of God.
    Not realising trouble about himself and his place in creation.
    Not realising that God offers all this and infinitely more.
The only way to reach heaven—Christ.
    The city, heavenly Jerusalem.

Often his outline might include reference to hymns or to a secular author from whom he noted a relevant quotation. In the above case he had scribbled in a corner the striking words of Dostoevsky: 'All the framers of social systems, from the remotest times up to the present year 187–, have been dreamers, tellers of fairy tales, simpletons who contradict themselves and know nothing of natural science and that strange animal called man.' Other quotations written in the margin of the same notes were these: 'Social systems which have no Christian basis (the only one capable of transforming man) inevitably become systems of violence and slavery.' And, 'Man is only an organ stop under the fingers of nature.' One can imagine the use he made of the latter words!

On Hebrews 13:8: 'Jesus Christ the same yesterday, and to day, and for ever', there are three different sets of outlines. Behind one of these sets there are a further two skeletons, offering different divisions of the text. The one that he settled for and subsequently elaborated for his final notes reads:

1. The changing scenes of time

     Yesterday: Superficial . . .

     Actual . . .

     Today: Superficial . . .

     Actual . . .

2. The unchanging task of the Church

3. The changeless Christ

     The one thing of which we can be certain –

          the Eternal Son of God.

In the elaborated form of this skeleton he added further points which make clear what he meant to cover in the past and present under the words 'superficial' and 'actual'. A hundred years earlier, he argued, the actual situation was worse than the superficial appearance. But today, with empty churches and a seemingly hopeless situation, the actual situation, with permissiveness, irrationalism and lawlessness, gave clearer support to the *truth* of the word of God than did the superficial religion of the Victorian age.

I must proceed now to give some reasons for the importance of the practice of skeletonising.

1. This is preparation that can be done at any time and in any place. Nothing more than a pencil and a scrap of paper is needed. No-one has ever been a great preacher or a greatly used preacher without living for preaching. A man sent to preach is a man whose mind is constantly turning to this one thing. Having lived with the work of writing Dr Lloyd-Jones's biography for several years there is nothing clearer to me than the fact that this was eminently true in his case. Once, for example, as he was dressing and preparing to shave one morning, several thoughts came strongly to him for a series which was subsequently published as *Spiritual Depression: Its Causes and Cure.* He immediately hurried down to his study and put down those first thoughts. Again, I recall meeting him alighting from a train which had just arrived in Edinburgh one cold night in April 1977. He was elderly and at the end of a long journey from London. When it was announced that the train was over an hour late I anticipated seeing a rather weary traveller late that evening. But not at all! He approached the ticket barrier where I was standing with his usual firm quick step, and was soon telling me how in enjoying working on the skeleton outline of a new sermon on 1 Timothy 3:15 he had scarcely noticed the time. I was so surprised I did not ask him for his 'heads', but I have since read them among his papers. Of course, by the 1970s, with a lifetime of preaching behind him, ML-J had no need to work on new sermons. But the practice had long since become such a central part of his life that he continued it almost until the end.

2. A clear skeleton is easily memorised and Dr Lloyd-Jones had his outline very clearly in his mind. As I have said, he often carried somewhat fuller notes with him into the pulpit but he was never dependent upon them. When his daughters were studying away from home he would very often in weekly letters to them give the outline of his morning and evening sermons of the previous Sunday. He was not copying from his notes but giving what was clearly fixed in his mind. In 1972 he was asked to speak at the Jubilee Assembly of the Fellowship of Independent Evangelical Churches. For this he prepared a new address, in part historical and in part expository. Shortly before he rose to speak on this rather special occasion, he discovered that his notes of what he had to deliver were not in his inside jacket pocket where he believed he had put them. I rather think that a deacon was sent to search his vestry desk (for the meetings were being held at Westminster Chapel) but the notes were not there and so he had to proceed to speak without them. Even he had some misgivings on that occasion but his method of preparation carried him through with no-one noticing anything amiss. Apart from getting one heading in the wrong order, he spoke freely from the outline which he knew by heart.

3. A logical outline has a great deal to do with simplicity in preaching. Simplicity is a very different thing from superficiality. ML-J's preaching enabled the hearer to carry an argument in his mind that was invariably clear. In part, of course, this is due to natural gift. Yet it was also due to the hard work which had gone into his first outline. The whole message was shaped and structured according to a few leading ideas which were logically connected and which carried the subject through to a very definite conclusion. It was sometimes said that he spoke more as a barrister than as a preacher. ML-J believed that Paul was the true model in this regard. Some preachers, he said,

> are difficult to follow because their sermons lack a scheme and order and arrangement. Other preachers are logical; they start with an introduction, then proceed to a first point, which leads in turn to a second point and to a third point, and finally to a climax and conclusion. The Apostle Paul certainly belonged to the second class.[1]

[1] D. M. Lloyd-Jones, *Romans: Exposition of Chapter 5, Assurance* (London: Banner of Truth, 1971), p. 174.

In another place he says that in Paul logic and eloquence are wedded together, and comments:

> There are foolish people who think that the moment you enter the realm of logic you have departed from eloquence. But that is not so . . . Indeed I would suggest that you can never be truly eloquent unless you are logical. You cannot be eloquent about nothing.[1]

Far more than is commonly realised, one of the main factors which make too many sermons hard to listen to is that they come from preachers whose cupboards are bare of the right kind of skeletons. When preaching loses confidence in the plain word of God it tends to be dressed up in fine phrases or telling anecdotes. These things were not to be found in Dr Lloyd-Jones's sermons. He handled the Bible as one who believed it utterly, and his one concern for the content of his sermons was that biblical principles should be set out and organised with compelling clarity.

Elsewhere in these pages I compare Lloyd-Jones and Spurgeon. As preachers they differed considerably yet on the question of the place of divisions in a sermon they teach the same lesson. Speaking of his Nonconformist contemporary, J. C. Ryle once wrote: 'I am not a bit ashamed to say I often read the sermons of Mr Spurgeon . . . We ought always to examine and analyse sermons which draw people together. Now when you read Mr Spurgeon's sermons, note how clearly and perspicuously he divides a sermon, and fills each division with beautiful and simple ideas. How easily you grasp his meaning!'[2]

I personally believe that it would be a great aid to ministers if a number of Dr Lloyd-Jones's outlines could be published – not for

---

[1] Ibid., p. 141.
[2] J. C. Ryle, 'Simplicity in Preaching' in *The Upper Room* (repr. Edinburgh: Banner of Truth, 2006), p. 42.

anyone else to attempt to use them but because they would show how he set about sermon-making.

I close with two more examples from ML-J's papers. When he was in the United States in 1969 more than one of his hearers testified to the powerful effect that was wrought by a sermon on 1 Corinthians 3:18-20: 'Let no man deceive himself. If any man among you seemeth to be wise in this world, let him become a fool, that he may be wise . . .' It was apparently preached from a one-and-a-half page outline which is beside me as I write. I think it was newly prepared in 1969, though as he drew it up he had with him notes of a sermon he had preached at Westminster Chapel on a parallel theme in 1 Corinthians chapter 2. Here are the main points of his outline:

Men's Wisdom

    1. Starts with man – humanism, sociology.

    2. Thinks problem is mainly intellectual.

       H. G. Wells and education. Gilbert Murray.

    3. Its view of man:

       His nature – developing. Not really bad. No sin.

       Wants good and ready to listen to it and respond to it.

    4. Man's need – Help.

       To be informed. Instruct by teaching and example.

       Change of environment from poverty and slums.[1]

    5. Man's inability to help himself.

       Has it in him. His power of decision. His mind.

       His will power.

       Good works and his own righteousness.

---

[1] His notes show that in revising this outline this fourth point was dropped and incorporated into his next point.

God's wisdom

1. Starts with God – all is from Him.
2. Problem much deeper than that of intellect and
      knowledge – at centre of personality. All wrong.
3. View of man:

   Fallen. Evil. Perverted. Rom. 7:14. At enmity against
      God. John 3:19. Hateful and hating one-another.

   Guilty under wrath of God. Dead and completely helpless.
4. Men's need.

   Forgiveness and reconciliation.

   New birth and nature.

   'Create within me a clean heart O God and renew . . .'
5. Way of salvation.

   Men completely helpless.

   Righteousness as filthy rags. Dung and dross.

   Salvation all of God.

What God does for us in Christ

   Miracle. All the exact opposite of what we expect: Christ's birth,
      occupation, death on cross.

   This needed by all and offered to all.

   This ridicules men's wisdom. It is wrong in theory and practice.

   Wrong about man, his need and ability; wrong about God.

   God's wisdom works and holds out hope for all.

   Men's wisdom seen to be most foolish when it rejects this . . .

   [illegible words follow and a reference to Matthew 11:25].

Only thing to do

   Recognise folly.

   Submit to this.

   Become a fool as Paul had.

Even in this mere outline form we can surely understand why, in hearing it, a woman wept unashamedly and said to Mrs Lloyd-Jones afterwards: 'That is an experience I shall never forget. I can't tell you what it has meant to me.'

Where the truth of God is concerned even bare bones have power! One dictionary I have consulted gives us the saying, 'No skeleton is allowed to remain peacefully in his cupboard.' Those of Martyn Lloyd-Jones certainly did not! They have now done their work but as God is pleased to bless his word in the future we may be sure that something very like them will be seen and felt again in the future.

Let the final word be from another outline, written in pencil on the text, 2 Kings 13:21: 'And it came to pass, as they were burying a man, that, behold, they spied a band of men; and they cast the man into the sepulchre of Elisha: and when the man was let down, and touched the bones of Elisha, he revived, and stood up on his feet.'

Elisha's Bones

Strange and extraordinary event. Accident. Obviously full of meaning.

1. To rebuke Israel for her condition.
    Weak and fearful and hopeless.
    Why – Disobedience. v. 2-3; 6-7; 11.
    Lack of faith. Now: Truth, Life, Lack of Faith.

2. To remind them of the glorious past.
    v. 23, Abraham, Isaac and Jacob. Covenant. Defeat of
        Moabites.
    Chap. 6, Syrians – Dothan.
    Chap. 4, Naaman. Same in 1904-5.

3. To teach them that it was not Elisha.

    v. 14. Our danger with E. R. [Evan Roberts]

4. To remind them of what He could still do.

    Passing of years makes no difference – or changed circumstances or conditions.

5. What He does.

    Life to the dead.

6. What we need.

    Elisha's spirit.

    Elisha's faith.

    Elisha's obedience.

But – and, to me, this is the thing that Whitefield tells us more than anything else – orthodoxy is not enough . . . To state the Truth is not enough, it must be stated 'in demonstration of the Spirit and of power'. And that is what this mighty man so gloriously illustrates. He was orthodox, but the thing that produced the phenomenon was the power of the Spirit upon him . . .

This power of the Spirit is essential. We must be orthodox, but God forbid us to rest even on orthodoxy. We must seek the power of the Spirit that was given to George Whitefield. That will give us a sorrow for souls and a concern for souls, and give us the zeal, and enable us to preach with power and conviction to all classes and kinds of men.

ML-J

'JOHN CALVIN AND GEORGE WHITEFIELD'

THE PURITANS: THEIR ORIGINS AND SUCCESSORS, pp. 126-127.

5

RAISING THE STANDARD OF PREACHING

NOTES OF A MEMORABLE ADDRESS

[Dr Lloyd-Jones preached for the last time as minister of Westminster Chapel on Friday, March 1, 1968. Illness (from which he recovered after surgery) then led to his retirement from that pastoral charge. But among the labours that he continued thereafter was his chairmanship of the Westminster Fellowship of ministers, and, on resuming public ministry one of his first engagements was at the Fellowship, meeting at Westminster Chapel on October 9, 1968. In the intervening months he had heard preachers in different places and of different denominations, some of them no doubt men who attended the Fellowship. As with a number of ML-J's addresses no record of this one was taken, by tape or shorthand, and what follows are only my hurried notes as a hearer. Even in this fragmentary form I believe they are worthy of preservation. The meeting was packed; love and thankfulness for the speaker were the paramount feelings, and his rousing words were long to be remembered by all who were there. The title above is my own and no subject was given in advance of the meeting.]

Dr Lloyd-Jones began by apologizing for the interruption to his presence at the Fellowship, although 'it had been beyond my control'. He would say only one thing about his operation. Before that he had enjoyed remarkable health, and he had found it difficult to visualise what one would be like when taken ill. 'I think I now know "the peace of God that passeth all understanding" as a very real thing. Something that cannot be put into words was given me in a way I shall never forget as long as I live. On the negative side, I have to confess, I wondered afterwards why I did not feel as Paul a "desire to depart and to be with Christ". It wasn't that I was craving to live, but looking back on it, there was a lack there. I knew I was going to get well. It seems to me I should have known something of that other aspect in facing death – a spirit of expectation. I regard the absence of that as a deficiency. Our relation to our Lord should make it otherwise. We should not be waiting for things to happen, for death to come; we should be preparing.' He endorsed the words of a minister dying from tuberculosis who urged those around him to love God with all their *strength*, for when illness comes strength is gone. 'We become too weak to read, even the Scriptures. We must use our strength, and lay up reserves for the day of trial.

'Our danger is to be victims of our routine, to get carried away by the momentum of the work. We need reminders of the words of Edmund Burke. In the midst of a parliamentary election campaign at Bristol, Burke was about to rise and speak when he was told that his opponent in the election had suddenly died: "What phantoms we are, and what phantoms we pursue!"

'Another thing has concerned me in these last months. The point at which my ministry was interrupted had a message for me. I was preaching on Romans 14:17, "For the kingdom of God is not meat and drink; but righteousness, and peace, and joy in the Holy Ghost." I had dealt with "righteousness, and peace" [the

latter on March 1], and there I was stopped. I was not allowed
to deal with "joy in the Holy Ghost". I have a feeling it was not
accidental. God intervened and I could suggest a reason why.
I was able to deal with "righteousness, and peace" (I had a fleet-
ing experience of it), but the third thing is the profoundest of all.
Why was I not allowed to deal with "joy in the Holy Ghost"?
Because I knew something, but not enough about it. As though
God said, "I want you to speak with greater authority on this."

'I am convinced this is the most important thing of all and it
leads me to what I want to put before you. For six months, until
September, I did not preach at all. I have been a listener and it
has been a most valuable experience. As a listener, through four of
those months, my general impression is that for people outside our
churches most of our services are terribly depressing! I am amazed
people still go. Most who do go are females, over the age of forty,
and I feel they go out of duty; some, perhaps, have the opportunity
to be important in their little spheres. There is nothing to make a
stranger feel he is missing something – instead he finds this awful
weight! And the minister, feeling this, thinks he must be short; thus
people come together in order to depart. I am speaking generally
about the churches, but in this respect there is very little difference
in evangelical churches.

'It is a great thing to be a listener. You want something for
your soul, you want help. I don't want a great sermon. I want to
feel the presence of God – that I am worshipping him, and considering something great and glorious. If I do get that I do not care
how poor the sermon is.

'I suggest to you that our greatest danger is the danger of
professionalism. We do not stop sufficiently frequently to ask ourselves what we are really doing. The danger is of just facing a text,
and treating it as an end in itself, with a strange detachment. Far
away from London, and in an Anglican church, we heard a vicar

preach on the words of Jeremiah 20:9 "Then I said, I will not make mention of him, nor speak any more in his name. But his word was in mine heart as a burning fire shut up in my bones, and I was weary with forbearing, and I could not stay." The preacher had taken great trouble preparing the sermon; it was well arranged, there was form to it; the one thing that was not there was *fire*. It was a cold douche. No-one could possibly go out of that service on fire! The preacher could not have asked himself, "What is this fire and is it for me?" Instead of asking such a question, he had just prepared a sermon and the vital thing was not there.

'You may think I was listening as a critic, I was not. At another location I heard a sermon on Galatians 3:1: "O foolish Galatians, who hath bewitched you, that ye should not obey the truth, before whose eyes Jesus Christ hath been evidently set forth, crucified among you?" We were told a lot about "bewitching", and the sermon was about things that could and do side-track us; but I was astounded that the preacher did not see the main thing in the text – these Galatians turned from this glorious thing, Jesus Christ who had been placarded before them. This is what we must be talking about!

'We can miss the wood because of the trees and lose the glory of the gospel. Our business is to send people away with the most glorious thing in the universe. This applies to people who come regularly. There is no hope of attracting outsiders while those inside are as they are. Those outside are already depressed, and, if not, they will soon be.

'One of the things of encouragement to me was a visit to a London church. Many who are not evangelicals say that the only thing to get people into church is to talk about things people are interested in – the war in Biafra and so on. I can testify from experience it isn't true. I went to hear Howard Williams, who is boosted by the Baptist Union and television as a man that "deals with practical problems" and "attracts thinking people". He has "one of the best pitches in London", yet I saw only 120 people. He had not many "thinking people" there that night! I came from there really encouraged. The people know it is useless. We have nothing to worry about with liberalism; it is dead and finished.

'Here is a wonderful opportunity for us. Well, what is wrong with us? Our approach is wrong. They [liberals] start with what people are interested in; our danger is to forget people altogether. Our ideas, and the results of our preaching, suggest we haven't thought about the people at all. We are too objective. (I am tired of hearing sermons about 'the church', denouncing the World Council of Churches, etc). Once evangelical preaching was too subjective; now it is too objective. This leads to a mechanical approach to preaching.

'I believe in a series [of sermons] but it can be done in the wrong way – not taking into account the state of the people listening, so that although we may deal with a passage excellently, there is no message for them. There is a difference between a running commentary on a passage and a sermon. I believe in expository sermons, not a running commentary. What is the difference?

'A sermon has a form about it; it has a message to be applied. This is much more difficult than a running commentary (I am not sure the latter even has a message). The concern of a preacher should be to have a *message* and he must labour to put it into the best form in which it can be delivered. This was the glory of a man like Charles Haddon Spurgeon. His sermons had form, thrust, and the impact of a message. *A running commentary is not a sermon*. The whole notion of a message – 'the burden of the Lord' – needs to be recaptured. There ought to be an impact; whereas just to give an 'exposition', in which no message comes through, is to make preaching intellectual only. Nor should it be just emotional – too often it is either one or other of these. No life! No power! We of all people ought to have it. And joy and power are intimately related, one without the other is spurious.

'The opposite of sociological preaching is not this running commentary. People say "It is biblical." It is not. Biblical preaching brings out a message. A mechanical explanation of the meaning of words – not fused into a message with point and power that leaves hearers glorying in God – is not preaching. It is not enough to make an affirmation of Christian truth; it may be heard as just one view against another. *We have got to bring a message.*

'Surely we have got to have "the demonstration of the Spirit and of power"! This is our greatest need of all, and I do not separate it from joy. Look at Robert M'Cheyne: what he knew is what ultimately counts. He had the burden of his people on his soul. He did not come to the pulpit having simply prepared a sermon. He came from God with a message.

'The time has arrived when we must assess the whole situation. It is entirely wrong to take *our* problems to the people; we have got to preach what is most profitable for them, what is really going to help them. The main problem of evangelicalism today (apart from slipping away from truth) is the lack of power – what do our people know of "joy in the Holy Ghost"? You will not win people to teaching if you are a dull teacher! The wife of a deacon said to me about someone she had heard, "He is unlike many of our Reformed preachers who are so dull." If you preach without moving people you have failed as much as others. If we do not know the joy of the Lord what is the value of what we say? We must start with ourselves. To hear of "excellent lectures on doctrine" being given on a Sunday night is truly appalling. Are you right in assuming those in front of you are enjoying the Christian life, and that they are able to convict others? These two things go together. Arguing about niceties will not help us. What is the value of anything if we are not "living epistles"?

'I have been giving you my experience, as a patient and as a common listener. I have been passing through a period of self-examination and I can thank God for giving me a pause to enable me to do this. What remains of life and vigour I am determined to use to bring out this particular aspect. Without this the situation is hopeless. It is not hopeless, but we must start with ourselves. Do I know anything of this fire and, if not, what am I doing in the pulpit?'

In discussion that followed this address, questions came up and additional comment from ML-J. One defect in his preaching, he believed, was that it had sometimes been too demanding in its content, and he spoke of two occasions when he had been corrected by older men for this fault. 'I shall have one point, and state it in three ways', he was told by an older friend with whom he was sharing services in his early ministry. The danger lay in preaching that addresses the mind and not the whole man. 'We must diagnose both ourselves and our people. If we cannot assess the condition of our people we have failed as preachers. I wasn't always a long preacher; we must bring the people up to it. The old preachers knew this; they were great exhorters.

'We are to be like a mother feeding her child: she studies both the food and the amount. There is nobody hopeless; all can grasp doctrines. But we have got to cook it well, and make it as attractive as we can. Use history and anecdotes as illustrations – I reacted too much against them – but in the right amount.'

During the above comments, he added in passing, 'I am not sure my progeny have been a credit to me, or whether they reflect a defect in me.'

'I am also troubled about our praying, and what passes as prayer. Prayer should not be a confession of faith – a recital of doctrine; that is spiritual poverty. No, in prayer, we are to assume all this doctrine.'

105

On the nature of sermons, he went on to say: 'There should be an element of concealment in effective preaching. When a farmer is going to buy cattle in a market, the ones that attract him are those where the skeletons are not showing.' Similarly, sermons should not show a preacher's reading; it is a 'fatal defect' for a preacher not to *assimilate* his reading. Rather it should 'pass through him' so that it comes out as a new thing. Some men, he feared, read the Puritans and then transmitted their reading like gramophone records. 'Don't read to get preaching material; reading is first to feed me, and to make me think originally.' Sermon preparation is 'a trying process. The hardest part of a minister's work is the preparation of sermons. That is why I feel so well at the moment; I do not prepare three sermons a week. There is an agony, an act of creation, in preparation. The burden of a sermon has to involve the whole of my personality.'

A medical specialist in Cardiff once said to ML-J that he had a problem over his preaching. It was how unconverted people could evidently enjoy it. This was no puzzle to ML-J: 'They are attracted by the presentation, and that should be attractive (as Whitefield's preaching was to Benjamin Franklin). Let us present the sermon the best we can – the best language, the best of everything. We have got the curious notion, "It's the doctrine that matters", and ignore this. With the message we have got, it is tragic if we can be cold, lifeless, and dull.'

With prayer and the announcement that the next meeting would be on the first Monday of November (1968), the meeting closed. Dr Lloyd-Jones was to chair the Fellowship for another eleven years, doing so for the last time on December 3, 1979.

The congregation of Westminster Chapel on a
cold December Sunday morning in the 1960s.

THE FUNERAL OF C. H. SPURGEON, FEBRUARY 11, 1892

Books written for the Master and his truth, though buried in obscurity are sure of a resurrection. Fifty years ago our old Puritan authors, yellow with age, and arrayed in dingy bindings, wandered about in sheep-skins and goat-skins, destitute, afflicted, tormented, but they have been brought forth in new editions, every library is enriched with them, the most powerful religious thought is affected by their utterances, and will be to the end of time. You cannot kill a good man's work . . . Deeds done in the power of the Spirit are eternal . . . Oh, the joy of knowing, when you are gone, the truth you preached is living still.

C. H. SPURGEON
METROPOLITAN TABERNACLE PULPIT,
1875, vol. 21, p. 119.

6

LLOYD-JONES AND SPURGEON COMPARED

There is a type of comparison-making which is condemned in Scripture. Paul said of some in Corinth, 'But when they measure themselves by one another, and compare themselves with one another, they are without understanding' (*2 Cor.* 10:12). It is no more our calling to adjudicate the relative positions of servants in the kingdom of God than it was that of the mother of the sons of Zebedee (*Matt.* 20:21). But the comparison I have in mind is of a different kind.

One reason that Lloyd-Jones said little about himself in speaking on the subject of the ministry was that he was afraid of implying that his life and programme should be a pattern for others. 'I am', he asserted, 'an opponent of universal set rules for all'; and that because men differ widely in temperament, nature, and constitution. He concluded, 'Nothing is more important than that a man should get to know himself.'[1] But if Lloyd-Jones was so used of God, would it not be the part of wisdom for men to imitate him as closely at they can? Not at all, for men equally used of God have not resembled him in a number of respects. 'Know yourself' is a primary axiom; or, in the language of Scripture, 'I say to

---

[1] *Preaching and Preachers*, p. 167.

everyone among you not to think of himself more highly than he ought to think, but to think with sober judgment, each according to the measure of faith that God has assigned' (*Rom.*12:3). On which William Plummer comments, 'We should know and understand what our endowments are and what they are not.' The God who has so varied creation has also varied leaders in his kingdom, and to compare them, and notice the differences between them, can be a healthy way of understanding the importance of individuality. After God makes a man, said Spurgeon, he breaks the mould; there are no genuine replicas. It was not entirely healthy 'that as a preacher Spurgeon set the model for hundreds of pulpits throughout the civilised world.'[1]

A comparison between eminent men should also bring home the truth that 'the best of men are men at best'. They not only differ in their gifts but in their understandings; none is always right, all are wrong at some points. Thankfulness for God-given leaders is ever to be conditioned by the warning, 'Do not be called teachers; for one is your Teacher, the Christ' (*Matt.* 23:10).

On some of the differences between Lloyd-Jones and Spurgeon there is no need to dwell. The one was Welsh, the other thoroughly English (with perhaps a touch of Huguenot ancestry). ML-J the twentieth-century man, lived eighty-one years; Spurgeon, born four years before the coronation of Queen Victoria (1838), died nine years before her death (1901) at the age of fifty-seven. Referring to Spurgeon's health, ML-J once said, 'That great man was subject to spiritual depression, and the main explanation in his case was undoubtedly the fact that he suffered from a gouty condition which finally killed him.'[2]

---

[1] *Charles Haddon Spurgeon, By One Who Knew Him Well* (London: Melrose, 1903), p. 120.
[2] *Spiritual Depression*, p. 18. Spurgeon was well aware of this. 'Our good fathers', he said, blamed the devil or their unbelief 'when frequently their depressions arose from want of food, or fresh air, or a torpid liver, or a weak stomach. A

110

It is interesting that both men came from Christian homes in the Congregationalist tradition, where Spurgeon was converted at the age of fifteen and Lloyd-Jones when he was approaching his mid-twenties.[1]

In their constitutions both possessed phenomenal memories. Spurgeon, it is said, knew not only the 5,000 members of the Metropolitan Tabernacle but the titles of the 12,000 books in his library. Lloyd-Jones could recall in detail a conversation that occurred many years earlier, and he regularly astonished by his ability to recognise at a second meeting individuals whom he scarcely knew. Both men had powerful and comprehensive minds. In the case of Spurgeon it would be a great mistake to draw a different conclusion from the simplicity of his preaching. His contemporary, Dr Richard Glover, could say of him: 'His intellectual qualities were of the supremest kind. I have met many great men, but never one so swift in perception, so rapid in seizing on the prime element in every case, so prompt in discussion.'[2] In Lloyd-Jones's case the thinking was more analytical and diagnostic – due both to the more 'legal mind' with which he was born and to his medical training. He had been drilled in such rules as, 'Look at the whole, before you look at the parts'; and 'First address the cause, not the symptoms.' I think it was largely the different cast of mind in the two men that explains ML-J's comparatively small interest in Spurgeon's books.[3] He may also have been influenced by

---

thousand things can cast us down, and we ought not to despise the body through which they act upon us.' *Metropolitan Tabernacle Pulpit*, vol. 28, p. 374.

[1] Spurgeon, of course, was to become a Baptist. There being no Congregationalist chapel in Llangeitho, the Lloyd-Jones family attended the Calvinistic Methodist cause, which was the Presbyterian Church of Wales.

[2] Quoted in W. Y. Fullerton, *C. H. Spurgeon, A Biography* (London: Williams and Norgate, 1920), p. 270. A medical doctor once said of Spurgeon: 'He is the most remarkable man I ever met . . . He would have made a splendid physician.' W. Williams, *Personal Reminiscences of Charles Haddon Spurgeon* (London: RTS, 1895), p. 79.

[3] The only time I find ML-J quoting Spurgeon is when the latter is dealing with

pastors he had known who sought to emulate Spurgeon's ministry but scarcely commended it. Of course, he admired him as an
evangelical leader, but he read him little and Spurgeon exerted no
influence on his own career. This may sound surprising, given
that their doctrinal convictions were so similar, yet the fact is that
ML-J came to his Reformation and Puritan beliefs through a different route. The Victorian period did not appeal to him, and,
except for occasional brief tributes to Spurgeon and one or two
other men, he was critical of the Victorians.

Spurgeon was a writer, with ability comparable to that of
William Tyndale or John Bunyan. Lloyd-Jones took no interest in
writing as such. Given the large number of ML-J titles now in print
it may seem near ludicrous to say he was not a natural author,
yet it is true. The spoken word absorbed his interest. By far the
greatest part of everything published under his name came from
transcripts of his preaching, either taken down in shorthand or,
from about 1953, by tape recordings. In the latter decade of his
life he spent a good deal of time in editing transcripts (with the
help of Mrs Lloyd-Jones and others) but this was drudgery for him.
Ideas were what appealed to him; the art of writing and the crafting
of words were not his concern. Thus the publication of his small
early books was genuinely the result of pressure from others and,
as I have already said in these pages, he was fifty-nine years of age
before the first of his two substantial volumes on the Sermon on
the Mount appeared.

Spurgeon, on the other hand, had the gift of writing appealing
and compelling prose and finished his first book when he was only
twenty-two.[1] Dr John Campbell (who had officiated at Spurgeon's

---

assurance of salvation, for instance, Sermons 241 and 384, in *New Park Street Pulpit*,
vols. 5 and 7. I rather think that someone drew his attention to those sermons.

[1] *The Saint and His Saviour* (1857). He says it had been 'more than two years in
hand' by the time of publication.

wedding), counselled the young man to keep to his pulpit, with the warning, 'The number who attain eminence both with tongue and pen is very small. It is Mr Spurgeon's wisdom to know his place and be satisfied to occupy it.' Instead of heeding the advice, writing became a constant part of Spurgeon's work; it led to a monthly magazine, and some 150 books. In addition to these were the volumes of annual sermons, largely produced from transcripts in shorthand, which reached a total of 63 volumes before their termination in 1917 – twenty-five years after his death.

That Spurgeon accomplished so much in this way is connected to another gift in which he also greatly excelled ML-J. As a born organiser and manager, he could both delegate and control. Some-one has claimed that Spurgeon initiated no less than sixty-six organ-izations, chief among them being an Orphanage, the Pastors' College, and the Colportage Society. Whatever the actual figure, it is certain he had responsibility for a considerable staff, includ-ing a personal secretary and editorial assistants. J. W. Harrald, in particular, was his invaluable right-hand man.

Lloyd-Jones could scarcely have been more different. He was known to say that he had only once started anything (the West-minster Fellowship). Staff at Westminster Chapel was minimal; he had no full-time secretary or editorial assistant. Those who did help were part-time and retired, with their careers behind them. Part of the explanation for this deficiency, perhaps, was a lack of finance, for more money went out from Westminster Chapel in the support of others than was ever spent within. But the truth is that ML-J would have been very slow to accept that there was any organisational 'deficiency' at Westminster. He feared that too many churches and organisations were running too much on their own activities; what he looked for was evidence of the work of God.

RESEMBLANCES

Both men served the church and their age in a manner contrary to the current of opinion. *Zeitgeist* – 'the spirit of the times' – was the popular word in the late nineteenth century. 'Spurgeon does not know whether there is such a thing', newspapers critically said of him; and it was equally true of Lloyd-Jones. Significantly, neither man had entered the ministry through the fashionable denominational channel of theological education. So Spurgeon was 'not a theologian', it was said; and Lloyd-Jones had 'no formal qualifications or academic standing as a biblical scholar'.[1] The words meant they were lacking education in the latest learning. The truth is they both believed, 'That man serves his generation best who is not caught up by every new current of opinion, but stands firmly by the truth of God, which is a solid, immoveable rock.'[2]

Both men regarded a living communion with God as the first priority in their lives. Their real strength was far more closely connected with private prayer than was always recognised. In the case of ML-J his wife was a witness to that fact, as I have already quoted. It was often the case that the way he spoke to God as he led in congregational prayer was as much a means of grace as the sermon that followed. Simply to hear a tape recording of a sermon from his Westminster Chapel days – shorn of the worship that

---

[1] For fuller quotation, see below, p. 197.

[2] *Metropolitan Tabernacle Pulpit*, 1892, p. 75. Sermon, 'His Own Funeral Sermon', on the text, 'For David, after he had served his own generation by the will of God, fell on sleep' (*Acts* 13:36). He warned: 'If any young man here shall begin to preach the doctrine and thought of the age, within the next ten years, perhaps within the next ten months, he will have to eat his own words, and begin his work all over again. But if you begin with God's Word, if you are spared to teach for the next fifty years, your testimony at the close will not contradict your testimony at the beginning.'

preceded it – is to miss much. The worshipper was often deeply moved before ever the sermon began. In so far as ML-J followed any mentors, his chief examples were the Calvinistic Methodist fathers of Wales, and in nothing were they stronger than in their insistence on the minister as a man of prayer. Henry Rees, one of them, addressing a candidate for the ministry told him: 'You will overcome all difficulties, if you but give yourself to prayer. Praying! Praying! Praying! How dimly do we discern even a thous-andth part of the power of praying upon preaching!'[1] It was the same lesson that Spurgeon urged upon his students at the Pastors' College: 'If the foundation of the pulpit be not laid in private prayer, our open ministry will not be a success.'[2] When the American preacher, Theodore Cuyler, visited Spurgeon's home at Westwood with a friend, it was their host's praying that left the uppermost impression upon their hearts, and they commented to each other, 'To-night we got into "the hidings of his power", for a man who can pray like that can outpreach the world.'[3]

But, let it be added, for these men prayer was a far greater thing than gaining influence for the pulpit. Prayer is communion with God. 'We lost sight of Spurgeon altogether', said a worshipper at the Metropolitan Tabernacle, 'in the reality of the Eternal Majesty and the Infinite Love.' As the First Epistle of John makes clear, a true consciousness of God and his love will be seen in relationships with other people. Spurgeon and Lloyd-Jones were humble, approachable individuals; ready in sympathy and compassion. Like Whitefield, they resembled 'a lion' in the pulpit but 'a lamb' out of it. Both men gave much time every week to

---

[1] A. M. Davies, ed., *Life and Letters of Henry Rees* (Bangor: Jarvis & Foster, 1904), p. 289.

[2] *The Soul-Winner*, p. 160.

[3] Theodore L. Cuyler, *Recollections of a Long Life* p. 184. Further on this subject, see Dinsdale T. Young's Introduction to *C. H. Spurgeon's Prayers* (London: Passmore & Alabaster, 1905).

the pastoral help of individuals. It is true they could not do this by house visitation, but the time they gave to this at their churches was very considerable. Lloyd-Jones would never leave the premises on a Sunday evening before he had seen everyone who wanted to see him and a notice, giving an invitation to see him after the services, was in every pew. Where longer interviews were needed he would appoint another time mid-week. Both men were conspicuous in the way in which young children were at home in their presence.

A test of Christian leadership is willingness to suffer unpopularity. Spurgeon and Lloyd-Jones both knew that a way to be unpopular with many is to be negative as well as positive. This involved serious controversy for both men towards the end of their ministries: Spurgeon in the 'Down-Grade Controversy',[1] and Lloyd-Jones in his protest that ecumenism was not a neutral issue, as I shall take up in chapter 8. Both believed that separation from error is part of a Christian's duty.[2] 'Few agreed with my father', Thomas Spurgeon was to say after the great preacher's death, and probably ML-J was on the minority side in the 1960s. They believed that the approval of God requires that a man be faithful.[3] Controversy is therefore sometimes inevitable; although they sought to avoid it as far as possible with fellow Christians, mindful of the aphorism, 'When good men quarrel, the devil cries, "Bravo!"' Both men lived disciplined personal lives; time was precious and

[1] I have described this controversy in *The Forgotten Spurgeon* (London: Banner of Truth, 1966, repr. often). The release of material, not previously available from the Baptist Union, has now thrown more light on the BU Assembly meeting of April 1888. See Mark Hopkins, *Nonconformity's Romantic Generation: Evangelical and Liberal Theologies in Victorian England* (Milton Keynes: Paternoster, 2004), pp. 223-226.

[2] For Spurgeon on this, see *Metropolitan Tabernacle Pulpit*, vol. 18, p. 706.

[3] 'Many a preacher has been ruined by his congregation. Their praise, their encouragement of him as a man, has almost ruined him as a messenger of God . . . He tends almost unconsciously to be controlled by the desire to have his people's good opinion and praise.' ML-J, *Sermon on the Mount*, vol. 2, p. 82.

they did not go in for socialising, dinner parties or entertainments. The only letter I have of Spurgeon's, written from Nightingale Lane, Clapham, reads: 'Mr Spurgeon thanks Mr and Miss Baxter for their kind invitation to dinner but he must decline it, first because he never dines out and secondly because it is his regular service night.'

Neither Spurgeon or Lloyd-Jones were 'committee men'. In part because of their belief in the saying, 'Many captains, and the ship goes on the rocks'; and more because they thought their usefulness greatly overrated. 'Have we not committees enough to sink a ship with their weight?', Spurgeon asked.

> As for patrons, presidents, vice-presidents, and secretaries, had not Christianity been divine it could not have lived under the load of these personages . . . If there should ever come a day when brethren go forth preaching the gospel, simply resting in faith on the Lord alone, I for one expect to see grand results; but at present Saul's armour is everywhere.[1]

From such sentiments it may be thought that these two men were individualists, who did not understand that the progress of Christianity involves the whole body of Christ. Spurgeon was accused of standing for a 'one man ministry' and, given our contemporary fondness for 'team ministry', Lloyd-Jones would no doubt face the same criticism. But while they certainly held that 'the minister of the word' is a distinct office, they believed that office is intended to raise all believers to usefulness: 'The plain and clear teaching of Scripture is that every single Christian person is an evangelist.'[2] 'The church is not meant to be a place where one man does everything and nobody else does anything. The church is not a place where one man alone speaks and the

---

[1] *Metropolitan Tabernacle Pulpit*, vol. 21, p. 515.
[2] *Sanctified Through the Truth*, p. 21.

others just sit and listen.'[1] Nor did they think that the pulpit alone was central in the work of the church; for them the gathering of members at the church prayer meeting was no less important. ML-J believed, as much as Spurgeon, that 'Great things are done by the Holy Spirit when a whole church is aroused to sacred energy: then there are hundreds of testimonies instead of one, and these strengthen each other.' It was said of the Metropolitan Tabernacle in Spurgeon's time: 'Probably no congregation in modern days ever sent forth so large a proportion of its members as ministers, evangelists, and home and foreign missionaries and workers of all kinds.'[2] The same may have been true of Westminster Chapel.

In their insistence on the vital role that literature plays in advancing the cause of Christ the two men were identical. None in their time gave more encouragement to publishers than CHS and ML-J. 'Week by week', said one of Spurgeon's students, 'we were advised what books to buy. To many this advice has proved of almost priceless value.' A good deal of this advice went into Spurgeon's *Commenting & Commentaries*,[3] a book which was to play a key role in the 1950s and 1960s in the reprinting of the Puritans. That there was sale for reprints in the twentieth century was, under God, due more to ML-J than any other man. His commitment to the spread of the best books was immense, and it was seen in the Puritan Conference (begun in 1950), the Westminster Chapel Bookroom, the Evangelical Library (of which he was president), the Banner of Truth Trust (begun at Westminster Chapel in 1957), and many other agencies.

---

[1] *Romans: The Gospel of God (1:1-32)*, pp. 238-239.
[2] *Spurgeon, By One Who Knew Him Well*, p. 119.
[3] Reprinted in *Lectures to My Students* (Edinburgh: Banner of Truth, 2008).

As Preachers

On the surface of things the difference in their preaching is easily apparent. It is not to disparage Spurgeon to quote his words, 'I owe more to variety than to profundity in my preaching.' It was the sustained average power and freshness of his sermons that was most notable. This is not to deny that he had occasional lapses, and one preacher (and friend) who heard him, was thankful that he did. Listening to Spurgeon on one occasion, William Williams 'thought it the poorest sermon I ever heard him preach, and for that reason it did me good, for I thought if he is not up to the mark sometimes, I will not be discouraged because I am not.'[1] The truth is that there is unevenness in all preachers. ML-J says of one of his predecessors at Westminster Chapel, Dr John A. Hutton, whom he admired, that 'he only preached really well about one out of every six occasions', and explains, 'he was a man who did not pay sufficient attention to the sermon.'[2] There is no resemblance between him and Lloyd-Jones in this regard, yet the latter, like Spurgeon, also had occasional lapses. I doubt whether he would have approved the printing of a few of his sermons published after his death.[3]

Whereas ML-J's preaching was accompanied by more 'action' in mid and later life, with Spurgeon it was the reverse. In early

[1] *Personal Reminiscences of C. H. Spurgeon*, p. 259. 'I have known his really great sermons to discourage preachers. One brother minister heard him on 1 Kings 4:33, and he declared on leaving the church that he could never preach again.'

[2] *Knowing the Times*, p. 271.

[3] Twenty sermons delivered in his series on Ephesians did not appear in the published volumes. This was at his decision; the reason was not, however, that he doubted the quality. It was because they developed subjects not strictly pertinent to the text and he wanted the volumes to be expositions of that epistle. Four of these excluded sermons were published posthumously, D. M. Lloyd-Jones, *Not Against Flesh and Blood* (Bridgend: Bryntirion Press, 2001)

years he walked about his spacious pulpit and gesticulated freely, whereas, as his health declined in later years, he did no more than raise an arm as he stood still behind a chair, a hand resting on its back. At times he had even to rest one knee on the chair. This does not mean that his preaching became in any way formal; he continued to 'blaze' in spirit, if not in body.

A difference between the two men with regard to the preaching of a series consecutively on a passage or book has been noted earlier. Rightly or wrongly, Spurgeon believed he did not have the gift necessary to make a series profitable for his Sunday hearers. He also thought that too many men supposed they had the gift, while wearied congregations doubted it; and he did not forget a series he had heard on Hebrews in his youth that had made him frequently wish the Hebrews 'had kept the epistle to themselves, for it sadly bored one poor Gentile lad'.[1] Williams remembered: 'He discouraged us as students from announcing a series of sermons on a given subject, and thought we ought to keep ourselves free for any subjects the Holy Spirit might suggest to us week by week.'[2] He did not want to preach on a text that did not 'bite'. At the same time it should be remembered that Spurgeon, in the public reading of Scripture (related to the chapter from which he was to preach), often gave brief, but illuminating, verse by verse comments.[3]

Spurgeon made frequent use of illustrations, often from history and biography, whereas Lloyd-Jones deliberately did not. In the

---

[1] 'On the Choice of a Text', *Lectures to My Students*, p. 106.

[2] *Personal Reminiscences*, p. 236. But Williams adds, 'He preached several series himself (yet without announcing them) on Thursday evenings with very great acceptance and effect.'

[3] For reasons unexplained these were not printed regularly in the *Metropolitan Tabernacle Pulpit* until the volume for 1892, where they begin to be listed in the Contents pages as 'Expositions of Scripture'. He lays down guidelines for this practice in *Commenting & Commentaries*, reprinted in the new Banner edition of *Lectures to My Students*, pp. 680-692.

United States in 1969, ML-J said, 'This whole business of illustrations and story-telling has been a particular curse during the last hundred years.' On the other hand, speaking to his own men at the Westminster Fellowship, the previous year, he exhorted us to use appropriate illustrations more than he had done, admitting he had reacted to their over use. He made no such concession in speaking to students in the States where he believed illustrations and stories had too large a place in sermons, bordering on entertainment and 'pandering to carnality'.[1]

The last statement leads me to say something on the use of humour in preaching. It was ML-J's belief that, 'The man who tries to be humorous is an abomination and should never be allowed to enter a pulpit.' Spurgeon he exonerated of trying to be humorous on the grounds that it was natural to him and 'bubbled out of him'. Nonetheless he does not commend his preaching in that regard, 'There was a great deal of humour – some of us would say too much humour.'[2] I believe that Dr Lloyd-Jones is here following a Spurgeon legend, rather than speaking from personal familiarity with Spurgeon's sermons. That Spurgeon had a store of 'sparkling humour', and 'an infectious gift of laughter', is true; his students and friends often witnessed it. But this was not carried into his pulpit. In the words of a friend, 'He thought it no sin to raise a smile in his sermon but to say that he joked in the pulpit would be altogether incorrect.'[3] His sermons prove this conclusively; nor is there the slightest evidence that anything humorous was ever edited out when published. Indeed the legend is directly contrary to his

---

[1] *Preaching and Preachers*, pp. 232-233. He particularly condemned the conceit of ministers who talked about their families: 'Why should people be more interested in the preacher's children than in those of other people?' If illustrations must be used, he urged, they must be accurate.

[2] *Preaching and Preachers*, pp. 240-241.

[3] *Spurgeon, By One Who Knew Him Well*, p. 173. The same author refers to the element of truth in the legend that misled ML-J, Ibid., p. 148. Both men suffered from the retailing of the apocryphal.

specific statements. His students were warned of the necessity of 'deep seriousness of heart' when it comes to preaching, and on the words, 'They that sow in tears shall reap in joy' (*Psa.* 126:5), he wrote:

> Our heavenly seed could not fitly be sown laughing. Deep sorrow and concern for the souls of others are a far more fitting accompaniment of godly teaching than anything like levity. We have heard of men who went to war with a light heart, but they were beaten; and it is mostly so with those who sow in the same style.[1]

In addresses on various occasions, not connected with the worship of God, Lloyd-Jones could also use the amusing story. To deduce from his preaching that he was lacking in a sense of humour would be a real misunderstanding of what he was.

On the fundamentals of effective preaching both men held the same priorities. 'A preacher should be borne away by the force of the truth he preaches', was Spurgeon's conviction, and he emphasised the need for the Holy Spirit as much as ML-J: 'The lack of distinctly recognising the power of the Holy Spirit lies at the root of many useless ministries.' He likewise believed in the need for what he called 'new baptisms of the Holy Spirit'. For both men evangelistic preaching was a 'burden' that moved them deeply, and they could not rest without seeing conversions.

At the same time there was an element prominent in Spurgeon's ministry that was missing in many of his followers, and which reappeared in Lloyd-Jones. Both men stressed the necessity of doctrinal Christianity. Strong Christians need to be well-taught Christians; a diet of random, unrelated devotional thoughts, with no system of belief, only leads to superficiality. Christians

---

[1] C. H. Spurgeon, *Cheque Book of the Bank of Faith*, reading for October 18.

need to know why regeneration precedes faith; why justification establishes the law of God; why a distinction is made in Scripture between everlasting, electing love and the universal compassion expressed in the gospel. They should understand such differences as those between Calvinism and Hyper-Calvinism; between gospel liberty and Antinomianism. These and many other points of doctrine were clearly enunciated in the commonly discounted Protestant and Puritan Confessions which ML-J and CHS both upheld. 'Let me strongly recommend to you The Assembly's Catechism', Spurgeon said to his people.

> Many a minister has derived his first doctrinal knowledge from that book; and, indeed it has in it the very life-blood of the gospel. Let our youths and maidens study the Scriptures daily, and let them use The Baptist Confession of Faith, which they will find to be a useful compendium of doctrinal knowledge.[1]

The resistance which Spurgeon encountered for this emphasis was similarly experienced by Lloyd-Jones who wrote:

> We are living in an age when definitions are at a discount, an age which dislikes thought and hates theology and doctrine and dogma . . . It is an age that dislikes strong men because, it says, they always cause disturbance.[2]

---

[1] *C. H. Spurgeon's Autobiography*, vol. 1 (London: Passmore and Alabaster, 1899), p. 306. There are many similar statements throughout Spurgeon's writings, e.g. C. H. Spurgeon, *Autobiography: The Early Years* (London: Banner of Truth, 1962, repr. often), p. 387.
[2] *Sermon on the Mount*, vol. 2, p. 161.

DIFFERENCE IN THE WORK GOD GAVE THEM TO DO

While the essential work they did was the same, the considerable difference in the times in which they lived influenced their
calling. Spurgeon was living at the end of an era: an era in which
the Bible had been widely known; when there were many full
churches, when church discipline was still practised, and when
Christian literature was widely available. But the tradition that
had given rise to these conditions – that came down from the Puritans and the Evangelical Revival – was being steadily displaced
by what claimed to be 'a better form of Christianity'. It professed
little interest in doctrine and was impatient with the Old Testament.
Spurgeon grew up in the Puritan tradition, surrounded by its literature from childhood, and his calling was to preserve and conserve
that heritage. But before he died he was commonly regarded as
'an echo from the past' and as 'the last of the Puritans'. The Rev.
Dr Henry Allon, preaching in London after Spurgeon's death,
regretted that 'Mr Spurgeon accepted a theology traditionally,
and resented any departure from it.'

The thirty-five years between Spurgeon's death and the start
of Lloyd-Jones's ministry demonstrated the false dawn of the 'better form of Christianity'. Church attendance was in marked decline and membership increasingly nominal; the Bible was being
side-lined in national life; Puritan theology was forgotten and its
literature no longer printed or even wanted. What was needed
now was not preservation but *recovery*. Lloyd-Jones had first to
rediscover for himself what had been lost; and he found it not in
theological colleges or religious journals but chiefly in secondhand
bookshops. His calling became to restore what had been thrown
aside and to inspire a new generation with a more biblical Christianity. In 1889 Spurgeon had said, 'For my part, I am willing to be

124

eaten of dogs for the next fifty years; but the more distant future shall vindicate me.'[1] His confidence was founded on Scripture and it would not be disappointed. In a sermon entitled, 'One Worker Preparing for Another', preached in the last twelve months of his public ministry, the pastor of the Metropolitan Tabernacle told his people:

> There will be somebody to carry on the work of the Lord; and so long as the work goes on, what matter who does it? God buries the workmen, but the devil himself cannot bury the work. The work is everlasting, though the workmen die. We pass away, as star by star grows dim; but the eternal light is never fading. God shall have the victory. His Son shall come in his glory. His Spirit shall be poured out among the people; and though it be neither this man, nor that, nor the other, God will find the man to the world's end who will carry on his cause, and give him the glory.[2]

---

[1] C. H. Spurgeon, *An All-Round Ministry*, (London: Banner of Truth, 1972), p. 360.
[2] *Metropolitan Tabernacle Pulpit*, 1892, vol. 38, p. 297.

The life-long reader.

7

A CONTROVERSIAL BOOK
JOY UNSPEAKABLE: THE
BAPTISM WITH THE
HOLY SPIRIT

As is apparent in earlier pages, a major theme in Dr Lloyd-Jones's ministry concerned the Holy Spirit in the life of the individual. Spiritual life begins with the Spirit's work in regenerat ion, and thereafter hisindwelling remains in every true Christian. There are not therefore, he taught, two classes of Christians, one with the Spirit and the other without. Yet there are significant differences between Christians, and for ML-J the most important of these differences had to do with assurance of salvation. A measure of assurance belongs to every Christian in their new life, but 'full assurance' is by no means common to all. Where it exists there is an enjoyment of the love of God, a radiance of life, a freedom in prayer and thanksgiving, and a readiness of witness, which is not true of every believer. Such assurance, he believed, is parallel to what is said in the book of Acts on being 'filled with the Spirit'.

ML-J's understanding of this point dovetailed with his whole view of spiritual priorities. In the face of an indifferent world, the church's first need was within – 'We must start with the Church if we are to evangelise the outsider' – and especially the need for

Christians to attain full assurance by a larger experience of the Holy Spirit. 'The greatest need at the present time is for Christian people who are assured of their salvation.'[1] He was sure that every true revival, and every powerful evangelistic advance in the world, began in this way.

Lloyd-Jones addressed this subject on many occasions. It figured prominently in his lectures on Christian doctrine on Friday nights in 1954; in his sermons on Ephesians 1:13 in 1955; and in his exposition of Romans 5:5 and 8:16 in 1958 and 1961 respectively.[2]

In 1964-1965 he took up the subject again, in sermons which were published in 1984-1985 in two paperbacks, *Joy Unspeakable, The Baptism with the Holy Spirit*; and *Prove All Things, The Sovereign Work of the Holy Spirit*.[3]

Before proceeding it is necessary to understand how ML-J understood assurance. He formulated it in terms of three grounds. First, the assurance to be gained by the Christian who, on coming to faith, rests on the promises of God. Second, assurance strengthened as the Christian observes the change in his life corresponding with what Scripture says on the marks of the children of God; they 'love the brethren' (*1 John* 3:14), etc. These two grounds of assurance, he says, 'taken together give strong grounds of assurance'.[4] But there is a third ground of assurance which is 'yet stronger and higher', which he called 'the ultimate', and 'The highest and the greatest form of certainty and assurance that one can ever have

---

[1] *Joy Unspeakable* (Eastbourne, Kingsway, 1984), p. 39.
[2] The special relevance of the subject to preachers he underlined in his concluding lecture at Westminster Seminary in 1969, published in *Preaching and Preachers*.
[3] (Eastbourne: Kingsway, 1985). The two titles were later to be published as one volume under the title, *The Baptism and Gifts of the Spirit* (Wheaton: Crossway, 1996).
[4] *God's Ultimate Purpose*, p. 263.

of the fact that one is a child of God.'[1] The difference between this form of assurance and the two former is that while the Spirit assists the believer in the former, here he acts *directly*. It is assurance 'done by the Spirit to us' – no longer assurance gained by any process of reasoning on our part ('I believe the promises; I love the brethren, therefore I am a Christian'). 'No longer indirect, but direct . . . this is entirely the action of the Holy Spirit – not our action.'[2] This assurance he came to designate 'the baptism of the Spirit', 'sealing of the Spirit', and 'witness of the Spirit', all of which, he believed, refer to the same experience and were therefore terms that he used interchangeably. 'We should try to forget labels', ML-J warned, but unless we understand the terminology he uses the case he argued cannot be followed.

In this chapter it is his book *Joy Unspeakable* that I am especially considering. As there will be many quotations from that title I will, from this point, include the page number references within brackets in the text rather than in footnotes. When published in 1984 it was the book that became the most controversial of his publications, and why that was so needs explanation. There had been little controversy when the sermons were first preached in 1964-1965; why now, three years after his death?

The answer lies chiefly in what had been happening in the twenty years between the preaching and the publication. The subtitle given to *Joy Unspeakable*, *The Baptism with the Holy Spirit*, coincided with what had become a popular phrase in the evangelical world, promoted world-wide by the charismatic movement. The

---

[1] *Romans: Exposition of Chapter 8:5-17, The Sons of God* (Edinburgh: Banner of Truth, 1974) p. 304.
[2] *Joy Unspeakable*, pp. 70–71. My summary here is drawn from the convictions of his later ministry. He spoke differently on assurance in a sermon of the 1940s in which he was 'anxious to emphasise that the indirect testimony of the Spirit is just as much a testimony as the direct testimony.' Sermon on Romans 8:16 in *The Christian in an Age of Terror*, p. 155.

excitement the book caused was connected with the idea that it was some kind of endorsement of the movement; and this idea was one which the two men who wrote the prelims to the book appeared to favour. In his Foreword, the Rev. Peter Lewis wrote of ML-J: 'God led him to welcome (though not uncritically) many aspects of the rising charismatic movement and to see its fundamental com-patibility with historic evangelicalism' (p. 9). In his own Introduct-ion, Christopher Catherwood, editor of the sermons, said that his grandfather 'believed that all the gifts existed today',[1] and that he was 'both reformed and charismatic, in the biblical sense' (p. 13).

THE CONTEXT OF THE *JOY UNSPEAKABLE* SERMONS

In reading any of the published sermons of Lloyd-Jones it can be helpful to be aware of the date when they were preached. Con-siderable changes occurred in the Christian scene during the years of his ministry, and his emphases were adjusted to meet those changes. For example, in his preaching during the 1950s and early 1960s there is sustained opposition to what he called the 'take it by faith' teaching promoted at the Keswick Convention and else-where. In essence this teaching was that the Christian is to 'accept' blessings, such as the 'victorious life', in faith and not to be over-much concerned whether his feelings undergo any change. But in 1974 ML-J could say, 'The Keswick message has virtually disap-peared . . . the Higher Life or Victorious Life teaching is not a live issue today.'[2]

Our recognition of the date when he preached particular sermons is especially important with respect to the sermons pub-lished posthumously as *Joy Unspeakable*. What was his intention in

---

[1] This statement was patently a mistake.
[2] 'Living the Christian Life', *The Puritans*, pp. 324-325.

these sermons and what prompted them? In addition to his continued concern to see believers knowing a greater assurance of their salvation, there were at least three reasons why he took up this subject in 1964. By numbering them I do not mean to put them in order of importance.

First, in July 1964, Inter-Varsity Press published a forty-page booklet by John Stott, Rector of All Souls, Langham Place, London, on *Baptism and Fullness: The Work of the Holy Spirit Today*. ML-J read and carefully annotated his copy. With one of its main premises he was in strong disagreement, namely, that all Christians are 'filled' with the Spirit at their conversion. The baptism of the Spirit, given to the church at Pentecost, it was claimed, now happens to every Christian at their regeneration.[1] This teaching was not new, for some time it had been 'the most popular and common evangelical teaching' (p. 269).[2] But it dismayed ML-J to see it cogently argued in an Inter-Varsity publication. He thought the teaching tended to promote satisfaction with existing spiritual conditions, and to preclude the need for a larger work of the Spirit. It explained, he thought, the absence of earnest prayer for the Spirit and for revival. If a Christian receives the fullness of the Spirit at conversion, what need can there be to seek anything more? 'There is nothing', he said, 'I am convinced, that so "quenches" the Spirit as the teaching which identifies the baptism of the Holy Ghost with regeneration.'[3]

A colleague of Stott's in the evangelical world, including the student work of Inter-Varsity, ML-J did not want this case to go unchallenged. He had read *Baptism and Fullness* in the summer of 1964; his series of sermons, later to be called *Joy Unspeakable*, began

[1] This assertion was in part based upon 1 Corinthians 12:13, and the belief that the language of the New Testament allows for no other 'baptising' work.

[2] That was no longer true twenty years later.

[3] Sermon preached on 'Quenching the Spirit', (1961); see *The Christian Warfare*, p. 280.

on November 15 of that year, and he gave quotations from what Stott had written, though without naming his friend.[1]

Secondly, there was now a problem arising from an altogether different direction, and it lay behind Stott's booklet. One of his curates at the church of All Souls was the Rev. Michael Harper. By 1964 Harper and a few other Anglican clergy had become deeply involved in a stirring that began among evangelicals in California and had reached England through visitors, including one man, introduced to a lunch for 'Christian leaders' at the Hilton Hotel in London, as 'the greatest Spirit-filled Christian in the world today'.[2] Here, suddenly, there was emphasis on *experiencing* the Holy Spirit and his gifts (of which 'tongues' would become, for a time, the most prominent). Stott's booklet sought to be an answer and refutation of this development which had caused difficulties in his congregation. (Harper's curacy at All Souls ended in August 1964).[3]

Lloyd-Jones reaction to the reports from California was different. He hoped there was a genuine element in what had been happening in the States, but thought that the explanation of the 'tongues' was psychological rather than supernatural. Tongues had come in under the influence of the older Pentecostal teaching that held that the gift of tongues always accompanies 'the baptism of the Spirit'. So in 1964 ML-J was ready to give some cautious encouragement to the new interest in the need for the Holy Spirit

---

[1] *Baptism and Fullness: The Work of the Holy Spirit Today* (London: Inter-Varsity Press, 1964), quoted on pp. 37, 39, 41.

[2] The words are quoted by David Watson. ML-J was not at this meeting, at which I was also present. John Flavel says: 'Erroneous teachers are great boasters: They usually give out to the world what extraordinary comforts they meet with in their way, which proves a strong temptation to young converts.' *Works*, vol. 3 (repr. London: Banner of Truth, 1968), p. 485.

[3] Further on this, see Timothy Dudley-Smith, *John Stott: A Global Ministry* (Leicester: IVP, 2001), pp. 21-23. After ten years promoting charismatic teaching, Harper became Canon of Chichester in 1984 and was received into the Orthodox Church in the early 1990s.

while, at the same time, he was also concerned to warn against what could discredit the whole idea of a greater work of the Spirit. This concern he stated explicitly in one of the sermons in the series (March 21, 1965), when he said:

> Let me say that one of my main objects in this whole series of sermons is to safeguard the doctrine of the baptism with the Holy Spirit. There is a tendency on the part of some [Stott's position], because they dislike the gifts and the manifestations and the excesses, to throw out the doctrine of the baptism of the Spirit with it. Let me underline this important fact – you must differentiate between the two. It is possible for a man to be baptised with the Holy Spirit without ever speaking in tongues.[1]

Thirdly, there was yet another factor prompting ML-J to preach this series in 1964-1965. He wanted to caution his hearers against forming a premature negative judgment with respect to those who were now insisting on the Holy Spirit and his gifts. He knew from history that a new work of God has often been accompanied in its early stages by things wrong and erroneous. Whitefield and Wesley, for example, had not been exempt from real mistakes; nor had the revival in Wales in 1904. He was concerned lest a zeal for orthodoxy would lead some to dismiss what was new out of hand. In that connection he thought that young men (over whom he had much influence) were too ready to judge everything by the Reformed text-books, and needed to exercise patience as well as critical discernment.

To deduce from this caution in the 1964-1965 sermons that Lloyd-Jones was open to the charismatic movement, and ready to give it a measure of support, is entirely illegitimate. There was no such name or movement in England *at the time* he started that series. All that existed in England were incipient beginnings among

[1] *Prove All Things* (Eastbourne: Kingsway, 1985), p. 146.

133

a comparative few. So little support did these beginnings have, at the time the sermons were preached, that in later years 'the courage' of Leonard Cutts of Hodder and Stoughton was praised for publishing Harper's *As at the Beginning* in 1965.[1]

By 1971, however, a very different situation existed as charismatic influence and publications were becoming commonplace. And at that date ML-J spoke openly in a very different manner of what had become a movement with a definite name:[2]

> There is a factor which to me is a very serious one at the present time, and that is what is known as the charismatic movement. I am sure that you are all familiar with this. This is a phenomenon that has been confronting us for the last fifteen years or so, and it is very remarkable. It began in America and it has spread to many other countries, most countries probably by now . . . The teaching of this movement is that nothing matters but 'the baptism of the Spirit' . . . they have their congresses and their conferences, and they are virtually proclaiming that doctrine does not matter at all.[3]

In a letter of August 20, 1970, on fanaticism at Chard, in Somerset, he identified it with 'part of the Michael Harper move

---

[1] *Fight of Faith*, p. 484, where I deal with this more fully. I believe it was not until November 1965 – months after the ML-J series concluded – that the first public meetings under the name 'charismatic renewal' were seen in London.

[2] I say 'openly' for it should be understood that ML-J had expressed serious criticisms back in 1963, when he was still hopeful that what was happening might yet prove to be of God. A man who heard him speak at the Evangelical Library meeting of members in 1963 complained, 'He presents what he terms a "recrudescence of interest in the gifts of the Spirit" in a wholly unfavourable light, and sets over against this the revived interest in the Reformed theology as being what really matters and which alone can meet the spiritual need.' See *Fight of Faith*, p. 483.

[3] An address, 'What is an Evangelical?' given at a conference of the International Fellowship of Evangelical Students, Austria, *Knowing the Times*, pp. 312, 314.

ment' and believed people should be shown 'the gross dangers and thoroughly unscriptural character of the whole thing.'[1]

Yet for years to come charismatic believers sought to claim his sympathy for the movement, and it was even circulated that ML-J himself spoke in tongues – an allegation he emphatically denied.[2]

THE ACTS OF THE APOSTLES AND THE CONTROVERSY

While it was not a little misleading for the sermons in *Joy Unspeakable,* published twenty years after they were preached, to be presented as in any sense an endorsement of the charismatic movement, there was one feature that could appear to give support to that claim. This was his argument that an understanding of 'the baptism of the Spirit' is dependent principally upon the Acts of the Apostles, because 'all the teaching of the epistles is based upon and presupposes the history of what happens in Acts' (p. 43). Certain passages in Acts (long highlighted in Pentecostal teaching), he regarded as crucial; these were the narratives on the 'receiving' of the Spirit by the believers in Samaria, Caesarea, and Ephesus (*Acts* 8:14-17; 10:44-46; 19:6). These incidents he held to be cases of a 'baptism with the Spirit', happening to those who were already converted. As already noted, he understood this 'baptism' to be the receiving of 'the highest form of assurance', in a sudden and direct manner. It was the same experience, he believed, as the 'sealing' of Ephesians 1:13 and 'the witness of the Spirit' in Romans 8:16 (pp. 39-40, 157). Those who have known

[1] *D. Martyn Lloyd-Jones Letters, 1919-1981,* (Edinburgh: Banner of Truth, 1994), p. 204.
[2] 'I have never spoken in tongues either in private or in public' (May 17, 1971). Ibid., p. 205. Charismatic opinion-formers made great efforts to claim the sanction of evangelical leaders; even John Stott was alleged to have changed his mind and to speak with tongues. *John Stott: Global Ministry,* p. 40.

this experience are marked by a profound consciousness of God, and boldness and authority in testimony. The Spirit is thus given so that believers, endued with power as at Pentecost, can truly be the effective witnesses promised in Luke 24:48-49.

At first sight, this may seem to be in line with the charismatic contention that 'all Christians today ought to receive "the baptism of the Spirit".' But further examination undermines the identity of his belief with Pentecostal teaching. The biblical instances from Samaria and Ephesus, quoted above, speak of the giving of the Spirit by the laying on of hands; in Caesarea there is no reference to the imposition of hands. It was important for ML-J to regard that Caesarea exception as the norm for today because he knew no scriptural authority for believing that any body of men now have the apostolic calling 'to transmit this blessing to others by laying their hands upon them' (p. 188).[1] The apostolic office has ceased. Referring to the evidence of church history he said, 'I do not know of a single instance among such men where they received the blessing as the result of the laying on of the hands of someone else; not a single one' (p. 189). This was a rejection of a major feature in Pentecostal teaching: 'They are virtually saying that truth has only

---

[1] He is more dogmatic on this in *Romans: The Sons of God (8:5-17)*, pp. 281-282. In *Joy Unspeakable* he is prepared to take the case of Ananias putting his hands on Saul (which he understands as another instance of baptism with the Spirit) as a 'special instance' of the practice by a non-apostle (p. 189); and therefore, though he did not know of such instances today, he was not prepared to rule out the possibility that a Christian might receive 'a definite and special commission to do so'. It is, however, very doubtful if what happened to Saul at Damascus (*Acts* 9) is the same as the three incidents of Samaria, Caesarea and Ephesus. Hands were put on individuals in the NT for more than one purpose. In Acts 6:6, 13:3, and 1 Timothy 4:14 the meaning is best understood as symbolical, without any miraculous agency being involved in the action. As Patrick Fairbairn writes on the text in 1 Timothy, the laying on of hands in miraculous communication 'belonged exclusively to an apostle'. In the case of Saul, John Stott may well be right in saying, 'I suspect that this laying-on of hands was a gesture of love to a blind man.' John Stott, *The Message of Acts* (Leicester: IVP, 1990), p. 175. There are some complex differences in the understanding of parts of the book of Acts, as every reader of commentaries will know.

come by them and that for 1,900 years the Church has dwelt in ignorance and in darkness. The thing is monstrous.'[1]

No less significant is ML-J's refusal to identify the 'baptism' with the gift of tongues, although tongues are explicitly mentioned in the cases at Caesarea and Ephesus (*Acts* 10:46; 19:6), and probably also in Samaria (*Acts* 8:17-18). Nor is this all. While, on the basis of the passages in Acts, Lloyd-Jones believed it likely that 'most' New Testament believers were baptized with the Spirit (and so baptized, when, it might be argued from Acts, they were still young converts), he did not want that to be seen as usual in the church today. Certainly, this 'baptism' (i.e. direct assurance of salvation) may be simultaneous with salvation (p. 30) but, more commonly, he seemed to suggest, it comes much later. Christians may have to be patient as they wait 'many years' (p. 225) – maybe more than 'twenty years' (p. 278). This kind of assurance may only come after a long period of faithful Christian service (he instances, John Flavel), or indeed, only at the very point of death (p. 242). The general impression which ML-J gives is that this high degree of assurance is more likely to belong to mature, tested Christians – to those, in the words of Charles Simeon, 'who after having believed have maintained a close walk with God' (p. 205). It is not common Christian experience but belongs rather to the 'heights of the Christian life'.

Such words agree with the *Westminster Confession of Faith's* view of full assurance,[2] but it is hard to see how they harmonise with the three passages in Acts ML-J used to support his teaching. He does not explain why, if so many young converts reached the 'heights' so rapidly in the apostolic era, that should not be the case today.

---

[1] *Spiritual Depression*, p. 188.
[2] 'This infallible assurance doth not so belong to the essence of faith, but that a true believer may wait long and conflict with many difficulties, before he be partaker of it' (*Westminster Confession of Faith*: XVIII:3).

But the charismatic does have a ready explanation. He knows the New Testament converts did not wait for years for 'the baptism' because there were apostles present to transmit 'the blessing' by the laying on of hands, and sees no reason why the power to convey the same gift should not exist and be used today. Accordingly, for the charismatic, Lloyd-Jones was mistaken in his emphatic insistence that the Christian cannot determine the time he or she receives 'the baptism'. Contrary to the charismatic position, ML-J affirmed: 'You can pray for the baptism of the Spirit, but that does not guarantee that it happens, as many of you know. You can live a good life, surrender yourself, do all you are told to do, but still you are not baptized with the Spirit' (p. 77). For this lack he does not blame the Christian, because 'the baptism of the Spirit' is solely God's work, given in his own time and manner. 'It is entirely his gift, and entirely in his hands' (p. 52). A believer should never say, 'It is no use, I have striven for many years. I have done everything you said but have not had the blessing . . . we must neither be impatient or discouraged' (p. 225).

By contrast, if charismatic believers are right, and men today have the ability to impart the 'baptism' (and tongues, too), then patience is no virtue. The modern Christian can go straight back to apostolic experience – there is no need to wait for 'twenty years', or even for a lifetime. Thus the genuine charismatic is bound to say, 'Dr Lloyd-Jones describes a great blessing and he tells us that most New Testament Christians possessed it, but then he asserts that, unlike the book of Acts, God has appointed no means to make it immediately available for all converts today!'

I think I have said enough to show that, on the central issue, the Lloyd-Jones position differs widely from that of the charismatic. Not only does it differ over how parts of the book of Acts relate to the present day, the disagreement is more fundamental. The charismatic movement teaches that 'baptism with the Spirit' is to be sought as a once-for-all crisis experience that introduces the Christian to a higher state of experience. But, understanding the experience in terms of 'the highest form of assurance of salvation that anybody can ever receive' (p. 157), ML-J held that 'This experience is not permanent' (p. 244); indeed, to claim that it is he calls 'a great error'.[1] For him there was no one *single* experience to be treated as making a unique and permanent difference. But if this is so, do not the incidents at Samaria, Caesarea and Ephesus prove too much for the case he argues? What were the apostles asking for when, in Samaria, 'they prayed for them [the disciples], that they might receive the Holy Spirit' (*Acts* 8:15)? Clearly it was not that the disciples should be regenerated – they were already believers. The prayer, ML-J says, was for full assurance; yet we are bound to wonder whether this was their need, given that they were already possessed of 'great joy' through believing in Christ (*Acts* 8:8). And, supposing their need had been for full assurance, why did not Philip himself pray they might receive that blessing (if it could be received that way)? Would petition for 'assurance' have made it necessary for apostles to come from Jerusalem? (*Acts* 8:14-15). Does the evidence not point to the prayer of the apostles being concerned with what belonged uniquely to their calling, 'they laid hands on them' (*Acts* 8:17); and what the believers then received was so visible that Simon coveted the authority to convey the same gift? Was it full assurance the erring Simon wanted? Was it not rather the sight of the 'miracles and signs which were done' (*Acts* 8:13) that motivated him? The clearest explanation of the passage would seem to be that by the laying on of the apostles'

---

[1] *God's Ultimate Purpose*, p. 291. Yet his teaching lacks some consistency here. Preaching 'the nature of the blessing', a year later (October 1965), he spoke of those 'who are suddenly lifted to another level, and go on living on the mountain tops of the Christian life.' D. M. Lloyd-Jones, *Spiritual Blessing: The Path to True Happiness* (Eastbourne: Kingsway, 1999), p. 67.

hands miraculous gifts (charismata), such as speaking in tongues, were received by believers in Samaria.

The 'baptism of the Spirit' defined as 'full assurance', without any necessary presence of miraculous gifts, does not well fit these Acts passages. *If* the Acts of the Apostles is normative in all things for Christians today, then the charismatic case stands on stronger ground than ML-J will allow. But if the apostolic office has ended, belonging only to the formation of the church (*Eph.* 2:20; *Heb.* 2:3-4),[1] then it would be natural to expect what Paul calls the 'signs of an apostle' (*2 Cor.* 12:12) to end also. This is why ML-J, while taking the Acts incidents as examples of 'the baptism of the Spirit', would not tie special gifts with the experience today. 'Special gifts', he said, 'were given to attest the authority of the apostles – these special gifts given at the beginning.'[2]

This leads to another problem over Dr Lloyd-Jones's position. If 'full assurance' is not to be obtained today in the way he believed it could be obtained in the book of Acts (by the laying on of hands), then how is it to be obtained? Nothing, he says, that the Christian may do, secures the reception of this blessing – hence perhaps the 'twenty years' waiting already quoted. But how does this harmonize with the New Testament directions that believers are responsible to attain assurance (*John* 14:21; *Heb.* 6:11; *2 Pet.* 1:10; *1 John* 2:5; *Rev.* 2:17 etc.)?

Further, New Testament believers are exhorted to be 'filled with the Spirit' (a continuous present imperative). On this ML-J says, 'Being filled with the Spirit (*Eph.* 5:18), is something which

---

[1] See his argument from these texts in *Great Doctrines of the Bible, vol. 2, God the Holy Spirit* (Wheaton: Crossway, 1997), pp. 268-271.

[2] Ibid., p. 271. Also, *God's Ultimate Purpose*, p. 281. This does not mean he denied the existence of the miraculous today, or that miraculous signs may not, at times, occur in church history – a different thing from saying 'all the gifts existed today'.

you and I can control.'[1] 'We ourselves are responsible for being filled with the Spirit . . . But we are not responsible for the baptism with the Spirit which is something we receive in a passive manner.'[2] Baptism with the Spirit, he emphasises, 'is something that happens to us, which we do not control' (p. 77). Now he also believed it is clear that in the book of Acts 'baptized' and 'filled' with the Spirit are terms 'used interchangeably'.[3] So, he noted, Christ's promise in Acts chapter 1, that the believers would be 'baptized with the Holy Spirit', is fulfilled at Pentecost in chapter 2, although it is only said that the disciples were then 'filled' with the Spirit. The difference, he sometimes suggested, between 'the baptism with the Spirit' and 'the fullness' is simply that the word 'baptism' is applicable to the first occurrence of the experience. These words only deepen the problem. If the experiences of 'baptism' and 'filling' are of the same nature, how can it be that we are responsible for the one (being 'filled', as *Eph.* 5:18) and not the other?

ML-J was conscious of an anomaly here, and offers two explanations: either the believers in Ephesus could obey the injunction of Ephesians 5:18 because they were already baptised with the Spirit (in which case the command did not apply to those not thus 'baptized'); or the 'being filled' in that text relates to a different kind of 'filling with the Spirit' from that which he believed resulted from the baptism in the book of Acts. These explanations are unconvincing.[4]

---

[1] *God's Ultimate Purpose*, p. 263.

[2] *Romans: The Sons of God (8:5-17)*, p. 273.

[3] *God's Ultimate Purpose*, p. 264.

[4] Again I have to say his thinking here is not consistent. Preaching in 1965 on the same subject, he likens receiving the blessing to the way the disciples received the wine that Christ had changed from water: 'Fill the waterpots', Christ commanded them. From which MLJ deduces that there is something for us to do to receive the blessing: 'There is no by-passing the commandments.' *Spiritual Blessing*, p. 48. 'We can be passive and active at the same time' (p. 55), but this is not what he has said in many other places. In seeking to establish his case on assurance, I believe he did not maintain the exegetical care that it was his custom to

THE BASIC PROBLEM

We have seen that Dr Lloyd-Jones believed it essential to defend his position in terms of 'the doctrine of the baptism with the Holy Spirit'. Yet difficulty was almost bound to arise due to the absence of any such phrase in the New Testament. There are six texts in the Gospels and the Acts of the Apostles which speak of Christ 'baptizing' with the Spirit. This activity is described by a verb, not a noun. No specific incident is identified as being 'the' or 'a' baptism with the Spirit. Why should not *all* the work of the Spirit in the believer come under the mediatorial work of Christ? He remains 'the baptizer with the Holy Spirit'. From him comes the on-going, abundant 'supply' of the Spirit, as the Authorised Version translates the term in Philippians 1:19.[1] Is it not easier to understand the New Testament as teaching that no one type of assurance is to be termed 'the baptism', rather *all* real assurance is the Spirit's work. Indeed, all the blessings we receive are of Christ and by the Spirit (*Eph.*1:3). The words of the hymn writer on Christ's gift of the Spirit resonate with Christian experience:

> And every virtue we possess,
>
> And every victory won,
>
> And every thought of holiness,
>
> Are His alone.

---

exercise. In four sermons on Abel, Enoch, Abraham and Moses (preached in 1963), he used the patriarchs to demonstrate 'direct' assurance, even to the point of saying that the believer, apart from Scripture, can be as certain of the voice of God as Abraham was. *Heirs of Salvation: Studies in Biblical Assurance* (Bridgend: Bryntirion Press, 2000), p. 73. If that were so, we could trust what we think God is saying to us as much as we trust what Scripture actually says. The publication of the two posthumous paperbacks cited in this footnote, in my opinion, is to be regretted. They are not ML-J at his best.

[1] 'There is an ἐπιχορηγια του πνευματος, Phil.1:19, "a supply of the Spirit", continually given out to believers from Christ, their head, Eph. 4:15, 16 . . . a sufficient provision administered unto a person for his work or business'. John Owen, *Exposition of Hebrews*, vol. 4 (Edinburgh: Banner of Truth, 1991) p. 219.

ML-J's objection to the above paragraph would be that it leaves no place for the extraordinary; and that there are extraordinary experiences of Christ and the Spirit that Christians may know, just as there are extraordinary periods in Christian history that we call revivals and for which we ought to pray. His burden was that the whole present tendency of the church was to accept present spiritual conditions as the 'normal', without recognising the possibilities (indicated by Scripture and church history) that there is much more. To counter this he thought it necessary to press a distinction between the things the Christian can do, and what only God can do for us – between what 'we can control' and what is 'immediate', 'direct', and sovereignly given. 'The baptism' and 'full assurance' are not in our hands, to attain as we will. And as he understood revival as many receiving 'the baptism' at the same time, it is equally true to say that revival also is sovereignly given.

The danger of Christians resting satisfied with low spiritual conditions is a real one. But, with respect to the memory of one to whom I owe so much, the remedy need not demand the formulation of a doctrine of '*the* baptism with the Spirit'. It is impossible to demonstrate such a doctrine consistently from the New Testament;[1] and this, at times, ML-J himself comes close to admitting, when he says it was not necessary for the doctrine to be written about in the epistles because 'all' those addressed *already* possessed the experience (pp. 36, 38, 43).[2] (If that were so, why the teaching

---

[1] There is no evidence to show that being 'sealed' by the Spirit (*Eph.* 1:13), and experiencing his 'witness' (*Rom.* 8:16) are to be interpreted as meaning full assurance. It is more probable that the 'seal' is the Spirit himself, indwelling every Christian; and 'the witness' (present tense) is not one great experience but an ongoing reality in varying degrees of strength.

[2] In a quotation given earlier he said 'most'; but here he says 'all' on the basis that the 'seal' and 'the witness' (which he identifies with 'the baptism') are spoken of as true of all the believers at Ephesus and Rome. That full assurance marked all the believers addressed in the epistles is surely not the case. The church at

in the epistles on fuller assurance? And would not that argument weaken the sufficiency of the epistles as guidance for all ages of the church?)

I think the danger he wanted to meet can be addressed by understanding that Christ's giving of the Spirit to the churches and to individuals is not uniform; there are variations, measures, and degrees of the Spirit's work, and thus always cause for believers to seek more. Only of Christ is it said, 'God gives not the Spirit by measure to him' (*John* 3:34). Sometimes the Spirit is 'poured out' in plentiful effusions (and, traditionally, that has understandably given rise to the use of the term 'baptisms'), but Scripture draws no clear line to warrant us to say '*this* is the baptism of the Spirit and that is not.' In Ezekiel's vision of the Spirit as water (47:3-6), the water 'was ankle deep', ' knee deep', 'up to the waist', and finally 'deep enough to swim in'. There are corresponding variations in the Christian's experience. Sometimes blessings are deeper and more intensely felt, but there is no warrant to say that one of these should be counted as *the* blessing.

Although Lloyd-Jones speaks of '*the* baptism', as though it stands uniquely apart in Christian experience, he does often qualify that impression by the very point I have just made. 'The intensity does vary considerably';[1] 'there are degrees of it' (p. 59); 'Some people tend to think that unless you have the maximum experience as it were, you have nothing at all' (p. 85). This he confirms by illustrations: 'When you receive a letter by post you look at the stamp on the envelope and also the postmark. You notice that the postmark is sometimes very clear, and at other times is so faint that you

---

Corinth, he says, far from possessing 'high spirituality', 'was in a most pathetic condition'. *Great Doctrines of the Bible, vol. 2, The Holy Spirit*, p. 270. If 'baptism with the Spirit' means the same in Acts as being 'filled with the Spirit', then all were not so ' baptised', for Luke speaks of those 'full of the Holy Spirit' (*Acts* 6:3) who could be distinguished from others.

[1] *God's Ultimate Purpose*, p. 286.

can scarcely tell where the letter was posted.' So the work of the Spirit which he identifies with the baptism, sometimes 'is faint . . . you must not say it is not there because it has not the intensity that you sometimes read of in the great classic examples.'[1]

> You may be walking along a country road and there may be a slight drizzle, but because you haven't got an overcoat you go on walking through this drizzle and eventually you get thoroughly wet; but it has taken some time because it was only a slight drizzle. But then you may be walking along the same road at another time and suddenly there is a cloud-burst and you are soaking wet in a matter of seconds. It is raining in both cases, but there is a great difference between a gentle drizzle, which you scarcely observe, and a sudden cloud-burst which comes down upon you' (p. 68).

In my mind, this qualification allowing a wide variation, instead of confirming ML-J's teaching, introduces more doubt. In quoting the experiences of those who had 'the baptism', he said: 'There was always an overwhelming element', God 'showering his love upon us, overwhelming us.' D. L. Moody 'felt that his body was cracking under the greatness of the experience'. Yet in the same sermon he goes on to face the question, 'Is it therefore correct to say that we have not been sealed with the Spirit until we have had some such overwhelming experience?' And, surprisingly, he answers it in the negative: 'The answer is that the intensity of the experience may vary considerably.'[2] But if both the 'slow drizzle' and the 'sudden cloud-burst' can be described in terms of 'baptism with the Spirit', is not the wisest thing to avoid the attempt to put such experiences into a separate classification? With the statement that the New Testament teaches that believers know

---

[1] *Romans: The Sons of God (8:5-17)*, p. 329.
[2] *God's Ultimate Purpose*, pp. 284, 286.

degrees of assurance there can be no dispute. It is calling any *one* experience '*the* baptism with the Spirit' that I am questioning.

PRAYER AND PROMISES

Can it be that the whole discussion above is simply a matter of words? To some extent I think that is true, especially whether being 'baptized' with the Spirit admits of a broader, experimental meaning, or can only be rightly used in speaking of union with Christ in regeneration (*1 Cor.* 12:13). But words affect practice, and it is one thing to believe the Scriptures warrant the broader understanding of 'baptizing', and another to apply it to one, specific post-conversion experience. A real danger, it seems to me, lies in the construction that ML-J wanted to establish. If a sudden, overwhelming experience of the love of God (which he calls 'the baptism') is the highest form of Christian experience – which only God can give, and which is not permanent – will not this teaching produce Christians either looking backward to such an experience in the past, or looking forward to the hope of obtaining 'it' in the future? ML-J was well aware of the danger of Christians living in the past and, referring to Wales, he said, 'I have known many such Christian people.' He went on to mention one minister he met in 1927, 'whose whole ministry was ruined' by the way he constantly recalled the blessing he had enjoyed in 1904. 'When the revival ended . . . he was still expecting the unusual; it did not happen. So he became depressed and spent about forty years of his life in a state of barrenness, unhappiness and uselessness.'[1]

How is this danger to be avoided? It is hardly enough to say 'the baptism' may be repeated, for in the above case, as in many

---

[1] *The Christian Warfare*, p. 195.

of the other instances that ML-J quoted from biographies in his sermons, the experience was only once in a lifetime. I do not think that ML-J squarely faced the problem.

We have already noted that he preached: 'In every single instance of the baptism with the Spirit it is something that happens to us, which we do not control. You can pray for the baptism of the Spirit, but that does not guarantee that it happens, as many of you know. You can live a good life, surrender yourself, do all you are told to do, but still you are not baptized with the Spirit' (p. 77). In a later sermon the problem I have raised comes up with reference to the promise of Acts 2:38, which ML-J also took as a promise of 'the baptism of the Spirit'. He then addressed the concern of a hearer who says, 'The promise is plain, "Ask and ye shall receive." I have asked, but I have not received' (p. 170). The answer he gives is, 'The promise is a general one accompanied by conditions.' How can this be if the 'baptism' experience is sovereignly given, with no 'conditions' for securing it?[1] I believe there is no answer short of abandoning the idea of a one-off experience as the supreme form of assurance, and believing that the Spirit is given to believers throughout life in varying degrees, according to their need and their obedience.

Or let this be put another way. The Christian's desires and prayers are to be regulated by scriptural promises. There is no promise of a special event for every Christian to be called 'the baptism with the Spirit', but there is a promise of the Holy Spirit being given to all who ask. In Luke 11:13 Jesus says not that the Spirit 'may be given', but 'how much more shall your heavenly Father give the Holy Spirit to them that ask him.' This promise is surely not for an event that may happen years in the future – it

---

[1] There is clearly a condition attached to Acts 2:38, but the condition is a saving receiving of Christ, shown by repentance and baptism. Believing in Christ is *the* condition for receiving the Spirit (*John* 7:37-38).

is a promise for present need and present duties. In the light of it, the believer has reason at all times to trust the ability of God to supply every need 'according to his riches in glory' (*Phil.* 4:19); so that he, 'always having all sufficiency in all things, may abound to every good work' (*2 Cor.* 9:8). The 'baptism of the Spirit' teaching, having the tendency that it does to put the believer looking for one special experience, does not induce that confidence. It has more hope for tomorrow than for today.

This has a clear bearing on the subject of revival. As already said, a revival, in ML-J's terms, begins with many receiving the baptism of the Spirit at the same time (p. 51). But as there is no promise of 'the baptism', neither is there promise of revival. As in the case of the individual and 'the baptism', ML-J stressed that revival is sovereignly given. For that reason he did not support 'tarrying meetings', that is, prayer meetings specifically to await the 'baptism with the Spirit' or revival. 'In "tarrying meetings" people who desired this blessing met together and decided they would stay until they had it . . . I do not accept that idea.'[1] 'I know of men, individual ministers, who have been teaching this for twenty years and more, trying to persuade their people to do it [i.e., receive the baptism by 'yielding and obeying']. They have obeyed, they have sacrificed, they have surrendered, they have had special prayer meetings every morning at seven o'clock; it has been going on for years but nothing has happened so far' (p. 278). ML-J said this for a very good pastoral reason. People who acted in that way only depressed themselves and others. 'I do not find it in the Scriptures', he said, and urged that Acts chapter 1 provides

---

[1] *Romans: The Sons of God (8:5-17)*, p. 281. The warning is repeated in many places. Speaking of those who teach 'You can get a revival', he said: 'I have known large numbers of men who have tried that with great thoroughness, but they have never obtained a revival.' *Authentic Christianity vol. 6, Acts 8:1-35* (Edinburgh: Banner of Truth, 2006), p. 142.

no example to be followed, for there the disciples were *promised* the Holy Spirit 'not many days hence'.

But is this a sufficient answer if passages in Acts under discussion teach there is a special experience that all Christians should seek? Why not tell such people to go on waiting 'patiently', as in the advice (quoted earlier) to those who had prayed long and not received 'the blessing'?[1] A better answer, as I have suggested, would appear to be that the promise of the Spirit's aid to every believer and church is sure for the present, in the measure of God's own determination. Certainly it is part of the nature of the Christian to long for the advance of Christ's kingdom – therefore, for seasons of special blessing, and, beyond them all, for the coming of Christ, when all things will be put under his feet. But 'the government' and the 'times and seasons' are on his shoulders. As Samuel Medley says,

> Too wise to be mistaken, He,
> Too good to be unkind.

Too often when there is prayer for 'revival' the blessing asked is for a repetition of 1904, or 1859, or 1740. But is the prayer for the Holy Spirit, taught us in Luke 11, not answered unless we see such great events? May we not rather say the prayer *is* answered in the measure of grace we presently need? At times the Spirit will be given above all that we can ask or think, and the awakening of churches has often come in that surprising way. Yet if we see no awakening or revival it does not mean that the prayer is unanswered, and that we must make do with a second best. To think in that way leads to the idea that only in receiving 'the baptism' or revival can there be true rejoicing. The 'baptism of the

---

[1] See above, p. 137.

Spirit' teaching is prone to lead to that conclusion. Unlike prayer that rests on promises, prayer based on that teaching can lead to disappointment. As already noticed, such disappointment ML-J often met with in Wales, and he sought to counteract it by warning against 'seeking experiences' and 'living on experiences'; but he did not seem to recognise how the people were disappointed because of the Pentecostal teaching they had believed. His own overall grasp of Scripture prevented him from falling into the conclusion that affected others. He would have agreed with the words of John Milne, a preacher much used at one period in revival in Scotland:

> The Holy Spirit is not intermittent; nor limited to revival seasons. Parents give good gifts at all times; and more so God. We are commanded to do all duties in the Spirit; to live, walk, pray, work in the Spirit. We should not be blamed for carnality if the Spirit were not always attainable. God is not impoverished by the abundance of bestowment.[1]

---

[1] Horatius Bonar, *Life of John Milne* (Edinburgh: Nisbet, 1868), p. 413.

Conclusions

1. The differing beliefs in this discussion should not be seen as distinguishing those who believe in the need for more experience of God and his love, and those who do not.

The difference is over whether or not the New Testament distinguishes distinct types of assurance, with 'the highest' to be understood as 'the baptism of the Spirit'. As we have seen, Dr Lloyd-Jones believed that his third ground of assurance had to be the most important, for it was bound up with enjoying the felt ('sensible'), presence of Christ. Yet he quoted William Guthrie's words:

> This sensible presence . . . is so absolutely let out upon the Master's pleasure, and so transient or passing, or quickly gone when it is, that no man may bring his gracious state into debate for want of it (p. 105).[1]

If that is true, it must follow that such assurance can only be intermittent and fleeting. But does that do justice to the New Testament and to the place it gives to faith in the possession of a settled assurance? Faith is not represented as supplying a second-best form of assurance; rather in faith there is 'full assurance' (*Heb.* 10:22); by faith there is 'joy and peace' (*Rom.* 15:13); 'the joy of faith' (*Phil.* 1:25); 'believing you rejoice with joy unspeakable and full of glory' (*1 Pet.* 1:8). In the epistle written that the joy of believers 'may be full', the instruction is to 'believe in the name of the Son of God' (*1 John* 5:13). Of course, this is not to set believing against 'sensible experience'; but there is no suggestion in the epistles that obtaining one experience, apart from the exercise of

---

[1] Quoting from William Guthrie, *The Christian's Great Interest* (repr. London: Banner of Truth, 1969), p. 109. Instead of speaking of the need of one extra-ordinary experience, Guthrie wrote, 'Full assurance will keep a man at work all his days' (p. 189).

faith, is the way to the greatest certainty. On the contrary, there is truth in the words of J. C. Ryle, 'Assurance after all is no more than a full-grown faith.'[1] On the same point, John Colquhoun, one of Scotland's ablest evangelical writers, affirmed:

> The spiritual comfort of the saints, *is according to their faith.* 'According to your faith', said the Lord Jesus, 'be it unto you.' It is according to the strength of their faith. If a man's faith is weak, his consolation is weak and unstable. In some happy moment, he may, indeed, feel a sudden transport of joy; but still, he has very little solid or lasting consolation.[2]

Ryle quotes many Puritans, showing their emphasis on the place of faith, including the maxim, 'Faith of adherence comes by hearing, but faith of assurance comes not without doing.' These writers are not discounting the value of sudden and extraordinary experiences of God's love, but they draw a distinction between temporary and permanent assurance, and believe that it is on the latter that the emphasis and directions of Scripture fall. The Christian's peace is not dependent on the 'sensible'; he can honour God without it and may often be called to do so. As Benjamin Morgan Palmer said, 'Our faith may be pleasing to our Heavenly Father when, without sensible comfort, there is nothing but this faith to which we can cling.'[3] On the same point Thomas Scott wrote:

> It is a common observation, that where (as in the case of Abraham), Almighty God has communicated strong faith, he subjects it to severe trials. If any persons can conceive of nothing superior to present comfort, to them this may be puzzling; but it need not

[1] J. C. Ryle, *Holiness* (repr. London: Clarke, 1952), p. 106.
[2] John Colquhoun, *Treatise on Spiritual Comfort* (Edinburgh: Ogle, 1814), pp. 29-30.
[3] B. M. Palmer, *The Threefold Fellowship and The Threefold Assurance* (repr. Harrisonburg, VA: Sprinkle, 1980), p. 133.

be so to others. The result, in such cases, proves honourable to God, and edifying to his saints.[1]

We may tell ourselves that the enjoyment of the felt presence of God is our greatest need; but God's dealings with his people suggest that a settled habit of faith, that can abide through trials and death itself, is the best for us in our present state. We are to 'live by faith', and to die affirming, 'I know whom I have believed' (*2 Tim.* 1:12). Which is what William Nevins meant by saying, 'Religion should not be a *rapture*, but a *habit*.'[2]

Of course, I am not implying that Lloyd-Jones gave little place to faith in the Christian life. A great deal that he preached shows that he did indeed emphasise this root grace; especially so in relation to justification and its close connection with assurance. 'There is no assurance apart from being clear on the doctrine of justification . . . without it we shall never really assume a truly Christian position and begin to enjoy its great blessings.'[3] There is need for assurance based on something outside of ourselves, because as ML-J said, 'I have despaired of myself a thousand times.'[4] From these con-

---

[1] John Scott, *Life of Thomas Scott* (London: Seeley and Burnside, 1836), p. 366.

[2] *Select Remains of William Nevins* (New York: Taylor, 1836), p. 386.

[3] *Sanctified Through the Truth*, p. 114. Thomas Charles, the Welsh evangelical leader in North Wales, noted: 'It is a mistake very injurious to us to set our feelings of comfort, or of no comfort, as our ground and rule in our communion with God, instead of the word of truth.' *Spiritual Counsels*, Edward Morgan, ed., (repr., Edinburgh: Banner of Truth, 1993), p. 445. Andrew Bonar writes: 'A minister, who had great joy in Christ, said on his death-bed regarding his peace and quietness of soul, "That he enjoyed these not from having a greater measure of grace than other Christians had, nor from any special immediate witness of the Spirit, but because he had more clear understanding of the covenant of grace."' *Gospel Truths* (Glasgow: Glass, 1878), p. 61. As ML-J constantly said, realising the truth is the basis of happy Christian living, and his teaching on justification continues to bring help to very many through his expositions of Romans, chapters 3 to 5, and other writings.

[4] Ibid., p. 151.

victions expressed in 1953, and in many other places, he did not move. But there was some change of emphasis. In preaching on assurance in the 1960s little place was given to faith.

I believe that was because his attention was set on opposing the 'take it by faith' teaching – the idea that all the Christian needs is 'bare faith'. That error encouraged him to present 'the baptism with the Spirit' as something outside the realm of our faith, and as the 'direct and immediate' work of the Spirit. Such a construction of assurance inevitably leads to treating faith as belonging to a lower level of assurance; as though to insist upon the exercise of faith is to miss what is more supernatural. Unlike the 'lower' assurance that may come by the use of means and the exercise of faith, 'the baptism' experience is wholly of God.

This seems to me to treat faith in a manner the New Testament does not recognise. All true faith is divinely energised. The distinction should not be between faith and the work of the Holy Spirit; it should be between a self-induced 'faith' (which may 'take' a blessing and receive nothing), and the faith wrought in the believer by which God himself works in him 'both to will and to do of his good pleasure' (*Phil.* 2:13).[1]

2. It was Dr Lloyd-Jones's rule that in facing any problem, the general should be looked at before the particular.

His general position in his theology of the Holy Spirit was that the Holy Spirit is the executor of the redemptive work of Christ. All that comes to us comes because of what the Saviour has done. The Spirit acts according to Christ's work and will, and the variations in his operations are never to be understood as being under the control of men. To make human decisions decisive is the characteristic of Arminian theology and leads to such language as, 'Chris-

---

[1] How often in the New Testament is faith linked with divine power, e.g. 'the work of faith with power' (*2 Thess.* 1:11; see *Eph.* 3:16-17; *1 Pet.* 1:5; etc.).

tians can obtain and promote revivals, and they can – by prayer, by "full surrender" or by other means – obtain "the baptism of the Spirit".' Lloyd-Jones's mind was closed to such teaching because it is opposed to the 'all important principle' of divine sovereignty (pp. 51, 231, etc.). As already noted, he will not even allow that prayer can secure revival. His definition of revival is the classic one of the older evangelicalism, an outpouring of the Spirit of God at 'special seasons of mercy'. In other words, it is not God's purpose that the church should always be in the experience of revival. He believed that teaching which would make revival normative violates 'the great principle and doctrine of the sovereignty of the Lord Jesus Christ'; and for the same reason he opposed any formula that offered to give 'the baptism of the Spirit'. He knew that all attempts to secure a great crisis experience (whether Wesleyan 'perfection-ism', the Victorian 'second-blessing', or the modern charismatic) proceed on the basis of an Arminian theology.[1]

If his particular teaching on the 'baptism of the Holy Spirit' is not understood in the structure of this theology as a whole, it will be misunderstood.

3. While ML-J differed from his own Reformed tradition on the present-ation of the doctrine of assurance, he did not differ from that tradition on its true nature.

Assurance makes Christ real to believers and leads to Christ-centred lives. It means the love of God shed abroad in the heart – the persuasion not of our love to God but his love to us. 'The

---

[1] For his conviction on the connection between Calvinistic belief and a right understanding of revival see, *The Puritans*, p. 211. It should also be remembered that the sermons published as *Joy Unspeakable* were preached to a congregation which received much instruction in the word of God. Several sentences remind us of this. Conviction and regeneration are 'of course' the work of the Spirit (p. 66). Again, 'We are all agreed that there is no need or necessity for spectacular signs' (p. 53).

hallmark of the saints is their great, increasing concern about the element of love in their lives.' That was his emphasis. At the same time he did not reduce assurance only to love and joy – counterfeits which mysticism may offer. He put weight on the Scripture that links 'the fear of the Lord' with 'the comfort of the Holy Spirit' (*Acts* 9:31). The more real assurance there is, the more there will be of reverence, awe, faith in Scripture, self-distrust and humility. The person who knows most of Christ is the last person to talk about himself; but the person with the 'false experience' shows it by his pride, his 'boasting', and his 'carnal self-satisfaction'.[1]

Distractions from holding to the centrality of Christ are repeatedly to be found throughout his sermons: 'Beware of regarding anything as the work of the Spirit in you, no matter how striking the phenomena may be, if it has not led you to the Lord Jesus Christ . . . Our great enemy tries to counterfeit these things, and he can produce phenomena, but he never leads to the Lord Jesus Christ.'[2] 'The devil turns people's attention to the phenomena, to the experiences, to the excitement.'[3] 'Any teaching or preaching which does not keep the Lord central and vital and overruling everything is already wrong teaching.'[4] The lesson of Christian biography, he reminds us, is that the saints 'were more concerned about holiness and about God and his love and the knowledge of him than they were about the experience' (p. 227).[5]

The claims of some that 'experience of Christ' supersedes any need for adherence to the word of God, and orthodox belief, he strongly denied. 'I am not interested in the experience of a man who is still wrong in his doctrine. The test of the baptism with the

---

[1] *Romans: The Sons of God (8:5-17)*, p. 367.
[2] Ibid. p. 24.
[3] *God's Ultimate Purpose*, p. 287.
[4] *Prove All Things*, p. 129.
[5] He emphasises this same truth elsewhere, 'We are not to seek experiences and phenomena as such.' *God's Ultimate Purpose*, p. 297.

Spirit is that it leads a man to the truth and to an understanding of the truth' (p. 111). It is to the word that the Spirit of truth directs attention. Thus, he would often say, revival comes,

> while God's people are met together and the word is being expounded and unfolded. That is the way in which it comes. And again let me make this clear; the expositions need not be about the Holy Spirit, or about the baptism of the Holy Spirit. Many friends need to be reminded of this at the present time (p. 235).

At the same time he warned against all who would confuse assurance with new gifts of revelation. 'Irrespective of what a man may say about a vision or an experience that he has had, if the teaching cannot be found in Scripture, or be reconciled with Scripture, it is to be rejected as false teaching. Even though the remainder of his teaching may be scriptural and accurate, he is in error and he must not be followed.'[1] 'Let us not forget what happened in the Irvingite movement', he urged in 1965, warning of disasters if the lesson was not learned.[2]

4. In so much that Lloyd-Jones preached and published he is to be found in the tradition of such men as John Flavel, Jonathan Edwards, George White-field, John Newton, Edward Payson, and others.

He quotes them freely, yet in his formulation of the doctrine of assurance he deviates from their teaching.[3] That does not of itself

---

[1] *Romans: The Sons of God (8:5-17)*, p. 177. See also p. 194 against subjective feelings being taken as proof of the leading of the Spirit.

[2] Arnold Dallimore, *The Life of Edward Irving: The Forerunner of the Charismatic Movement*, (Edinburgh: Banner of Truth, 1983)

[3] Flavel believed in a post-conversion 'sealing' but he did not teach assurance in terms of an 'immediate and direct' experience – 'if such a thing be at all, it is but rare and extraordinary' *Works*, vol. 4, pp. 219-221; vol. 5, p. 433; vol. 6, p. 354). Edwards is definitely against identifying full assurance with an immediate witness' (*Works*, vol. 2, Banner of Truth, 1974, pp. 448, 450. See also vol. 1, p. 243.) On Whitefield, see my *Jonathan Edwards, A New Biography* (Edinburgh: Banner of Truth, 1987), p. 490.

mean that the older tradition was right; but they did not see any scriptural justification for making a distinction between a 'direct' work of the Spirit and his other work in the believer.

The reason ML-J wanted to insist on the superiority of the 'direct' and the 'immediate' was that he believed it was the answer to the problem of 'cold, intellectual believism'. But did not these authors (whose profound spiritual experiences he often quoted) also have an answer to that danger? They declined to take the line he took because history had shown them that to classify some of the Spirit's work as immediate and indisputable is to open the door to fanaticism. In 1964-1965 ML-J was conscious of the danger of fanaticism, and repeatedly warned against it;[1] but his main concern was with countering the low spiritual conditions. Instead of the supernatural being exaggerated he feared that far too little attention was being given to that dimension. A sudden rise of interest in the work of the Holy Spirit gave him some hope that brighter days might be approaching, and I believe this inclined him to be more tolerant towards some ideas than he was at an earlier date. In particular, if – as began to happen – some now claimed to have the endorsement of the Holy Spirit's direct leading for what they were doing or saying, instead of reasserting that the church is not to be led by 'the vagaries of subjectivism', he was inclined to allow some liberty. Having said previously that the laying on of hands for the 'baptism of the Spirit' belonged to the apostolic office, he went on to say in 1965, 'No man should lay his hands upon another unless he has received a definite and a special

---

Letters of John Newton, Josiah Bull, ed., (repr., Edinburgh: Banner of Truth, 2007), pp. 74-75; 371; 389, are also helpful.

[1] The warnings are very clear in his 1953 sermons from John 17: 'It is a great fallacy to think that God must always work directly or he is not working at all.' 'While we thank God for subjective experiences and realise their great value and importance in the work of sanctification, we must never rely upon them.' *Sanctified Through the Truth*, pp. 58-60. Why then should experiences be given the highest place in assurance?

commission to do so' (p. 189). But how is a 'special commission' to be challenged if the person claiming it professes to have the definite call of God? 'Consider', wrote Flavel, 'how difficult, yea impossible it is for a man to determine that such a voice, vision, or revelation is of God; and that Satan cannot feign or counterfeit it; seeing he hath left no certain marks by which we may distinguish one spirit from another.'[1]

A door was left open and through that door the 'Irvingite disaster' was to be repeated, even within Westminster Chapel itself. I am thankful ML-J did not live to see it, but within twenty years of his retirement from Westminster in 1968, a great deal that he had once taught from its pulpit was being thrown aside. Dr R. T. Kendall, having begun with a Reformed profession as minister of Westminster Chapel in 1976, relapsed first into Pentecostalism and finally into the full-blown charismatic confusion of the Kansas City prophets and the 'Toronto Blessing'. How was this possible? 'Westminster Chapel has not exactly been a card-carrying charismatic church', wrote Kendall in a considerable understatement; but the change came because he was 'open to the Spirit'.[2] He explains that this change at the Chapel was not easy to effect. Although there had been removals and deaths in the congregation since ML-J's retirement in 1968, there were enough old members to be a source of opposition. But he faced their concerns with the claim that he was being loyal to ML-J: 'Had it not been for Dr Lloyd-Jones's teaching on the "immediate and direct" baptism of the Spirit – he insisted on those very words – I would never have survived at the Chapel.' He continued:

[1] *Works*, vol. 3, p. 484.
[2] R. T. Kendall , *In Pursuit of His Glory: My 25 Years at Westminster Chapel* (London: Hodder and Stoughton, 2002), p. 258. I reviewed this title in *The Banner of Truth*, March 2004, pp. 25-32.

This made it easier for me. By openness to the Spirit I therefore mean the 'immediate and direct' witness of the Spirit, a phrase Dr Lloyd-Jones would use again and again. It means that we want to know the Holy Spirit directly – not simply through the Word. I have taught that we must be open to any way God would choose to turn up, whether it has to do with the gifts of the Spirit or signs, wonders or miracles . . . It was a good while before I could say we had truly become a 'Spirit' church.[1]

Not all that Kendall tells us in his autobiography can be taken at face value, but there is some truth in the above words. Faithful members of Westminster Chapel were deceived into thinking that nothing significantly novel was being introduced. When numbers did awake to the situation it was too late.[2] By the 1990s, with almost all the old leaders in the congregation gone, Kendall tells us he 'was willing to do *anything* [his italics] for true revival'.[3] Visions, prophecies, tongues, 'slaying in the Spirit', a 'Jesus cheer', all came in. 'Manifestations of falling and laughter came to be expected in our services.'[4] The introduction of the laying-on of hands, he notes, as one turning point, though personally he lacked success in that practice: 'I wish I had Rodney Howard-Browne's or Charles Carrin's gift to impart power via the laying on of hands. When they pray for people God touches them so powerfully they often

---

[1] Ibid., pp. 31, 231-232.

[2] In 1986 six of the twelve deacons charged Kendall with Antinomianism; they lacked only one vote for the charge to be upheld, which would not have been the case if one of ML-J's trusted men had not been too old to recognize the situation. Antinomianism had arisen in the seventeenth century in connection with the teaching of assurance by an 'immediate witness'. In such 'assurance' there was no need of Scripture, and by this means, Flavel noted, 'swarms of errors have been conveyed into the world' (*Works*, vol. 3, p. 484). After the six deacons were dismissed, one of them, Richard Alderson, published the evidence of their charge in *No Holiness, No Heaven!* (Edinburgh: Banner of Truth, 1986).

[3] *In Pursuit of His Glory*, p. 255.

[4] Ibid., p. 113.

fall down; when I pray for people they usually stay standing like the Statue of Liberty!'[1]

A number of the 'prophecies' at Westminster Chapel are given in Kendall's autobiography; what he does not report is that these prophecies repeatedly proved their falsehood by their non-accomplishment. Among the many visiting preachers to the Chapel, Paul Cain prophesied a coming revival, and also the healing of ten members of the congregation by name, 'without apparent effect'. Gerald Coates prophesied that revival would come to the whole of Westminster by October 1996, promising that the Chapel would be 'totally unrecognisable'.[2] Instead of admitting the falsehood when no such revivals occurred, Kendall claimed the 'prophets' simply had their dates wrong. He professes no regrets over the confusion: 'I am not sorry that we have done our best to get God's attention, for we are no worse off for it . . . I hope we haven't gone too far. I only know that, if bringing revival were left to us, there is nothing more we could have done that I know of.'[3]

Dr Kendall continued to claim that he was following Lloyd-Jones, and that he had his predecessor's support up until the latter's death in 1981. The truth is that things that happened at Westminster Chapel in the 1990s were the very kind of things that ML-J had spoken of as prompted by demons.[4] Instead of retaining ML-J's support, the latter, when dying, deliberately excluded Kendall from speaking at his funeral and memorial service.[5] This piece of history is too important in its lessons to be ignored.

---

[1] Ibid., p. 233.

[2] For this and other information, see *CRN Journal, The Journal of Christian Research Network*, Spring 1998, 'The Theology of Dr Kendall', part 2, by Richard Alderson (one of Kendall's former deacons).

[3] *In Pursuit of His Glory*, p. 256.

[4] If the reader thinks I am exaggerating let him read *The Christian Warfare*, pp. 266-268, preached in 1961 and published in 1976.

[5] Dr Alderson writes that Dr Kendall himself told him this; I also know it is true. Such facts are carefully excluded from the Kendall autobiography.

5. Dr Lloyd-Jones believed that those who did not accept 'the baptism with the Spirit' teaching, as he understood it, were thereby encouraging low views of the Spirit's work and discounting the need for revival.

Hence the seriousness with which he spoke. I do not understand why he was so definite in making this connection. Men such as John Flavel and Jonathan Edwards opposed the way he was to formulate assurance, not because they did not believe in revivals as 'effusions of the Spirit', but just because they did. They feared that the 'direct and immediate' teaching, lessened the place of the word of God, and was prone to introduce the kind of excess that must discredit the work of the Spirit.

I believe it was a mistake to make an issue of terminology that cannot be substantiated from Scripture. A few have heavily criticised ML-J on this account, almost to the point of questioning the value of his work as a whole. I think that is absurd. If he went too far in his remedy for what he saw as the main need, the manner in which he drew attention to the need of the Holy Spirit did much good. It may also have influenced John Stott to write what he left unsaid in 1964. In his second and much-enlarged edition of *Baptism and Fullness,* published in 1975, the Rector of All Souls, while not altering his theological position, underlined the truth which ML-J had pressed. He wrote in his new Introduction:

> The general picture remains one of steadily diminishing Christian influence in an increasingly secular community. The dead, dry bones need the living breath of God . . . We are thankful indeed for what God has done and is doing, and we do not want to denigrate his grace by denying it. But we hunger and thirst for more. We also long for true revival, an altogether supernatural visitation of the Holy Spirit in the church, bringing

depth as well as growth; and meanwhile we yearn for a deeper, richer, fuller experience of Christ through the Holy Spirit in our own lives.[1]

Many of the works of ML-J – especially those published in his own life time – have joined with those of the tradition to which he belonged as a permanent heritage for the Christian church. To accept that there was a flaw in his presentation of assurance is not to question that he was drawing needed attention to a vital subject; and if he failed to prevent excess in some quarters, we may believe this episode in history will serve to make others more watchful in the future.

[1] John R. W. Stott, *Baptism and Fullness: The Work of the Holy Spirit Today* (Leicester: Inter-Varsity Press, 1975), pp.13–14. Lloyd-Jones's annotated copy of Stott's first edition remained, of course, private. It is now in the National Library of Wales at Aberystwyth. Stott also wrote in 1975: 'I think I may say with truthfulness that it has been my practice for many years to pray every day that God would fill me with his Spirit and cause more of the Spirit's fruit to appear in my life' (p. 118). See also his words in *John Stott: Global Ministry*, p. 156.

The first of two sides of notes for ML-J's Evangelical Alliance address, at Westminster Central Hall, October 18, 1966.

8

'THE LOST LEADER', OR 'A PROPHETIC VOICE'?

These headings summarize the two very different understandings of the most important controversy in the life of Dr
LloydJones. It came in the 1960s and brought on him the severest
criticism he ever faced from other evangelicals. Most who have
since gone into print on the subject have treated him as the blame-
worthy party. My concern here is not to defend his reputation.
What is of abiding importance is to assess the principles on which
he acted. All his ministerial life ML-J had sought to do nothing
that would hinder the gospel; when he came to the 1960s, in the
opinion of his critics, it was here that he failed. For his part, he
believed it was the gospel itself that was at stake in the controversy
of that decade. He saw it as a cause for which, if need be, he was
willing to lose influence and popularity. Perhaps I will not change
the minds of some in the following pages, but at least I hope to
show that something major was involved. I shall not argue that he
was wholly right, but that he was right on the heart of the issue.

Part of the confusion attached to this controversy is related
to the way in which separate events have been treated as though
they happened simultaneously. This in turn affects the way they
are interpreted. I begin therefore with a summary of the events in
which ML-J was principally concerned and their dates.

The best-remembered event took place on October 18, 1966, when ML-J was the opening speaker at the two-day 'National Assembly of Evangelicals', organised by the Evangelical Alliance at the Central Hall in London. He was announced to speak on 'Christian Unity'. The case he presented was that if evangelical belief represents essential Christian belief, then the priority of evangelicals ought to be their unity with one another, not with denominations heading for an ecumenical unity unsympathetic to the gospel.[1] John Stott, who chaired the meeting, feared that the address would be understood as calling Anglican evangelicals to an immediate withdrawal from the Church of England, and before closing the meeting he told the Assembly why he disagreed with his senior friend.

It should be understood that the two men had already talked of the subject in private and the difference between them was not personal. When Stott was once asked to name the individuals who had influenced him, the two ministers most prominent in his list were L. F. E. Wilkinson and Martyn Lloyd-Jones.[2] An anecdote from Stott's life illustrates his esteem. One Sunday evening, when he was saying goodnight to members of his congregation of All Souls in London, he spoke to a student whom he recognised and thought to be a visitor: 'Hello, I thought you went to Westminster Chapel.' Shy and embarrassed the young man said, 'No, I'm not a follower of the great Doctor.' To which John Stott at once replied, 'Aren't you? I am.'[3]

---

[1] The way ecumenical debate dominated the Christian scene in the 1960s needs to be remembered as the context in which evangelicals were to disagree. In that connection my article, 'Evangelical Reaction to the Ecumenical Movement in England,' *The Banner of Truth*, January 1968, pp.1-9, may be helpful.

[2] Timothy Dudley Smith, *John Stott: The Making of a Leader* (Leicester: IVP, 1999), p. 260.

[3] Ibid., pp. 233-234.

While what the 1966 Evangelical Alliance meeting meant remains debated (and I will discuss it further below), there is no doubt that it brought into the open a division between those who believed in remaining in denominations where evangelicals were suffered rather than welcomed, and those who believed that the times called for an open separation from those unfaithful to Scripture.

A second important event followed. The Westminster Fellowship of ministers, of which ML-J was chairman, was inter-denominational in its make up, and in this monthly forum the issues connected with his call for evangelical unity at the Evangelical Alliance meeting had often been discussed. No consensus was reached and, rather than spend more time on the issue, ML-J urged the preparation of a new statement as the basis of future membership. This 'Statement of Principles' regretted 'compromise on the part of many evangelicals in the doctrinally mixed denominations', and saw 'no hope whatsoever of winning such doctrinally mixed denominations to an evangelical position'. At some point, it believed, separation from denominations linked with the World Council of Churches 'is inevitable'.[1] Timothy Dudley-Smith, in the conciliatory account he gives in his biography of John Stott, strays somewhat beyond the evidence in saying 'the Westminster Fellowship ceased to offer a welcome to Anglicans.'[2] Some Anglicans did remain in the Fellowship; the 'Statement' required no instant withdrawal from denominations committed to the ecumenical movement; but those assenting to the new basis were accepting an understanding of the church scene contrary to the optimistic view of the Anglican evangelical majority. That view, in the words

---

[1] Document headed, 'Statement of Principles governing membership of new meeting. Drawn up and agreed at Westminster – January 23 and March 13, 1967.' The wording was not the work of ML-J but he obviously endorsed it.

[2] *John Stott: Global Ministry*, p. 69.

167

of Alister McGrath, was that they were seeing 'a remarkable period of renaissance within evangelicalism in England.'[1]

The public difference between Lloyd-Jones and John Stott in 1966 marked a divide in English evangelicalism, but another separation came later. For four years after that event Dr James Packer continued to share with ML-J in the organisation of the annual Puritan Conference that had met at Westminster Chapel since 1950. The Conference was convened as usual until 1970 when, in July of that year, ML-J and two other Nonconformist members of the committee decided that the public co-operation could not continue. Writing to Jim Packer as 'My Dear Friend' on July 7, 1970, ML-J, 'with a very heavy heart and deep regret', proposed that 'no conference be held this year'. He concluded: 'I sincerely hope that we shall be able to maintain some personal contact.'[2]

For the separations that came about through all these events ML-J has been blamed. Packer in 1986 had this comment on the question of withdrawal from 'doctrinally mixed church bodies': 'The way that in the last 15 years of his life Dr Lloyd-Jones highlighted this issue, and the pressure he put on Anglicans in particular over it . . . disrupted the evangelical community . . . and it diminished the Doctor's overall influence in England, which is at least a pity and perhaps a tragedy.'[3] As ML-J died in 1981, Packer's '15 years' go back to 1966 as the starting point. Alister McGrath, Packer's biographer, says more. He describes the controversy following John Stott's public disagreement with ML-J in 1966 as 'bitter', and continues: 'Rightly or wrongly, Lloyd-Jones was criticised for wrecking evangelical unity . . . Lloyd-Jones was now subject to serious criticism from within evangelical circles, on

---

[1] A. M. McGrath, *To Know and Serve God: A Biography of James I. Packer* (London: Hodder & Stoughton, 1997), p. 99.

[2] As this important letter is hitherto unpublished I will include it below, p. 205.

[3] 'A Kind of Puritan' in *Chosen by God*, C. Catherwood, *ed.*, (Crowborough: Highland Books, 1985), pp. 45-46.

the grounds that he had made denominational affiliation of decisive importance to evangelical identity . . . He became increasingly a voice in the wilderness.'[1] Morgan Derham, General Secretary of the Evangelical Alliance in 1966, believed ML-J was guilty of 'a monumental error'.[2]

Dr Gaius Davies, writing under the heading, 'The Lost Leader', described the closing of the Puritan Conference and the end of ML-J's public association with Packer as 'the *putsch* which ousted Packer and others who did not share the required beliefs about separation and a pure church'. He calls it 'very scurvy treatment'.[3]

But the fullest criticism did not come until a book was published in 2002. This was John Brencher's *Martyn Lloyd-Jones (1899-1981) and Twentieth-Century Evangelicalism*, a doctoral thesis revised for publication. There are some helpful things and sympathetic observations in Dr Brencher's well-researched work. There is also repeated censure of Dr Lloyd-Jones, based on the claim that the policy he came to adopt on church issues was 'sectarian'; he 'divided those whom God had united on the basis of Scripture and who had a common purpose and trust'.[4] 'While he favoured unity among believers, his separatist ecclesiology only exacerbated the situation and left evangelicals more divided than before.'[5] 'Lloyd-Jones's insistence on separation as a fundamentally biblical position alienated a body of opinion which was just as evangelical and loyal to Scripture. To separate from genuine evangelicals was, in our view, schismatic. In the broader sense, to cut oneself off

---

[1] *To Know and Serve God*, pp. 125-127.

[2] *John Stott: A Global Ministry*, p. 67.

[3] Putsch = attempt at revolution. Gaius Davies, *Genius, Grief and Grace* (Fearn, Rosshire: Christian Focus, 2001), pp. 368, 366.

[4] John Brencher, *Martyn Lloyd-Jones (1899-1981) and Twentieth-Century Evangelicalism* (Carlisle: Paternoster, 2002), p. 226.

[5] Ibid., p. xiii.

from other Christians in order to create a separated, holy society was a form of Christianity that was no longer acceptable.'[1]

In a final summary Brencher writes:

> His core beliefs never varied and, in his day, his contribution to evangelicalism was outstanding: he became a touchstone of orthodoxy. Unhappily he manoeuvred himself into a corner over the issue of separation and caused a breaking of fellowship when it was within his grasp to bring evangelicals together. He knew there was substantial agreement between separatist and non-separatist on gospel essentials yet he allowed a secondary issue – church affiliation – to over-ride what was fundamental. Not only was this an opportunity lost: it established a legacy of intolerance and perpetuated divisions among British evangelicals for years to come.[2]

John Brencher's book also quotes several evangelicals who were basically supportive of his critique. These include men who thought highly of ML-J, as did Jim Packer. Packer has written some of the finest tributes to ML-J as a preacher. This should make us cautious about being dismissive of the criticism; we need rather to try to understand why such a consensus ever arose. The answer is not perfectly straightforward. Why liberals and others should have been opposed to Dr Lloyd-Jones presents no problem; in the case I am now considering the difference was with evangelical Christians.

---

[1] Ibid., p. 230.
[2] Ibid., p. 231.

Two Considerations towards Clarity

1. In so far as the controversy of 1966 became public, it was aggravated and confused by a lack of reliable information.

ML-J's address at the Central Hall in that year was the occasion of division, yet by his own decision no recording or transcript was released, although the Alliance requested that it might be. More than twenty years were to pass before it was printed.[1] The non-availability of the full text of that speech has at least some relevance to the way much of the Christian press misreported its intention. *The Life of Faith* said that 'Dr Martyn Lloyd-Jones made an eloquent plea to evangelicals to leave their denominations and join a United Evangelical Church.' The magazine of the Free Church of Scotland said he put forward a passionate plea 'for the formation of an evangelical church'.[2] Others said the same.

It is noteworthy that Timothy Dudley-Smith, the biographer of John Stott, can write that the report asserting that Lloyd-Jones was urging men to '"leave the major denominations and to form a united church" was quite mistaken.'[3] But this rejection of the contemporary press reports did not appear until 2001. How, then, was such common misinformation printed at the time? The purpose of the Evangelical Alliance meetings in October 1966 was to discuss the published findings of a Commission of the Alliance which had concluded, among other things, 'There is no widespread

---

[1] An accurate summary of the Lloyd-Jones address was given in *Unity in Diversity: Ten Papers Given at the National Assembly of Evangelicals* (London: Evangelical Alliance, 1967), pp. 7–13. The full text was printed in *Knowing the Times*. Morgan Derham later alleged that ML-J made 'a forceful appeal in the words of Revelation – "Come out of Babylon".' I have seen the original copy of the address, taken down from the tape recording, and no such words were spoken. See *John Stott: Global Ministry*, p. 465.

[2] Documentation is in my *Fight of Faith*, p. 527.

[3] *John Stott: Global Ministry*, p. 67.

demand at the present time for the setting up of a united evangelical church.' It was in response to this report that ML-J was assumed to be speaking. He was known to be dissatisfied with a mere maintenance of the *status quo* among evangelicals; he believed that a much closer unity was urgently needed, and therefore it was possible for it to be thought that 'a united evangelical church' was what he was seeking.

Why, then, did ML-J not want his Central Hall address printed? Some people have offered this reason: he had really wanted the setting up of a new denomination, as most of the press reported; and it was only the lack of support following that meeting that led him to back off. This opinion is too absurd to be refuted.[1]

I believe the reasons he did not want it printed are no mystery. For one thing, it was because his address was part of a much larger discussion and that, without the context of that larger discussion, he could not set out his thinking adequately in one short address. Nor, given all the pressure on his time, had he any opportunity to edit his address or prepare something larger. As I have already said, discussion of the issues had been going on under his chairmanship at the Westminster Fellowship regularly for several years, and to a more limited degree at the Puritan Conference. In the Fellowship discussions it was abundantly clear he saw no need for a secession from *all* denominations, and that he was not intending to organise or lead any new denomination.[2] Had notes of discussions at the Fraternal been kept and published they would have

---

[1] Brencher writes on the events of 1966: 'Whether he would have formed a new denomination given the chance is a moot point. Publicly he denied any such intention, though some who were close to him are not so sure. R. T. Kendall, for example, feels that, when nothing happened, "he was very disappointed. He could have done it. I think the only reason he did not have the courage to do it was that he thought it might fail."' Brencher, *Lloyd-Jones*, p. 132. This, and a similar remark quoted on p. 224, show how little Kendall understood ML-J either then or later.

[2] See *Fight of Faith*, pp. 530, 536.

been helpful by way of clarification; but nothing was kept, and the same is true of discussions at the Puritan Conference (where only the papers given by speakers were printed). I do not doubt that the non-availability of records contributed to the confusion. As already noted in these pages, gifts of organisation and administration were not part of ML-J's make up.

There is another reason why ML-J did not want his address published. I question whether he expected the Central Hall meeting to constitute the crisis that it suddenly became. He was not, as alleged, calling ministers in what became known as the 'mixed denominations' to immediate secession, and for a very good reason. He knew that pastors are responsible for their people, and people had first to be prepared if they were to follow their teachers in a secession. Most congregations in the main and mixed denominations were not ready for such a step.[1] Yet, not without reason, John Stott, listening to the address, feared the possibility of immediate secessions from the Church of England; so he intervened as chairman to disagree with what had been said. It was this action that turned the meeting into a kind of Rubicon. It polarised discussion before, in the wider Evangelical context, it had ever really begun. True the Alliance had provided time for discussion the day after ML-J's address; but, with the lines already apparently publicly drawn, a subdued silence prevailed the next day. It was as though further talk was pointless, and with the Evangelical Alliance leaders dismayed at the public division of the previous night they had no wish for the main issue – evangelical versus ecumenical unity – to be addressed.[2] As with many significant events in history, the

---

[1] Kenneth Howard recorded this conversation with ML-J in 1965: 'I asked if the Doctor thought that congregations were ready to follow ministers if they seceded. He thought not and that perhaps the task of the next five years would be to prepare people quietly for such a step.' That was still ML-J's thinking in 1966. Ibid., p. 507.

[2] For the sake of maintaining the membership of Anglican evangelicals, and

two speakers never intended the night of October 18, 1966 to be a crisis that would be talked about around the world. If John Stott is to be criticised for turning the meeting into a public drama by his intervention, it may be that ML-J also showed some misjudgment in launching his case at a public rally instead of in a debate where there was time for extended discussion and clarification. ML-J's reply to this would be that if he had discussed the issue, rather than given the address that he did, it would have made no difference. He believed the mind of the other side was already made up. 'I did not expect anything different', he said, commenting on the majority Anglican evangelical response.[1]

2. There is another consideration that throws some light on the criticism of ML-J.

As already noted, opponents of his case argued that he was ending a unity that evangelicals had long recognised. The traditional position was that, although evangelicals belonged to different denominations, on essential truths they were united. Only on the secondary question of denominational allegiance did they differ, and this difference did not constitute disunity, for they had always believed that unity is primarily spiritual, not organisational and external. This is what ML-J himself argued effectively in his *The Basis of Christian Unity*. published in 1962. Christians, he said, are 'Not to produce a unity, not to create a unity, not to try to arrive at a unity, but to "keep the unity" . . . The unity is inevitable among all those who have been quickened by the Holy Spirit out

others, the Evangelical Alliance had adopted a position of 'benevolent neutrality' on the ecumenical movement.

[1] D. M. Lloyd-Jones, *Unity in Truth* (Darlington: Evangelical Press, 1991) p. 167. ML-J's wish, expressed in 1965, and reported by Dudley-Smith, that Stott might be his successor at Westminster Chapel, should be understood in the same light. He knew it was not a real possibility. See *John Stott: Global Ministry*, p. 464, note 69.

of spiritual death . . . The invisible Church is more important than the visible Church.'[1] Elsewhere he said: 'The one thing that matters is that we are found in this mystical, unseen, spiritual Church which alone is the body of Christ.'[2]

If this is so, the argument against ML-J ran, why was he now apparently urging a different kind of unity for evangelicals? This brings us to the first of two reasons which he believed justified secession from doctrinally mixed denominations. Without taking such action, he argued, evangelicals would be guilty of schism. As this charge of schism came into his 1966 address, the nature of schism was inevitably to be part of the ensuing controversy. ML-J defined schism as 'a division among members of the true visible Church about matters which are not sufficiently important to justify division'.[3] Among things not justifying division he had long placed differences over church government and similar things. He now argued that, because of their denominational attachments, many evangelicals were in visible unity with men who did not hold to the essentials of the faith, while in most of their work they were divided from other evangelicals. This led to his charge: 'for us to be divided from one another in the main tenor of our lives and for the bulk of our time, is nothing but to be guilty of schism.' There was therefore, he argued, a separation required of some in order to unity and he pressed the question at the Evangelical Alliance meeting, 'What reasons have we for not coming together?' Later he would press the same point in the words: 'For brethren who are agreed about the essentials of the gospel, and who are sharing the same life, to be divided by history, tradition, or any consideration, is the sin of schism, and it is a terrible sin.'[4]

---

[1] D. M. Lloyd-Jones, *The Basis of Christian Unity* (London: Inter-Varsity Fellowship, 1962), pp. 24, 60, reprinted in *Knowing the Times*, and as a separate paperback, (Edinburgh: Banner of Truth, 2003).

[2] *Christian Unity*, p. 53. The volume consists of sermons preached in 1957.

[3] 'Evangelical Unity: An Appeal,' in *Knowing the Times*, p. 253.

[4] *Unity in Truth*, p. 60. The words come from an address given in 1968.

The logic of this schism argument is that there must be a visible association of churches in order to true evangelical unity. But how was this consistent with the long-held belief that true Christian unity is not dependent upon any external ordering of churches? As he had long preached, all true believers are in real unity with one another irrespective of their denomination; they all belong to 'mount Zion, the city of the living God, the heavenly Jerusalem' (*Heb.*12:22). Christian unity can and does co-exist with differences over how churches are ordered. In the words of A. A. Hodge: 'If the Church be an external society, then all deviation from that society is of the nature of schism; but if the Church be in its essence a great spiritual body, constituted by the indwelling of the Holy Ghost through all ages and nations, uniting all to Christ, and if its external organization is only accidental and temporary, and subject to change and variation, then deviation of organization, unless touched by the spirit of schism, is not detrimental to the Church.'[1]

As soon as Lloyd-Jones spoke of the need for separation, in order to the avoidance of schism, it became necessary for him to state in what the proposed unity would consist: if it was to be more than the already existing spiritual unity what would it be? Would it not have to be a new denomination of one kind or another? There was a problem for ML-J in answering this question, for if a new body or association of churches was organised, with the claim to represent true Christian unity, then it would indeed look as though all Christians failing to adhere to it were persisting in 'schism'.

[1] A. A. Hodge, *Evangelical Theology: A Course of Popular Lectures* (1890; repr., Edinburgh: Banner of Truth, 1976), p. 181. The spirit of schism is a spirit contrary to the fundamentals of Christian truth and love. In John Owen's words: 'Among all the churches of the world which are free from idolatry and persecution, it is not different opinions, or a difference in judgment about revealed truths, nor a different practice in sacred administration, but pride, self-interest, love of honour, reputation and dominion, with the influence of civil or political intrigues and considerations, that are the true cause of that defect of evangelical unity that is at this day.' Quoted by ML-J, *The Puritans*, p. 98, from Owen, *Works*, vol. 13.

What in fact happened, as is now well known, was that the 'new body' became the British Evangelical Council to which only churches outside 'the mixed denominations' could belong.[1] But as a considerable body of evangelicals, both ministers and people, still remained in these denominations it could only mean that, *if the BEC was the necessary body for unity*, then evangelical unity was indeed fractured. On the basis of this reasoning Jim Packer wrote: 'He [ML-J], rather than I, was the denominationalist for insisting that evangelicals must all belong to this grouping and no other.'[2] With the same argument, in the words already quoted, John Brencher claimed ML-J 'allowed a secondary issue – church affiliation – to override what was fundamental'.

The call for secession in order to the avoidance of schism was, I believe, a mistake and it contributed to confusion over what the issues were. If there was misunderstanding among evangelicals in 1966, the blame does not lie entirely with those who disagreed with ML-J. But more than one argument was contained in his 1966 address. In the subsequent controversy, those who disagreed with him concentrated on what was not his main point. To this main point we now turn.

---

[1] The BEC was not a denomination, but an association of denominations. In 1967 ML-J encouraged Westminster Chapel to move from its Congregational Union connection to the Fellowship of Independent Evangelical Churches. Although he had long since ceased to be involved in the denominational affairs of the Presbyterian Church of Wales, his ministerial status formally remained with that denomination.

[2] *Chosen Vessels: Portraits of Ten Outstanding Men*, Charles Turner, ed. (Ann Arbor, MI: Servant Publications, 1985), p. 112. 'By contrast [with ML-J]', Packer wrote, 'I believed that the claims of evangelical unity do not require ecclesiastical separation.'

THE MAIN POINT

Lloyd-Jones knew very well that evangelicals had long associated across denominational lines. For many years this had been traditional and, of course, it was his own practice. But by the mid-twentieth century mainline Protestant denominations in Britain were changing dramatically and aiming to be 'one Church . . . not later than Easter Day, 1980'. Contrary to their denomination's original creeds, the leaders were no longer advocates of historic Christianity. Liberal unbelief was dominant. 'If there is anything that is more evident than anything else in the modern world', ML-J would say in 1973, 'it is the failure of liberalism and modernism in the church. It has emptied the churches and reduced the country to its present moral level.'[1] Anglican evangelicals, however, were now beginning to act as though the danger from unbelief in the ministry was past, or that it could be curtailed by an alliance with Anglo-Catholicism. Contrary to their history, contending for the Protestant faith against Anglo-Catholic teaching and practice now became a thing of the past. In 1927 one thousand evangelical Anglican clergy 'joined in a solemn pledge to leave the Church of England if the Prayer Book Measure were passed'.[2] This was a measure designed to give greater liberty to the Anglo-Catholic position, and the evangelical challenge at that date succeeded. But by the 1960s a very different standpoint was being adopted by Anglican evangelical leaders. It was now decided that everything should be done to avoid the impression that evangelicals were only

[1] *Unity in Truth*, p. 159.

[2] Marcus L. Loane, *These Happy Warriors: Friends and Contemporaries* (Blackwood, South Australia: New Creation, 1988), pp. 3-4. Loane describes this as 'the high-water mark of Evangelical strength and achievement between the two World Wars', and comments, 'Not a single Evangelical known to have stood out against the Prayer Book Measure was destined to become a Bishop.'

'a party' within the Church; instead, more effort should be made to co-operate with others. Thus when the National Evangelical Anglican Congress met at Keele in 1967, it was a liberal Anglo-Catholic, Archbishop Michael Ramsey, who was invited to speak.

Something of this new policy was already apparent in the book, *All in Each Place: Towards Reunion in England,* edited by Jim Packer, and published in 1965. The policy was officially expressed when the Keele Congress published its report in 1967. It was agreed at Keele that all who professed the World Council of Churches brief Basis of Faith 'have a right to be treated as Christians.'[1] The objective was that evangelicals should no more appear as a 'party'; 'comprehensiveness' was the term now in vogue. This was a very major decision. Some have even called Keele the most important event in twentieth-century English church history. The Rev. John King, a former editor of the *Church of England Newspaper* and an apologist for Keele, was pleased that that 'monolithic evangelical unity' had given way to a new 'church consciousness'. 'The outstanding effect of Keele', he wrote, 'was to deal a death-blow to the idea of an evangelical unity existing as a kind of alternative to the ecumenical movement.'[2] Hitherto, as Oliver Barclay comments, 'Evangelicals had their own ecumenism, bounded by the authority of Scripture.'[3] In practice it was *that idea of Christian unity* that Keele was rejecting.

How did this new Anglican evangelical policy relate to Dr Lloyd-Jones's address of 1966? The important fact is that, although the policy was not announced till Keele met a year later, it was being put in place before ML-J's appeal, and its existence – known

---

[1] P. Crowe, ed., *Keele '67: The National Evangelical Anglican Congress Statement* (London: Falcon Books, 1967), p. 37.

[2] John C. King, *The Evangelicals* (London: Hodder & Stoughton, 1969), pp. 120, 122, 150.

[3] Oliver Barclay, *Evangelicalism in Britain, 1935-1995* (Leicester: IVP, 1997), p. 74.

to him – was the background to his address. As I have already said, in speaking as he did in that address, he had no expectation of success, or that the Anglican evangelical leaders would think again. He argued that Christian unity arises out of a common faith in the centralities of the gospel. The New Testament puts doctrinal truth before fellowship. Evangelicals professed this, but the new policy was encouraging evangelicals to co-operate and work alongside those who did not preach a saving gospel and who in many cases denied it. This was to act as though the gospel was a non-essential for unity. The plea of ML-J in 1966 was that evangelicals in the mixed denominations should give their time to working alongside fellow evangelicals, not with those who were no guardians of the faith.

It was because ML-J's thinking so cut across the course already set by Anglican evangelical leaders that it provoked the disturbance that it did. Unlike the resistance of Anglican evangelicals in 1927, secession was not even to be considered as a possibility at Keele.[1] His 1966 address was the *occasion* more than the *cause* of the division. The cause was the changed evangelical policy towards those who were not evangelical, a policy about which the Evangelical Alliance sought to be neutral.

How was it that this new policy came to be promoted by evangelicals who had previously stood alongside ML-J? The answer (as I have explained more fully in my book *Evangelicalism Divided*) is not that they wanted a weakening of gospel belief; on the contrary, they acted as they did because they thought the times offered the opportunity for a major evangelical recovery in their denomination. The signs pointing that way were the participation of non-evangelical clergy – even the former Archbishop of Canterbury – in the Billy Graham crusades, and the promise of ecumenical leaders

---

[1] 'We do not believe secession to be a live issue in our present situation.' *Keele '67*, p. 38.

that evangelicals would surely be given much wider influence if they 'came out of their ghetto'. Anglican evangelical leaders understood that their former 'exclusiveness' within their denomination had given major offence. They also thought that while liberal leadership and control was passing in the Church of England, their own numbers were multiplying.[1] So by adopting a new 'openness' (as it was called) they believed that a recovery of the gospel in their denomination was a real possibility.

While the evangelicals who supported the new thinking spoke of the 'welcome' now being shown to them in ecumenical discussions, they also noted 'the prejudice and even hostility . . . directed particularly towards those known to be connected with the Inter-Varsity Fellowship.'[2] This was because the IVF, taking a stand on Scripture, was known to stand against co-operation with non-evangelicals. The ecumenical leaders in the British Council of Churches understood the need to detach men from the IVF position, and, as Leith Samuel has written, 'the key man to get hold of was Martyn Lloyd-Jones', together with John Stott.[3] They failed to gain Lloyd-Jones, but he understood why other evangelicals responded to the approach. They thought that a cautious measure of comprehension should be practised in order to a greater ultimate gain. Their danger was in not recognising that the offence previously given by Anglican evangelicals was mainly on account of the exclusiveness of the gospel itself. Did the New Testament permit the 'openness' that was now being advocated? Is union with Christ crucified, by faith alone, the only way of salvation, or may other

---

[1] Speaking of the 1960s, McGrath believed, 'Liberal evangelicalism had ceased to be a meaningful organised presence within the church [of England]. Conservative evangelicalism has, quite simply, eclipsed it.' *To Know and Serve God*, p. 132. It had ceased to be 'organised' as a pressure group because liberal belief was now to be found across the denomination.

[2] J. D. Douglas, ed., *Evangelicals and Unity* (Abingdon: Marcham Manor Press, 1964), p. 5.

[3] *Lloyd-Jones: Chosen by God*, p. 198.

understandings also be permissible? Are the deity of Christ, and the propitiation of the judgment of God by his death, to be considered 'views', or are they essential to the gospel? Were the one thousand Anglicans of 1927 extreme in their readiness to leave the Church of England rather than accept the sacramental teaching of Anglo-Catholicism? Above all, can there be agreement on such questions where there is no common submission to the sole authority of Scripture?

Packer, identified with the Keele decisions, argued that he was supporting both ecumenical *and* evangelical unity. For Lloyd-Jones there was a fundamental inconsistency in that position; it meant toleration, if not acceptance, of different meanings of 'Christian', and that when 'the great battle today is for the whole of the Christian faith. It is being queried, denied and ridiculed almost as never before.'[1] The mainline denominations had largely contributed to this situation. Thus, at a time when the recovery of true Christianity was the most urgent need, he saw the new policy, which encouraged men to co-operate with those who denied the gospel, as a most serious mistake. He said to the evangelicals following this policy, 'You are virtually saying that though you think you are right, they also may be right, and this is a possible interpretation of Scripture.'[2] Such a policy of 'openness' could only promote the doctrinal indifferentism that had already so weakened Christian testimony in the whole nation. As Oliver Barclay has observed of those who opposed ML-J's call: 'There was often an assumption that sheer force of numbers would somehow shift the churches in an evangelical direction, when there was no strategy to ensure that they themselves remained solidly evangelical in the face of growing

---

[1] *Unity in Truth*, p. 75.
[2] Ibid., p. 41.

pressure from those with whom they sought to work.'[1] The truth is that the policy adopted prevented any such strategy.

THE END OF THE PURITAN CONFERENCE

The position of the mixed denominations in the 1960s was far from static. On account of the ecumenical movement, the whole future of denominations was under discussion as it had never been before. When ML-J raised the great Reformation question, 'What is a Christian?', it was directly relevant to the current discussion. As members of the World Council of Churches the mainline denominations were all committed to the ecumenical quest for 'one world church'. He observed: 'Though one hand is held out to us, we must notice that the other is held out to Roman Catholics.'[2]

In the 1960s the term 'Protestant' had almost dropped out of evangelical usage. Certainly it was uncommon for anyone to say, as ML-J did, that Rome taught 'another gospel' and that 'there can be no compromise with sacerdotalism.'[3] While it was becoming customary for many evangelicals to regard such language as out-of-date, for him the danger was real. It entered into his reason for asking evangelicals at the 1966 Evangelical Alliance meeting whether their association with men of other beliefs was more important than giving their time and strength to a common cause with fellow evangelicals. Instead of waiting until united action might be forced upon a weakened evangelicalism in the future,

---

[1] *Evangelicalism in Britain*, p. 101. Barclay argued that wherever evangelicals ceased to have close connections with one another in a denomination there followed a 'steady erosion of the doctrinal clarity of evangelical witness' (p. 119).

[2] *Unity in Truth*, p. 181.

[3] Ibid., p. 40. 'Sacerdotalism' = 'The Church [Roman] affirms that for believers the sacraments of the New Covenant are *necessary for salvation.' Catechism of the Catholic Church*, (1994), p. 259 (para. 1129). Emphasis in original. ML-J regularly read contemporary Roman Catholic literature.

they should face the main question now whether they would be 'content with just being an evangelical wing in a territorial church that will eventually include, and must, if it is to be a truly national and ecumenical church, the Roman Catholic Church'.[1]

One of the contributing factors to confusion in the 1960s was the effort of the Second Vatican Council to soften the Church's former language on Protestantism, and to speak as though the disagreement was not as radical as was traditionally believed. There were not lacking non-Roman Catholics, impressed by this presentation, who adopted a similar approach. In the words of ML-J in 1969, 'There are foolish Protestants who seem to think that the way to win Roman Catholics is to show them there is practically no difference between us.'[2] He did not know when he spoke these words that conciliation had proceeded far enough for evangelicals to share in a book that would blur some of the main differences with Rome. In *Growing into Union* (1970) four Anglicans – two evangelicals and two Anglo-Catholics – professed to have found a unity between themselves which they believed would be permanent. They wrote, 'We now present our work as those who are still definitely and confessedly Catholics and evangelicals, even as strong and uncompromising men of such persuasions. But equally we are not what we were.' This book endorsed the ecumenical position that there should be no two denominations in the same locality; it allowed that 'both Scripture and Tradition must be seen as deriving from Christ'; held that the bishop in his diocese 'presents in his own person a small scale image of the ministry of Christ himself'; and claimed that baptism entitles a person to 'the riches of his Father's house'; 'The gospel makes us one in the Second Adam by baptism.'[3]

---

[1] 'Evangelical Unity: An Appeal,' *Knowing the Times*, p. 251.
[2] *Preaching and Preachers*, p. 140.
[3] C. O. Buchanan, E. L. Mascall, J. I. Packer, G. D. Leonard, *Growing into*

One of the four authors in this concession to Anglo-Catholic thinking was J. I. Packer. It was the publication of this book that brought the letter of ML-J to Packer of July 7, 1970, already quoted, and *Growing into Union* terminated the work in which the two men had been associated through twenty years. To represent this event as Packer being 'frozen out of the Lloyd-Jones circles', or as his being a 'casualty of the advancing separatist movement' is to ignore what caused the break.[1] The issue, as ML-J wrote to Packer, was that 'the views expounded in the book concerning Tradition, Baptism, the Eucharist, and Bishops, not to mention the lack of clarity concerning justification by faith only, could not possibly be acceptable to the vast majority of people attending the Puritan Conference.'[2]

In their belief that saving grace is conveyed through the sacraments Anglo-Catholic belief was the same as that of Roman Catholicism. The disagreement that ended the Puritan Conference involved the teaching against which the Reformation had been a protest. I do not think it was a new relationship with Roman Catholicism that Packer and Anglican evangelicals intended in 1970,[3] but ML-J saw this alliance of evangelical and Anglo-Catholic as the opening of a door that would open yet wider. That his apprehension was not unfounded is a matter of history. The follow-up to Keele (Nottingham, 1977), taught evangelicals to regard 'Roman Catholics as fellow-believers'. Packer acceded to this; and, the same year, he was the senior contributor to *Across the Divide*, a publication which acknowledged 'the most striking change of stance

---

Union: Proposals for Forming a United Church in England, (London: SPCK, 1970), pp. 64, 76, 34, 58.

[1] The opinions quoted on the breach are from McGrath, *To Know and Serve God,* p. 234, and Brencher, *Lloyd-Jones,* p. 110. The Conference was reconstituted, without Packer, as 'The Westminster Conference' in 1971.

[2] See below, p. 206.

[3] The alliance with Anglo-Catholics grew out of a common wish to defeat the proposals for Anglican-Methodist reunion.

. . . in relation to the Roman Catholic Church'.[1] The nature of this change was not clearly stated. It was *not* that Protestants now recognised that a Roman Catholic may be a Christian; that had never been questioned. The historic issue between Protestantism and Rome was whether a true believer should remain in that Church. In the words of Richard Baxter: 'I affect no union with any that are not united to Christ, or appear so to me . . . I will not close with a Papist, as a Papist; but if I meet with a Christian that goeth under that name, I will own him as a Christian, though not as a Papist and I would endeavour to undeceive him that I might fuller join with him.'[2] No such qualification accompanied the indiscriminate endorsement Anglican evangelicals now gave to Roman Catholics as 'fellow believers'. On the contrary, in 1980 Packer would write the Foreword to George Carey's book in favour of reunion with Rome;[3] and a decade later he was the leading theologian from the evangelical side in the Evangelicals and Catholics Together movement. It was not without reason, in 2005, that Mark Noll and Carolyn Nystrom dedicated their book, *Is the Reformation Over? An Evangelical Assessment of Contemporary Roman Catholicism*, 'To J. I. Packer, discerning pioneer'.[4]

Out of seemingly small beginnings, greater things thus grew. The controversy over the publication of *Growing into Union* was not prompted by some trivial difference. It was not about 'separatism or Anglicanism'. Indeed the Anglican Thirty-Nine Articles were one of the main casualties in the new policy.[5] Yet the alleged cause of the end of the Puritan Conference, as presented by

---

[1] *Across the Divide* (Basingstoke: Lyttelton Press, 1977), p. 14.

[2] Richard Baxter, *Confession of Faith* (London: 1655), p. 26.

[3] *A Tale of Two Churches: Can Protestants & Catholics Get Together?* (Downers Grove, IL: IVP, 1985).

[4] I have included a review of the Noll/Nystrom title below in Part 2, p. 251.

[5] The authority of the Articles, with its clear Protestant teaching, had already been flouted in the Church of England, but until the 1960s the evangelicals in the denomination had professed their adherence.

McGrath (on behalf of Packer), has been blindly followed by many others. Don J. Payne, one of those who has accepted the McGrath explanation, wrote: 'Packer followed the lead of George Whitefield, Charles Simeon, and J. C. Ryle in choosing to stay in the Church of England for the sake of facilitating reform. Lloyd-Jones found this intolerable.'[1] It was not the 'reform' of the Church of England that was advanced in the pages of *Growing into Union*. 'Separatist', was a label given to ML-J but he knew it had an honoured use at the time of the Reformation. Commenting on John 10:2, Calvin wrote:

> We ought not to form or maintain intercourse with any society but that which is agreed in the pure faith of the Gospel. For this reason Christ exhorts his disciples to separate themselves from the unbelieving multitude.

Packer has argued that, in ML-J's eyes, even 'opposing and repudiating' error within a mixed denomination, 'does not clear one of guilt unless one actually withdraws.'[2] I do not know any documentation to show that was Lloyd-Jones's belief; it was certainly not his main point. His call was not separation from denominations as such; it was for separation from error and unbelief. In 1978 Packer argued that the existing doctrinal comprehensiveness in the Church of England had to be accepted 'reluctantly and with sorrow'. He believed this was better than 'an unlovely perfectionism and self-sufficiency' which supposes 'God would never show Catholics or non-conservative Protestants anything he had not first shown evangelicals.'[3] In another place he writes:

[1] D. J. Payne, *The Theology of the Christian Life in J. I. Packer's Thought* (Bletchley: Paternoster, 2006), p. 70.

[2] *Chosen Vessels*, p. 112.

[3] J. I. Packer, *The Evangelical Anglican Identity Problem* (Oxford: Latimer House, 1978), pp. 31-32.

Any who lapse into this intellectual perfectionism will be sharp, no doubt, against their brothers who go into dialogue about divine things in the hope that new insights into the meaning of Scripture will come to them from their non-evangelical partners.[1]

This admission and defence of the changed position towards non-evangelicals does not appear to be recognised anywhere by Packer when he refers to his difference with ML-J. Thankfully, when Packer and Stott are not constrained by ecumenical or denominational considerations, the evangelicalism of their writings has benefited very many. But the consequences of the course they set in the 1960s are also still with us.

THE GOSPEL MAKES THE CHURCH

As I have said, I believe Lloyd-Jones's call for some evangelicals to secede had two strands to it. One strand was the argument from schism. I believe that argument was mistaken, for it was to make a visible, organisational relationship necessary to unity. It gave those who opposed his thinking some grounds for saying that the issue was really denominationalism. Even Christopher Catherwood has written: 'Sadly, as Jim Packer's writings have shown, the Doctor's views on ecclesiology led to a parting of the ways and to a severing of old friendships.'[2]

---

[1] Ibid., p. 11. ML-J marked these words in his copy of the booklet with the comment: 'Fatal admission!'

[2] Christopher Catherwood, *Martyn Lloyd-Jones: A Family Portrait* (Eastbourne: Kingsway, 1995), p. 172. This is to accept the distortion about which ML-J complained: 'If you today make a plea for evangelical unity you will be charged with dividing evangelicals. The man who stands for the truth is the troubler in Israel.' *Unity in Truth*, p. 157.

But this judgment leaves entirely to one side the major strand in ML-J's thinking, namely, if the choice for evangelicals was to treat non-evangelicals as colleagues in the ecumenical quest, or secession, then the right course was secession. A deliberate aligning with non-evangelicals meant a condoning of error and raised, as he said in one address, 'the question of guilt by association'.[1] Some seized on that one quotation, intending to represent him as teaching that belonging to a 'mixed denomination' was sinful *per se*. That was not his case. It was working alongside and accepting false teachers that he condemned as sinful. His thinking has been presented as though he broke off fellowship with all evangelicals in the mixed denominations, especially the Anglicans. It is not true. He maintained many contacts after 1966 (and to the end of his life) with Anglican clergy who were opposed to ecumenism. One of the 'many' was Dr Gerald Bray, who could write in 1998:

> I can testify that Dr Lloyd-Jones was not anti-Anglican as such, because when he found out that I was going to seek ordination in the Church of England he came to see me and encouraged me in my vocation. The one thing he warned me about was the danger of becoming an ecclesiastical politician.[2]

Contrary to what has been alleged, the division of the 1960s was not over a 'perfectionist' view of the church. A speaker at the Alliance meetings of 1966 supposed he was opposing ML-J when he argued that 'a perfectionist/individualist outlook will never make any headway in the matter of unity.' And, he asked, 'how long would a united Evangelical Church last before it was shattered into fragments?' ML-J's call for separation was represented as based on the illusion of obtaining a 'pure church'. The latter knew too

[1] *Unity in Truth*, p. 41.
[2] Gerald Bray, reviewing McGrath's biography of Packer, *Churchman*, vol. 111 (1998), p. 360.

much of history and of Scripture to adopt such a position. What he asserted was that a church ought to be a body of Christians, and it must uphold the gospel that alone makes people Christian. His opposition was to the acceptance of the ecumenical (and Keele) premise, 'We are all Christians', when in reality it was often 'another gospel' that was commonly preached in the churches. If the alternatives were comprehension without real spiritual unity or separation, was it not clear which course was the biblical one? Dr Brencher criticises ML-J with the words, 'To make rejection of the ecumenical movement a core belief of Christianity was too narrow: in fact it was sectarian.' This would only be true if it were shown that ML-J's gospel was narrower than the gospel of the New Testament. Yet the strange thing is that Brencher can also write in a way that throws doubt on the very criticism he advances. He writes:

> It is true that there was doctrinal woolliness in contemporary ecumenism and Lloyd-Jones had little in common with most of its leaders . . . Given the theology of Lloyd-Jones, the idea of biblical unity which he advocated was a perfectly valid one and his disagreement with those who held a more syncretistic view of the church was not unexpected . . . Lloyd-Jones's doctrine and practice was so closely defined, at least in the essentials, that it left him no room for manoeuvre.[1]

In the light of Brencher's whole thesis, this is an extraordinary admission. For it leaves entirely in the air the key question, Was ML-J's understanding of 'essentials' true or was it not?

---

[1] Brencher, *Lloyd-Jones*, pp. 135, 140-141.

CONTROVERSY BETWEEN CHRISTIANS

In his controversy with fellow evangelicals Dr Lloyd-Jones was aware of the need both to contend for the faith and to maintain a catholic spirit. He did not suppose that all true Christians would think as he did. He would say: 'We honour and respect evangelicals who disagree with us. We do not criticise them as individuals. We do not impute wrong motives to them. We grant that they are as sincere as we are and as honest as we are, and that they believe the gospel as we believe it.'[1] I have already said that ML-J did not break off fellowship with all evangelicals in the mixed denominations, but, regrettably, some who supported him thought that he did, and that is how they acted. It cannot be denied that, whatever the reason, relationships between many Anglican evangelicals and those who stood on the Lloyd-Jones side largely broke down. No sympathy towards Anglicans became evident among our Nonconformist ranks.

Divisions among Christians are ever liable to produce alienations, animosities and prejudices injurious to the gospel and the name of Christ. This undoubtedly happened on both sides of the divide in the 1960s. If there was the alleged 'bitterness', I doubt if it was general on either side; there was certainly sadness, not least at the loss of Packer's presence alongside ML-J. What we owed to Packer was not forgotten. Both sides suffered in the separation, and a lesson to be remembered is that every effort should always be made to maintain a degree of communion among believers, even when their differences are such that they cannot publicly work together or belong to the same denomination. Some of the finest words in the *Westminster Confession of Faith* are in the little-read chapter 'Of the Communion of Saints', which begins:

---

[1] *Unity in Truth,* p. 67. At the same time he spoke of some who disagreed with him as 'those who are not truly evangelical'. Ibid., p. 158.

All saints that are united to Jesus Christ their head by his Spirit, and by faith, have fellowship with him in his graces, sufferings, death, resurrection and glory. And being united to one another in love, they have communion in each other's gifts and graces.[1]

Does this mean that an evangelical can have fellowship with a true Christian who is still in the Roman Catholic communion? It does; but as I comment further in later pages, the grace of God finds individuals in that Church in spite of the anti-Christian teaching which it represents in its documents and practice. Friendship at the individual level is not inconsistent with speaking against remaining in a Church where the official doctrine is contrary to the gospel. If the difference between the two things is blurred then evangelical belief becomes inconsequential.

The words of John Howe to Nonconformist churches in the late seventeenth century, when the Puritan movement had become fragmented, are ever relevant:

Whereas a right scheme of gospel doctrine is the thing pretended to be striven for, I beseech you consider the more entirely, and the more deeply, the true scheme of gospel doctrine is inlaid in a man's soul, the more certainly it must form it all into meekness, humility, gentleness, love, kindness, and benignity towards fellow Christians of whatsoever denomination; not confined, not limited (as that of the Pharisees) unto their own party; but diffusing and spreading itself to all that bear the character and cognizance of Christ. The Spirit of our Lord Jesus Christ is a Spirit of

---

[1] For practical application of this, see, 'Communion with Brethren in Other Denominations,' Andrew Bonar, ed., *Memoir and Remains of R. M. M'Cheyne* (repr. Edinburgh: Banner of Truth, 1966), pp. 605-612.

greater amplitude; extends and diffuses itself through the whole body of Christ.[1]

Catholicity too easily gets lost in controversy. Wrong attitudes damage the cause of Christ as well as errors.

The Universities and the Church – 'Athens' or 'Jerusalem'?

The leaders whose differences I have discussed were closely involved in the impact that the Inter-Varsity Fellowship made in England in the 1950s. One reason for that impact upon a rising generation was the definiteness of the message, and the refusal to allow either leaders or speakers in the Christian Unions who did not adhere to the evangelical basis of faith. As I have already said, this 'exclusiveness' was the main reason why IVF was viewed with hostility by non-evangelicals in the denominations. The latter, instead of recognising that the IVF was seeking to stand for a biblical principle, caricatured the 'dogmatism' as stemming from the lack of intellectual competence and scholarship. This looked a reasonable assumption given that the university theological faculties were almost entirely dominated by non-evangelicals.

For some evangelicals this situation admitted of no reversal unless evangelicals themselves could get teaching posts in the universities. But the 'intellectual respectability' necessary for appointment to theological departments could not be gained by anyone who meant to teach the Inter-Varsity basis of faith (although that basis states no more than historic Christianity). At the very

---

[1] 'The Carnality of Religious Contentions', in *Works of John Howe*, vol 3 (London: William Tegg, 1848), p. 146.

least, an acceptance of the legitimacy of other 'views' would be required.

The difficulty involved was recognised by those who formulated the policy of the Tyndale Fellowship, the branch of the Inter-Varsity Fellowship which, in the mid-1950s, was offering grants for the training of research students who might counter liberal scholarship and compete in the academic scene. Once qualified, such men would gain 'a certain standing' and, it was hoped, reverse 'the incredible prejudice there is against the IVF and the rising cold war against "fundamentalism".'[1]

In the 1960s the 'openness policy' promoted at Keele was a crucial step in seeking to solve the anti-evangelical stance in the academic world. It encouraged more evangelicals to seek access to teaching at the university level, but at the cost of surrendering boldness to broadness. At the same time the position of the former generation of evangelicals (who had avoided taking theological degrees) was reversed, and the possession of such degrees came to be regarded as one of the best ways for evangelical ministers to gain status. Even Bible colleges, previously intent on producing preachers and missionaries, began to think their credibility had to be connected with the number of their students obtaining degrees. This, in due course, contributed to an increasing unease with the 'dogmatism' of Scripture in the wider evangelical scene.

Once again Lloyd-Jones found himself almost alone when he spoke out against the danger of pursuing acceptance in the world of academic theology. At the opening of the new building of the London Bible College in 1958, when he was the main speaker, he made himself unpopular by warning of the danger: 'You may have more BD's than any College in the land, but only if the result is

---

[1] The words quoted are those of Andrew Walls writing to Douglas Johnson (May 19. 1955), T. A. Noble, *Tyndale House and Fellowship: The First Sixty Years* (Leicester: IVP, 2006), p. 90.

that your people know God better.' All the faculty knew that he did not think the London BD was conducive to such a result. To this note he often returned, as in 1964 when he said:

> We are so anxious to be thought intellectually respectable and afraid of being charged with being non-intellectual, that we are in grave danger of worshipping scholarship in the wrong sense . . . this tendency to worship scholarship is landing us in a position in which the whole training for the ministry is being determined by secular universities.[1]

For Lloyd-Jones this was no small matter. He knew that the main cause of the spiritually weak state of the church and nation was the disbelief in the authority of Scripture 'sown in the minds of the masses of the people'. The universities had played a major part in this process, and for evangelicals to seek influence by not implementing the teaching of Scripture on false teaching had to be a disastrous mistake. It involved disregard for biblical commands:

> We are to avoid people who do not believe in the Bible as the Word of God, for they will do you harm; they will take from your energy and you will eventually become diseased. How often has this happened! How often have we known young men, truly converted, full of passion for souls, and zeal and enthusiasm, who after they have been to a theological college come out quite use-less! What has happened is that their faith in the Word of God has been undermined . . . Have no fellowship with people who do not believe the Bible to be the Word of God. I am talking about people who call themselves Christians. Of course, you have to deal with others; but if a man says he is a Christian and claims to be such, and yet undermines the very basis and foundation of the faith, have no fellowship with him. I am not saying this

[1] *Knowing the Times,* pp. 211-212.

on my own authority; there is scriptural warrant for what I say. The Apostle John in his Second Epistle says: 'If there come any unto you, and bring not this doctrine, receive him not into your house, neither bid him God speed.' We must act on this principle . . . The preacher is a man who is called upon to placard notices warning people of dangerous, infectious, spiritual diseases. The Church should put false teachers into quarantine and isolation hospitals, but until she does so, I say, Avoid such men and their teaching.[1]

Dr Brencher's book on Lloyd-Jones illustrates the very danger of which the latter warned. Brencher conceded that 'given the theology of Lloyd-Jones, the idea of biblical unity which he advocated was a perfectly valid one'. If that is so, then as an evangelical Christian he should have proceeded in his thesis to examine whether Lloyd-Jones's theology *was true or not* according to Scripture. That he did not do this was surely due to the fact that the academic world, whose approval his doctoral thesis required, allows no such final appeal to Scripture.

It is also relevant to note how evangelical leaders who worked in the academic scene appear to have been influenced by that ethos in their disagreement with ML-J. As Christopher Catherwood has observed: 'Packer was essentially an academic, to whom co-operation with those whose views differed from his own was quite natural . . . Packer believed in preaching the Gospel – and also in academic dialogue.'[2]

There has surely been a remarkable change when an Inter-

---

[1] *The Christian Soldier*, pp. 151-53. According to Christ (*John* 7:17) spiritual obedience is necessary for true knowledge. This vital connection has no place in university theology.

[2] C. Catherwood, *Five Evangelical Leaders* (London: Hodder and Stoughton, 1984), p. 189. It is my opinion that preachers, used to dealing with human nature at the pastoral level, are more cautious judges than those whose time is spent more largely with ideas.

Varsity book in 2006 could put ML-J down in the same way that liberals put down all evangelicals in the 1950s. Thomas Noble writes:

> Martyn Lloyd-Jones had undertaken no formal study of theology, but neither had he any formal qualifications or academic standing as a biblical scholar . . . Like an intellectual but deeply conservative Christian layman, he had tended to be rather suspicious of "Higher Criticism".[1]

Few people can have been better placed than Oliver Barclay to comment on the university and student scene. His book, *Evangelicalism in Britain, 1935-1995,* shows very clearly how the refusal of the earlier generation of evangelicals to seek acceptance by an unbiblical comprehensiveness was linked with a much stronger adherence to Scripture.[2] In an important article, 'Where is Academic Theology Heading?', published in *Evangelicals Now,* in December 2006, Barclay followed this up by arguing that university theology is no preparation for preachers. 'The foundational Christian conviction that God has spoken, and that the task of theology is first of all to understand better what he has said, fits badly into the intellectual climate of the modern university. As a history of the English Free Churches put it: the prophetic "Thus says the Lord" tends to be replaced by "It may be reasonable to suppose," with disastrous consequences.' In the academic world, he continued, theology, 'stripped of its spiritual and eternal

---

[1] *Tyndale House,* p. 70.

[2] Barclay was a leader in IVF (now UCCF) from 1938 to 1980, and followed Douglas Johnson as General Secretary from 1964. For Johnson's position see his book, *Contending for the Faith* (Leicester: IVP, 1979). In his conclusion to that book Johnson warned: 'In the light of its past history, and the experience of Christians everywhere, the biggest single danger to the Evangelical Movement at each stage comes not from its declared opponents, but from some of those who claim to be its friends' (p. 342).

significance . . . is spiritually dry . . . Though it may produce lec-
turers, it produces very few good preachers.'[1]

WHAT WERE LLOYD-JONES'S CHIEF MOTIVES?

When discussing what led ML-J to make the stand he did, several writers raised the question of his motives. It has been suggested that it was his Welsh mind-set that led him to choose some
of his targets. Again, he has been interpreted as a man who was
eminently an individualist. Worse, he is even accused of arrogance,
dogmatism, and of reaching decisions with an air of infallibility.
His letter to Dr Packer, which terminated the Puritan Conference,
is likened by Gaius Davies to 'a Papal Bull', and the same author
says:

> Dr Lloyd-Jones was very high on the trait of dominance.
> Whether he required submission consciously is immaterial: that
> is what he obtained from any true follower . . . Why did he always
> have to be right about everything, and why was he so combative,
> so aggressive?[2]

The critics of Dr Lloyd-Jones all praise him at various points
but, in common, they downplay the chief feature of his life, his
profound faith in the truth and finality of the word of God. Adherence to Scripture was the mainspring of his life. From this came

---

[1] In the correspondence columns of *Evangelicals Now* (Feb. 2007), Mr J. D.
Brand, as Director of an international mission agency, followed up Barclay's
article by writing of his certainty that 'one of the most negative factors in training for the Christian ministry in the last generation has been the rush by Bible
Colleges to seek accreditation by secular academic bodies whose agenda and
worldview is totally different . . . Many of the people leaving Bible Colleges today are far less biblically literate than those who left 25 years ago.' This whole
issue needs major examination. Financial considerations, including government
requirements for student grants, are part of the picture.

[2] *Genius, Grief and Grace*, pp. 366, 371, 373.

the governing direction of his ministry. Many-sided as his gifts were, it was his closeness to Scripture that made him pre-eminently an evangelist with a passionate regard for the salvation of men and women. This was the main explanation for the part he played in the controversy we have considered. It was not that he had taken a sudden interest in church issues. Rather he was persuaded that compassion for souls required the protest he made against a policy that was compromising the truth. He was not against a 'territorial church' because, as a Welshman, he disliked an English institution, as has been said. He spoke against it because it is a deception to suppose entrance into the church of God is according to the country in which anyone happens to be born. In the same way his hostility to Roman Catholic teaching rested upon the way it presents false grounds of salvation to sinners. His concern that Protestantism was being lost was no bigotry. He grieved deeply that at a point in history, when the churches and the nation were in a state of marked transition, there were so few safe guides to heaven.

The charge that he was always 'so aggressive' might have some justification if more had shared with him in giving the warnings that are so common in the New Testament; instead he was again and again left to stand alone. The reason he was prepared to do so was that he was held by the authority of Scripture and knew something of the compassion of Christ for people as 'sheep without a shepherd'.

To read the accusation that pride entered largely into ML-J's motives is painful to anyone who knew him well. The exercise of power was not what he sought. Professor F. F. Bruce was no natural ally of ML-J, yet he could say of him:

He was a thoroughly humble man. Those who charged him with arrogance were wildly mistaken. His assurance was based in the God whose message he was commissioned to proclaim.[1]

Dr C. Stacey Woods, Inter-Varsity leader in North America, who saw ML-J chair meetings on many occasions said: 'He never imposed his personal opinions and convictions except in so far as they represented his understanding of Scripture. Then, of course, there was authority.' The present writer, who had the privilege of serving as his assistant at one period, differed with him on some occasions and yet never knew him to use his superior gifts and position to bring me into line. His patience with the young and headstrong, with rare exceptions, was outstanding.

Lloyd-Jones was generally conscious of his own limitations. It may be that on occasions he needed his wife's reminder not to 'crack a nut with a sledge-hammer'. While never ill-tempered in debate, he could at times, in the words of his friend Douglas Johnson, 'hold tenaciously to an opinion when he might be wrong'.

There were certain things he knew he was not called to do. 'I am not an organiser – it is probably one of my greatest defects.'[2] This is part of the explanation for why he was not more explicit over the form that evangelical unity at the church level should take. But, as noted above, his motives have been questioned on that account. The truth is he believed he knew the *direction* evangelicals should take, but laying out or organising a programme was not his calling.

Ultimately his actions were bound up with his faith that the church is God's church. God needs none of us. All that is required of us is faithfulness to God's word in our callings. He shrank from any 'success' that was not of God. It has been repeatedly said that

---

[1] Review of *Fight of Faith* in *Evangelical Quarterly*, 1991, p. 71.
[2] *Fight of Faith*, p. 505.

the stand he took in 1966, instead of leading to success, led to his own loss of influence in the Christian world. He was 'the lost leader'. This is a short-sighted judgment. In the last fifteen years of his life before his death in 1981, when he had more quietness than would have been the case had he remained active at the centre of English evangelicalism, he was working on the books that, in their millions, were to touch all the ends of the earth from Brazil to Korea. On the world scale Lloyd-Jones's influence was to be far greater after 1966 than it had ever been before. Indeed the influence was to be still greater after his death.

Ultimately it was not the thought of national or world influence that concerned him. His aim was not success and popularity. Reflecting on one occasion on the explanation of Paul's ministry, he included an explanation of his own:

> I know that a day is coming in my history and in yours when the trumpet shall sound and the dead shall rise, and you and I will be amongst them. We must all appear before the judgment seat of Christ to give account of the deeds done in the body, whether good or bad.[1]

To be found faithful to the Saviour, who would also be his judge, was his great purpose here.

---

[1] *Unity in Truth*, p. 82.

PART 2

The Evangelical Library, London, with Geoffrey Williams.
Along with the pulpit of Westminster Chapel and the Puritan
Conference, the Library was one of the main agencies in the
recovery of interest in the Puritans.

9

THE END OF THE PURITAN CONFERENCE: LLOYD-JONES TO PACKER[1]

[Rev. Dr James I. Packer
133 Pembroke Rd, Bristol 8]

[July 7, 1970]

My dear Friend,

It is with a very heavy heart and deep regret that I write this letter. I do so on behalf of John Caiger and David Fountain as well as myself.

The three of us as the Free Church members of the committee of the Puritan Conference met together yesterday during the lunch interval of the monthly ministers' Fellowship.

In the Fellowship we spent morning and afternoon in discussing Growing into Union. The general opinion there, without a single voice to the contrary, was that the doctrinal position outlined in that book cannot be regarded as being evangelical, still

---

[1] See above, pp. 183-188.

less puritan. The three of us therefore feel, most reluctantly, that we cannot continue to co-operate with you in the Puritan Conference. To do so would be at the least to cause great confusion in the minds of all Free Church evangelical people and indeed also a number of Anglican people.

We suggest therefore that no Conference be held this year and that a simple notice to that effect be inserted in the Report for 1969 and also in the Evangelical Magazine and in the Evangelical Times list of meetings for December.

This I feel sure will not come as a surprise to you as you must have known that the views expounded in the book concerning Tradition, Baptism, the Eucharist and Bishops, not to mention the lack of clarity concerning justification by faith only, could not possibly be acceptable to the vast majority of people attending the Puritan Conference.

Your mind is made up and you have stated clearly that no wedge shall be driven between you and your Anglo-Catholic associates.[1]

There is no purpose therefore in any discussion and the last thing we would desire would be to do anything that could in any way harm our personal relationships.

I could write much but I must not weary you. You have known throughout the years not only my admiration for your great gift of mind and intellect but also my deep regard for you. I had expected that long before this you would have produced a major work in the Warfield tradition, but you have felt called to become involved in ecclesiastical affairs. This to me is nothing less than a great tragedy and a real loss to the Church.

---

[1] 'We are all four committed to every line in the book . . . and we are determined that no wedge should be driven between us' (*Growing into Union*, p. 19.) In interpreting the meaning of the book, the fact that G. D. Leonard, one of its two Anglo-Catholic authors, was received into the Church of Rome in 1994 is not without significance.

After all these years I am saddened at the thought that we shall not meet regularly year by year at the Conference and at other odd times; but I sincerely hope that we shall be able to maintain some personal contact. I shall always be interested in you and your career and in you as a family, and what I say for myself is true of us as a family. We have often disagreed about people but never about you.

With warmest regards and good wishes from John Caiger, David Fountain, and myself and the family,

Yours ever sincerely,
D. M. Lloyd-Jones

Dr Packer and the Rev. G. S. R. Cox were the Anglican members of the Puritan Conference committee. In his reply of July 9, 1970, Packer agreed to the termination of the conference and wrote:

> I naturally regret that you and David and John have felt bound to take this line, but I recognise it as one more application of the principles of co-operation which you have been advocating so strongly in recent years (and which, as you know, have never convinced me) . . . My respect for you and my gratitude for what God has given me through you in the past remains undimmed.

The two men met in October to discuss the above issue but the difference of judgment was never resolved. Packer believed that ML-J's position represented a withdrawal from the historic fellowship which evangelicals had always shared on essentials;[1]

---

[1] See *Martyn Lloyd-Jones: Chosen by God*, pp. 45-46.

ML-J held that it was Anglican evangelicals who were introducing serious change for they were acting as though the evangelical understanding of how an individual comes into the possession of salvation was not uniquely different from contrary teaching. Packer responded to a call from Regent College, Vancouver, in 1979, and his teaching and writing contributed largely to the recovery of interest in the Puritans which has taken place in North America. Wendy Zoba writes of his difference with ML-J:

> Ten years after their estrangement in 1970, Packer wrote his friend and colleague Martyn Lloyd-Jones asking to visit him on his forthcoming trip to England. Lloyd-Jones, who had been ill, encouraged him to come. 'I never saw him', Packer says. 'He died before I could get there. It didn't make a great deal of difference', he says. 'There's always heaven.'[1]

---

[1] 'Knowing Packer: The Lonely Journey of a Passionate Puritan', *Christianity Today*, April 6, 1998, p. 40.

10

SOME CONVICTIONS OF LLOYD-JONES IN MINIATURE[1]

GOD

In every view of salvation the place given in it to the glory of God provides the ultimate test. The proof that it is truly script-ural is that it gives all the glory to God.

These modern teachers do not believe in the wrath of God; they say it should be banished. But in the Old Testament this idea is put before us 580 times. That God is angry against sin, that God hates sin, is a basic proposition.

I say with reverence that even God can never show his love in a greater manner than he did on the Cross on Calvary's hill when he delivered up his own Son for us all.

---

[1] These brief notes were taken by myself and my late friend, Richard Alderson, from ML-J's sermons. The preacher would have preferred they should be heard or read in the context of what he was preaching; yet I believe they disclose some of his basic thinking. For an anthology of quotations see *Gems From Martyn Lloyd-Jones*, Tony Sargent, ed. (Milton Keynes: Paternoster, 2007).

The Bible's view of man as a lost, condemned, hopeless sinner is not common today, and this is simply due to the fact that we have not started with God.

There is a right fear of God, and we neglect and ignore that at our peril; but there is also a wrong fear of God. People regard God as a taskmaster, they regard him as Someone who is constantly watching to discover faults and blemishes in them, and to punish them accordingly.

The purpose of God is certain; nothing can stop it – nothing whatsoever! That is the great message of this Epistle to the Romans, as indeed of the whole Bible. God has set this plan of salvation in process, and neither devils nor hell nor the whole universe can stop it.

We know things about God, but our real trouble is our ignorance of God Himself – what He really is, and what He is to His people.

Paul says, 'the love of God is shed abroad in our hearts'. I am convinced that there is no aspect of the Christian truth that has been so sadly neglected in this century.

The men who have accomplished most in this world have always been theologically minded.

A butterfly type of Christian never knows much about glorying in God. That is always the result of facing the great doctrines, looking at them frequently and dwelling on them in your mind.

ASSURANCE

The Christian does not go round boasting about it; it is the 'hidden manna', it is the 'white stone'.

The greatest characteristic of the greatest saints in all ages has always been their realisation of the love of God to them.

Modern Christians seem to be more frightened of emotion than of anything else. This is due to their failure to draw the distinction between emotion and emotionalism.

There is nothing that is so encouraging to holiness, so stimulating, so uplifting, as to know the certainty of my final salvation and glorification.

THE BIBLE

I either submit to the authority of Scripture or else I am in a morass where there is no standing.

We must never read the Scriptures without praying.

A mere hurried and cursory reading of the Scriptures profits but little and never leads to true joy.

We must use these Confessions of Faith as guides and not allow them to be tyrants.

The whole case of the Bible is that the trouble with man is not intellectual (in the mind) but moral (in the heart).

The Christian

Oh, the privilege of being a Christian! Can you imagine anything higher or greater! We are not only in Christ, Christ is in us. 'I live, yet not I, but Christ liveth in me, and the life which I now live in the flesh I live by the faith of the Son of God, who loved me and gave himself for me' [*Gal.* 2:20].

By definition a Christian should be a problem and an enigma to every person who is not a Christian.

The Christian who does not know his own sinfulness and the blackness of his own heart is the merest child in the Christian faith. I am tempted to say that modern Christians are much too healthy.

No man ever became a Christian without stopping to look at himself.

The first sign of spiritual life is to feel you are dead.

The Christian is sorrowful, but not morose; serious, but not solemn; sober-minded, but not sullen; grave, but never cold or prohibitive; his joy is a holy joy; his happiness a serious happiness.

The great need in the Christian life is for self-discipline. This is not something that happens to you in a meeting; you have got to do it!

A man is not a Christian unless he can say with Paul, 'I am what I am by the grace of God.'

Most, if not all, of our problems in the Christian life would be solved if only we realised the greatness of our salvation.

The man who does not realise that he himself is his own biggest problem is a mere tyro!

Do you think that you deserve forgiveness? If you do, you are not a Christian.

The Christian is eager, but he is never excitable.

The Christian is the greatest thinker in the universe.

The more Christian a person is, the simpler will that person's life be.

The Christian is not 'a good man'. He is a vile wretch who has been saved by the grace of God.

The more spiritual we are, the more we shall think about heaven.

We are all so lop-sided. Some people are full of head knowledge, the theoretical knowledge of doctrine, and they never move any further. Others have no doctrine, but they talk about their activities and their lives – they are equally defective.

Look back and think of the times when you were unhappy and you will find that it was almost certainly due to something you said and which you regretted perhaps for days.

At the final bar of judgment the gravest charge that will be made against us Christians will be that we were so unconcerned.

CHURCH UNITY

Putting all the ecclesiastical corpses into one graveyard will not bring about a resurrection!

To me one of the major tragedies of the hour, and especially in the realm of the church, is that most of the time seems to be taken up by the leaders in preaching about unity instead of preaching the gospel that alone can produce unity.

If all the churches in the world became amalgamated, it would not make the slightest difference to the man in the street. He is not outside the churches because the churches are disunited; he is outside because he likes his sin, because he is a sinner, because he is ignorant of spiritual realities. He is no more interested in this problem of unity than the man in the moon!

DEATH

The Christian is a man who can be certain about the ultimate even when he is most uncertain about the immediate.

To me there is nothing more fatuous about mankind than the statement that to think about death is morbid. The man who refuses to face facts is a fool.

The first thing the Bible does is to make a man take a serious view of life.

If a philosophy of life cannot help me to die, then in a sense it cannot help me to live.

THE DEVIL

I am certain that one of the main causes of the ill state of the church today is the fact that the devil is being forgotten.

You may know that an attack comes from the devil and not from yourself, (a) if it appears to come from outside; (b) if you hate the suggestion made; (c) if it leads to anxiety, depression, doubts, over-concentration on self. Therefore 'resist the devil'.

The devil is anxious to produce counterfeits and cause confusion. He turns people's attention to the phenomena, to the experiences, to the excitement; and there are always people who look only for such things.

What fools we are if we listen to the devil and allow him to depress us!

DISUNITY

There is no union unless there is agreement about the truths of the gospel. It is a spiritual union, but it is also a union of faith. The Roman Catholic Church has been more guilty of the sin of schism than any other church the world has ever known. The division between Roman Catholic and Protestant I am prepared to defend to the death.

Some are ready to think that all that join not with them are schismatics, and they are so because they go not with them. What the cause of unity among the people of God has suffered from this sort of men is not easily to be expressed.

DOCTRINE

Doctrinal correctness, they maintain, has been over-emphasised in the past. Indeed, to hold doctrinal views strongly and to criticise other views is virtually regarded as sinful and is frequently described as sub-Christian. This is how the phrase 'speaking the truth in love' is being commonly interpreted.

Our main trouble as Christians today is a lack of understanding and knowledge. The man whose doctrine is shaky will be shaky in his whole life.

One almost invariably finds that if a man is wrong on the great central truths of the faith, he is wrong at every other point.

I always find that those who are driven with every wind of doctrine are those who are too lazy to study doctrine.

There is nothing so fatuous as the view that Christian doctrine is removed from life. There is nothing which is more practical.

I spend half my time telling Christians to study doctrine and the other half telling them that doctrine is not enough.

ERRORS

There is a very wrong belief which is a kind of fatalism, very often a misunderstanding of the sovereignty of God, a belief which says, 'Oh, this is a time of declension. This is not a time to expect blessing either individually or for the church, so don't ask for it.'

Calvinism without Methodism tends to lead to intellectualisation and scholasticism – that is its peculiar temptation. The result is that men talk more about 'the Truth we hold', rather than about 'the Truth that holds us'.

We divide ourselves into young people, middle-aged, old people. We do not find such divisions in the early church; they were all one. Age differences did not count; they should not count now.

How does one become a Christian according to Roman Catholic teaching? The answer is that you become a Christian merely by giving your intellectual assent to the doctrine of the Church. If you say, 'I am prepared to accept the teaching of the Church', you are immediately and of necessity a Christian.

If the 'grace' you have received does not help you to keep the law, you have not received grace. If you claim to love Christ and yet are living an unholy life, there is only one thing to say about you. You are a bare-faced liar!

EVANGELISM

There is a group of people who accept the wrath of God in theory, but they deny it in practice. 'Oh, yes', they say, 'we believe in the wrath of God, but you have to be careful. You don't put that first.' So, in the interests of evangelism, in the interests of attracting people, they deliberately do not start, as Paul does, with the wrath of God [*Rom.* 1:18]. The tragedy is that we do not believe in the power of the Holy Ghost as the Apostle Paul did. Paul did not stop to ask, 'Will the Romans like this doctrine?' He knew it all depended on the Holy Ghost.

The message preached in evangelism must be essentially a simple message, but it must also be a full message. It must have content; it must never give people the impression that all they have to do is to say they believe in Christ, and all is well. That is an incomplete message, ultimately a non-ethical message. True evangelism is always ethical.

If an evangelistic meeting does not lead to holiness it has failed.

Far too often evangelism takes the form of saying, 'Are you in trouble, are you unhappy, are you failing somewhere, do you need some help? Very well, come to Christ and you will get all you need.' Thank God, it is very true, if you come to Christ, you will derive many benefits; but I do not find the gospel presented in that way in the New Testament itself.

You cannot receive Christ in bits and pieces.

I do not preach decisions – I preach regeneration.

[To an undergraduate snob] You are common clay like the rest of us and in as much need of God's salvation as the local crossing-sweeper.

FAITH

This is our whole trouble. We do not believe in God as we should, in his glory, his love, his concern for us and his intervention in our lives.

Faith always includes the element of obedience. There is no value whatsoever in a supposed faith that does not lead inevitably to a changed life.

No difficulty in believing the gospel is intellectual, it is always moral.

Miracles are not meant to be understood, they are meant to be believed.

Faith may not only have to fight, faith does fight, faith can fight; and faith always fights victoriously in this matter of justification. The greatest saints have testified that even to the end of their lives the devil would come and raise this matter of justification with them and try to shake them. It may be a desperate fight at times, but faith can always deal with him, faith can always silence him.

MORALITY NOT CHRISTIANITY

If you try to imitate Christ, the world will praise you; if you become Christlike, the world will hate you!

To expect Christian conduct from a person who is not born again is rank heresy.

Some tend to think that Christianity is a matter of being nice. But niceness is purely biological. One dog is nicer than another dog!

Anyone who thinks he can live the Christian life himself is just proclaiming that he is not a Christian.

Affability is what most people mean by saintliness today. The man who is idolised today is a man who is an aggregate of negatives. The absence of qualities constitutes greatness today. People do not believe in true greatness any longer. They do not believe in goodness, in manliness, in truth itself. It is the smooth, nice, affable man who is popular.

The nicest people are often the most impatient.

PRAYER

If you have never had difficulty in prayer, it is absolutely certain that you have never prayed.

Everything we do in the Christian life is easier than prayer.

Sometimes we are praying when we should be resisting Satan.

People come to me and say, 'I am praying God to deliver me from this sin . . .' But what they really need is to realise that the Holy Ghost is dwelling in their hearts. That is the way to meet the devil.

There is no better index of where we stand than the amount of praise and thanksgiving that characterizes our lives and our prayers. Some people are always offering petitions or making statements.

Self-examination is the high road to prayer.

The ultimate test of the Christian life is the amount of time we give to prayer.

A horrible term called 'prayer backing' has appeared, as if prayer is something that 'backs' what we decide. Instead of starting with prayer, and discovering God's will, and putting ourselves at his disposal and waiting upon him, we decide and act.

In the Epistle to the Hebrews it is Christians who are exhorted to approach God 'with reverence and godly fear; for our God is a consuming fire.' Why is it, I wonder, that these great declarations of Scripture seem to have dropped out of our modern evangelical vocabulary? Reverence was the great characteristic of the prayer life and worship of our fathers, and it seems to have gone. Whatever boldness we have as we go to the throne of grace, it should never be at the expense of these tremendous truths about the being and character of God.

SANCTIFICATION

The New Testament method and way of sanctification is to get us to realise our position and standing, and to act accordingly. In other words, 'Be what you are.' Because you have been 'made free from sin' and become 'servants of righteousness' [*Rom.* 6:18], therefore, be what you are.

The New Testament way of handling sanctification is never an appeal, it is a command.

I would rather make bricks without straw than try to live the Sermon on the Mount in my own strength.

As Christians we should never feel sorry for ourselves. The moment we do so, we lose our energy, we lose the will to fight and the will to live, and are paralysed.

If you are not holy, you are not a Christian.

Holiness is not an experience that you have; holiness is keeping the law of God.

There are no short cuts in the Christian life, no patent remedies.

The ultimate test of our spirituality is the measure of our amazement at the grace of God.

Sin

'Man is just a poor creature who has never had a chance, and to whom therefore you should be very sympathetic and very lenient.' That is the modern idea. The biblical doctrine of sin really went out of man's thinking some sixty or seventy years ago, and psychology came in its place. That is why discipline and punishment have gone. The idea now is that we are all, essentially, very good. We do not believe in law and moral sanctions.

Sensitivity about self – is not this one of the greatest curses in life? It is a result of the Fall. We spend the whole of our life watching ourselves.

The whole trouble in life is ultimately a concern about self.

The intellectual critic is soon answered. We have but to ask him to explain the meaning of life and death.

The natural man is always play-acting; always looking at himself and admiring himself.

I remember a man who had been converted, but who fell into sin. I was very ready to help him until I found he was much too ready to help himself. In other words, he came and confessed sin, but immediately he began to smile and said: 'After all there is the doctrine of grace.' I felt he was too healthy; he was healing himself a little too quickly. The reaction to sin should be deep penitence. If you can jump lightly to the doctrine of grace, I suggest you are in a dangerous condition.

Intellectual pride is the last citadel of self.

The tragedy of sin is that it affects man in his highest faculties. Sin causes us to become fools, and behave in an irrational manner.

The trouble with man is not that he does certain things that are wrong; it is that he ever has a heart to do them.

When a man truly sees himself, he knows that nobody can say anything about him that is too bad.

TRIALS

Our behaviour in times of need and crisis proclaim what we really are.

Christian people are generally at their best when they are in the furnace of affliction and being persecuted and tried.

THE WORLD

The Christian is a man who expects nothing from this world. He does not pin his hopes on it, because he knows that it is doomed.

We have come to realise that a man can be educated and cultured and still be a beast!

The state of the world today is nothing but an appalling monument to human failure.

A man finally proclaims whether he is a Christian or not by the view he takes of this world.

A sketch of ML-J in the pulpit one Friday night circa 1960, by Andrew Anderson, and showing one of many facial expressions.

ML-J preaching to an estimated 4,000 at the Kelvin Hall, Glasgow,
April 23, 1963.

11

THE LLOYD-JONES SERMONS

It should be understood that the record and inventory that follows constitutes nothing like a full catalogue. After the retirement of Dr Campbell Morgan in 1943, ML-J annually undertook the entire ministry at Westminster Chapel. He was never out of his own pulpit, morning or evening, with the exception of a summer break of eight weeks, and occasionally, one Sunday around the New Year period. An interruption on account of illness was almost unknown. Given over forty Sundays of preaching each year at Westminster, the sermons which made up series (which I record below) by no means constituted all his preaching; in addition, there were many single sermons which I do not list. Some of these occurred at Christmas, and other times in the Christian year, when he would take a text particularly relevant to the occasion. It is significant that he had been twenty years in the ministry before he undertook the consecutive exposition of a book (2 Peter, begun in the autumn of 1946), and, although many expository series were to follow – especially on Sunday mornings – he never made the consecutive method of preaching a matter of principle. The longer series were the result of his development and his consideration of the needs of the people. The listing I give below, being incomplete, thus provides no sure estimate of the extent of Scripture that he covered. A full listing would need to include not only the individual, single sermons, but much other material, such as his sermons on the book of Revelation, preached on Friday evenings in the course of his 'lectures' on biblical doctrines (see vol. 3, *The Church and the Last Things*, Crossway, 1998).

I do not know of an instance where ML-J used the same sermon twice at Westminster; but he would return to texts, and preach from them a second time with much more fullness. An example would be his sermon on Psalm 107, listed in the year 1937, and then the eight sermons on the same psalm preached in 1957. Again, his sermon of 1941 on Numbers 11 developed into a series of five sermons on the same passage in 1957. His treatment of Ephesians and Romans 8, in the 1940s, gave way to his fullest expository series on those epistles in the 1950s and 1960s.

After his retirement from Westminster in 1968, Lloyd-Jones continued to preach regularly in many places until 1980; this ministry included new sermons until almost the end of his life. No record of these exists; some are available from Martyn Lloyd-Jones Recording Trust.

Lloyd-Jones's doctrinal convictions were largely settled during the period of his first ministry in Wales, with the exception of his understanding of certain passages of Scripture.[1] But there were to be changes in what he emphasised. In his own words he went to Wales in 1927 as a 'missioner', understanding his initial calling to

---

[1] Perhaps the most significant for him was the understanding of Romans 6 which he reached in 1954, as he writes in his Preface to his sermons on that chapter when published in the *Romans* series in 1972. The significance he now gave to 'died to sin' (*Rom.* 6:2), then affected his interpretation of Romans 7:14-24, which he had previously seen as descriptive of on-going Christian experience (*Sermon on the Mount*, vol. 1, p. 57). Some of his words when preaching on Romans 6 were moderated when he edited the sermons for publication. That he was right on Romans 6, and wrong on Romans 7, is possible. He would have said, with Paul, 'Let every man be fully persuaded in his own mind.'

be that of an evangelist. This is clearly reflected in all the sermons published from his early ministry. To preach for conversion was his great aim. To that emphasis, however, a stronger doctrinal note was added as the need for Christians to be taught grew more clear to him. He came to see the failure of evangelicals to recognise the importance of doctrine as a besetting weakness. A teaching role thus became a prominent part of his ministry. In his first two books, *Why Does God Allow War?* (1939) and *The Plight of Man and the Power of God* (1942), he demonstrated that it is only in the understanding of doctrine that a Christian gains the ability to live aright in this present world. This note was to remain prominent through the 1940s and 1950s. The church had been unprepared for World War II, he said, because

> Precise thinking, and definition, and dogma have been at a serious discount. The whole emphasis has been placed upon religion as a power which can do things for us and make us happy. The emotional and feeling side of religion has been over-emphasised at the expense of the intellectual. Far too often people have thought of it [the Christian religion] merely as something that gives a constant series of miraculous deliverances from all sorts and kinds of ills . . . The impression has often been given that we have but to ask God for whatever we may chance to need and we shall be satisfied . . . The great principles, the mighty background, the intellectual and theological content of our faith have not been emphasised, and indeed, oftentimes, have been dismissed as non-essentials.[1]

Not feelings, but the objective certainties of the Christian faith, thus came to the fore in the way he preached to believers. The Christian is not to think of sanctification as 'a gift to be received';

---

[1] *Why Does God Allow War?* pp. 45-46.

rather, 'Do you long to be holy? First, understand the doctrine', and believe what is already true.[1] Christians 'come to me about some problem or difficulty and they say: "I have been praying about this", and I say, "My friend, do you realise that your body is the temple of the Holy Ghost?" That is the answer. I say it again at the risk of being misunderstood, but such friends in a way need to pray less and to think more.'[2]

In the 1960s there was no change in his belief but, as I have already commented in these pages, there was change in emphasis. In the many circles where his influence was strong (not least in Westminster Chapel itself) his call to doctrinal understanding had been heard; and books with the same message were being read again as they had not been read for a long time. But such is the weakness of human nature, even in the Christian, that a loss of balance in the opposite direction to a previous fault was the new danger. Now it was necessary to insist that orthodox belief is not enough; the purpose of light is to lead to greater love and con-formity to Christ, and ML-J was afraid of Christians resting satis-fied with only mental attainments. Accordingly, he pressed the need for the experimental work of the Spirit, and especially with regard to personal assurance of salvation. This kind of adjustment in emphasis was all part of his wisdom as a pastor.

I note this variation so that the reader of his sermons can bear it in mind as he reads the dates when they were preached. To get the real balance of his ministry one needs to read him across the decades. When his books began to be published in numbers after his retirement (1968), I believe his decision on what should go into print was influenced by his assessment of the general needs in the English-speaking world. Today, with so much of his ministry now in print, the reader is faced with the need to be selective and

[1] See *Romans: Exposition of Chapter 5, Assurance*, pp. 156-58.
[2] *Spiritual Depression*, p. 173

I would recommend that *first attention* be given to the titles that he endorsed for publication before his death (1981). So in the listing below it is not only the dates sermons were preached that is interesting, but the dates of publication.

One area of exception needs to be added to what I have just written. I believe it would be right to say that no books of his evangelistic sermons appeared in his lifetime. That was because it was envisaged that Christians would want the sermons he preached for them.[1] This omission in publishing has contributed to a measure of distortion with respect to his memory. He is thought of as 'the great expositor', who preached long series at Westminster Chapel. But the truth is that, while other emphases were added to his original preaching, his original compulsion to be an evangelist never varied throughout his life. Through fifty years, he preached more evangelistic sermons that those of any other kind.

In ML-J's later Sunday morning preaching to Christians, as is well known, he increasingly preached consecutively through a passage of Scripture over a period of time. But he was much slower to do this in preaching to the unconverted. On a Sunday night, or when he was preaching around the country, as he often did, he had to treat each occasion as possibly the only one he might have with his hearers. He had therefore to be sure that they heard the complete message of the gospel. The idea that he was always 'expository' in the sense of consecutive is therefore erroneous. For evangelistic preaching he mainly used individual, single texts – texts likely to bring to mind the necessity of salvation even when all else was forgotten. Not only were his Sunday night sermons invariably evangelistic, but so also was the greater part of the mid-week ministry he exercised as he travelled in all parts of Britain.

---

[1] This is not to imply that Christians are not also in need of hearing and reading gospel preaching, and they did benefit from it throughout his ministry. But his evening sermons were specifically for the unconverted.

That ML-J has been followed by other ministers more as an 'expositor' than as an evangelist is, in part, due to a misunderstanding of his view of the Christian ministry. For a recovery of a more biblical evangelism today, the reading (and perhaps, even more, the hearing) of his evangelistic sermons is greatly desirable. The distinction between the two sides to his ministry will be clear in the listings below.

One other observation is important. The reader will notice that in all his sermons nothing will be found with a title such as 'The Five Points of Calvinism'. This is significant and warrants explanation. He believed that the best way of presenting doctrine is to teach the *text* of Scripture; the preacher's concern should not be that people take up a name or label, but that they gain a spiritual understanding of the word of God. His hearers, who knew what Calvinistic belief was, could recognise his theology; but the name, as such, was never paraded by him. He confined its use, as necessary, to addresses at conferences, or when speaking to ministers and students.

It has also to be said that, while he believed 'The Five Points', he did not believe they merited equal prominence; and, in the case of preaching to unbelievers, he did not think that some of the Points warranted prominence at all. Few have ever preached the first of the Five Points – man's total depravity – more strongly than he did: the corruption, vanity, impotence, blindness and folly of the unregenerate in rebellion against God, was his constant message, and drawn from all parts of Scripture. But the second of the Five Points – 'unconditional election' – did not follow in his preaching to the unconverted; indeed, he argued, it ought not to follow, 'To discuss election and predestination . . . with a man who is an unbeliever is obviously quite wrong.'[1] What that person needs

---

[1] *Sermon on the Mount*, vol. 2, p. 189.

is, first to be smitten by the consciousness of his sinfulness, and then to hear the willingness of Christ to justify freely, by faith alone. The message to the lost is that God now commands all men everywhere to repent (*Acts* 17:30), and John 3:16: 'For God so loved the world, that he gave his only begotten Son, that whosoever believes in him should not perish, but have everlasting life.' Others of the Five Points could be learned later; to treat them all as a formula for evangelism is to forget the saying of John Bradford, repeated by George Whitefield, 'Let a man go to the grammar school of faith and repentance, before he goes to the university of election and predestination.'

For the present writer, Dr Lloyd Jones's preaching ministry, continued in two congregations for more than forty years, is a wonderful confirmation of the fullness of the word of God – a revelation never diminished in freshness and power. And more than the man, we see the grace of Christ, promised to all his servants, so that, with only 'five loaves and two small fishes', the banquet never ends.

ABBREVIATIONS

WR, Westminster Record, a monthly publication of Westminster Chapel. From 1939 it contained a sermon either by Campbell Morgan or Lloyd-Jones, occasionally by both. This arrangement was continued by ML-J for over ten years after Dr Morgan's retirement in 1943.

BT, Banner of Truth.

IVF/IVP, Inter-Varsity Fellowship/Press

H&S, Hodder and Stoughton.

Sermons marked + are in *The Miracle of Grace* (Grand Rapids: Baker, 1986); a book made up largely from reporter's notes. Fuller versions of the same texts, corrected by the preacher, are in most cases in the WR.

Sermons marked * were originally published in WR and are now republished as *The Christian in an Age of Terror, Sermons for a Time of War*, M. Eaton, ed., (Chichester: New Wine, 2007).

NOTES

As well as the many Lloyd-Jones sermons now in print, there are also large numbers of them available on CDs and other formats. Almost all his ministry at Westminster Chapel from 1953 onwards can be heard through the ministry of the D. M. Lloyd-Jones Recordings Trust, 2 Caxton House, Wellesley Road, Ashford, Kent TN24 8ET (www.mlj.org.uk; or, www.mlj-USA.com).

As none of ML-J's sermons were given titles when first delivered, reporters and some publishers gave their own. Titles in WR, and in the books published in his lifetime were approved by the preacher, although seldom chosen by him.

The date of a sermon in WR does not necessarily indicate the year the sermon was preached. For example, the sermon 'Conquest of the Fear of Death', published in WR Jan. 1945, was preached on July 14, 1940, about the darkest time in World War II. For exact dating of ML-J's sermons a researcher would need to consult his sermon notes, now in the National Library of Wales, Aberystwyth. I am not sure how far the record book of sermons preached at Westminster Chapel was kept up-to-date during World War II. After that date the book was maintained at the Chapel.

PREACHED 1928-1937

Evangelistic Sermons at Aberavon (Edinburgh: BT, 1983).

Old Testament Evangelistic Sermons (Edinburgh: BT, 1995).
Eleven of the twenty-one sermons in this volume were preached in this early period. All the published sermons of the early period were from his MSS prepared for the pulpit. Thereafter he discontinued the practice of writing one sermon in full every week.

Luke 17:12-19, 'The Ten Lepers', reported in *Sunday Companion*, March 16, 1935.

Matthew 7:13-14, 'The Narrowness of the Gospel', WR April 1936 (his first sermon at Westminster Chapel, Dec. 29, 1935, three years before he settled there). Also *Christian World Pulpit*, Jan. 16, 1936, shorter and unrevised.+.

PREACHED 1936-1946

2 Timothy 2:4-6, 'How to be a Happy Christian', (a very non-Lloyd-Jones title!) reported in *Christian Herald*, Aug. 5, 1937.

Psalm 107, reported in *Christian Herald*, Sept. 2, 1937. In full in *OT Evangelistic Sermons* and WR, Aug. 1937, with simple title, 'Psalm 107'.

2 Kings 4:1-7 at Marylebone Presbyterian Church, London, Jan. 2, 1938, published in *Christian Herald*, Oct. 1938.+

Luke 7:11-16, report of evening sermon at Marylebone, Jan. 2, 1938. *Christian Herald*, March 17, 1938.+

Hebrews 6:11-12, 'The Hope of the Christian',+ undated reported sermon at the Metropolitan Tabernacle, London.

Romans 10:1-2, 'Zeal Without Knowledge', WR Aug. and Sept. 1938.

2 Kings 4:1-7, 'The Shunammite Woman', WR Dec.1938, Jan.1939. Fuller and different from the same text at Marylebone Presbyterian Church above, *Christian Herald*.+

Hebrew 12:9-10, 'Life's Preparatory School', WR, March 1939.

2 Timothy 2:8, 'Corner Stone of Christian Faith', reporter's notes, *Christian World*, July 13, 1939; WR, May 1939.

Why Does God Allow War? Five sermons preached October, 1939 (London: H&S, 1939; Bridgend: Evangelical Press of Wales, 1986). The first published book and of permanent relevance.

Acts 9:32-35, 'The Science of Sin', WR, April 1940.

James 1:5-8, 'One Supreme Need Today', reporter's notes, *Christian Herald*, Oct. 31, 1940. WR, July, 1940.+

2 Kings 5:1-3, 'A Little Maid's Testimony', WR, Dec. 1940.

1 Thessalonians 5:1-2, 'The Signs of the Times', WR, Jan. 1941.

Mark 4:35-41; Matthew 26:36–46, 'Asleep in the Hour of Crisis', reporter's notes, *Christian Herald,* April 3, 1941.

Numbers 11:4-6, 'The Nature of Sin', WR, Aug. 1941. Abridged.+

Acts 12:1-3, 'Religious Persecution', WR Sept. 1941.*

Acts 12:4-5, 'The Nature of the Conflict', WR, Oct. 1941.*

Acts 12:6-10, 'God Answering Prayer', WR Nov. 1941.*

Acts 12:10-12 'Where Miracle Ends', WR, Dec. 1941.*

Acts 12:23-24, 'The Church Triumphant', WR, Jan. 1942. *

The Plight of Man and the Power of God (London: H&S, 1942; Baker, 1982). Although four out of the five chapters are designated 'lectures', as expositions of Romans 1 they are closely akin to preaching, and were delivered in 'the hope' to 'serve in some measure to give a further impetus to the revival of that sadly neglected discipline.'

Romans 10:9, 'The Fact of the Resurrection', WR, July 1942. Abridged.+

1 Corinthians 16:13–14, 'Paul's Order of the Day (1) Introduction', WR, Sept. 1942.*

1 Corinthians 16:13-14, (2) 'Watch ye', WR, Nov. 1942.*

1 Corinthians 16:13-14, (3) 'Stand fast in the faith', WR, Jan. 1943.*

1 Corinthians 16:13-14, (4) 'Quit you like men', WR, March 1943.*

1 Corinthians 16:13-14, (5) 'Let all things be done with charity', WR May 1943.*

Hebrews 1:1-3, 'A Synopsis of Christian Doctrine, (1) Revelation', WR, Sept. 1943.*

Hebrews 1:1-3, (2) 'Revelation', WR, Nov. 1943.*

Hebrews 1:1-3, (3) 'From Glory–To Glory', WR, Jan. 1944.*

Hebrews 1:1-3, (4) 'Supreme Revelation in Christ,' WR, March 1944.*

1 Timothy 5:23, WR, May 1944.

Matthew 11:15, 'Hearkening to the Gospel', WR, June 1944.

Matthew 10:28, 'The Conquest of the Fear of Death', WR, Jan. 1945.

Ephesians 1:9-10, 'God's Plan for World Unity (1) General View.' WR, March 1945.*

Ephesians 1:17-23, 'God's Plan for World Unity (2) The Centrality of Christ', WR, May 1945.*

Ephesians 2:1-3 'God's Plan for World Unity (3) The Cause of the Discord', WR Aug. 1945.*

Ephesians 2:1-3, God's Plan for World Unity (4) Original Sin', WR Oct. 1945.*

Ephesians 2:1-3, 'God's Plan for World Unity (5) The World into which Christ Came', WR,1945.*

Ephesians 4:4-7, 'God's Plan for World Unity (6) 'The Only Hope', WR, Feb. 1946.*

Ephesians 2:13-18, 'God's Plan for World Unity (7) The Wondrous Cross', WR, April 1946.*

Ephesians 2:19-22, 'God's Plan for World Unity (8) The New Kingdom', WR, June 1946.*

Ephesians 4:4-6, 'God's Plan for World Unity (9) God Over All', WR, Aug. 1946.*

Psalm 42:3, 10, WR, Dec. 1946.

Revelation 4:1-2, 'A Preview of History (1) The Right Perspective', WR, Feb. 1947.*

Revelation 4:1-11 'A Preview of History (2) The Throne in Heaven', WR, March 1947.*

Revelation 5:1-4 'A Preview of History (3) The Two Types of History', WR, April 1947.*

Revelation 5:1-5 'A Preview of History (4) The Lord of History', WR, May 1947.*

Isaiah 35:4, 'He Comes Himself to Save You', WR, Dec. 1947.

PREACHED 1947-1968

From this point a more detailed record of his ministry is possible. Below I am listing all series that contain three or more sermons that he preached at Westminster. The first number given in the bracket is the number of the sermons in the series. The series that have been published are indicated by giving the Scripture passage in small capitals. Publishers commonly (I think regrettably) did not make the passage of Scripture dealt with the main title in publishing a volume; I am putting the Scripture text first, and giving the publishers' titles in footnotes. Often a published series has both a UK and a US publisher. I have not attempted to list every publisher or dates of reprints. The main titles probably all remain in print at the present time.

Series listed, but not in small capitals, are as yet (2008) unpublished. Throughout these years (as in his earlier ministry), Sunday evening sermons were always evangelistic and are indicated below by p.m. It will be seen that by far the greater part of series preached on Sunday mornings are now in print. As noted above, from 1953 most of his sermons at Westminster were recorded and remain available.

The listing below does not include lectures and addresses. His monumental *Romans* series, delivered on Friday evenings (14 vols., BT, 1970-2003) were often more sermons than lectures, and they constitute some of his most important work.

1946 2 Peter . . .

1947 2 Peter (25; BT, 1983). Philippians . . .
p.m. Romans 8:9-15 (6; New Wine, 2007).[1] Acts 26 (6)

1948 Philippians (40; H&S, 2 vols. 1989-1990).[2] 1 John . . .
p.m. Matthew 11:2-30 . . .

1949 1 John . . .
p.m. Matthew 11:2-30 (14; Crossway, 1991).[3]
Isaiah 9 (3); Luke 14:15-24 (3)

1950 1 John (67; Crossway, 2002).[4] Habakkuk (8; IVF, 1953).[5]
Matthew 5-7 . . .
p.m. Psalm 51 (4; Bryntirion, 1997).[6] Isaiah 55 (5);
Acts 17 (4); 1 Thessalonians (6)

1951 Matthew 5-7 . . .
p.m. John 14:2-3 (8; Vine, Michigan, 1995; reprint pending, Crossway, 2009);[7] Ecclesiastes 1-2 (5). Acts 16 (8)

1952 Matthew 5-7 (60; 2 vols., IVF, 1959-60).[8] John 17 . . .
p.m. [no record of a series]

1953 John 17 (48; Crossway, 2000).[9]

---

[1] *The Christian in an Age of Terror.*
[2] *Life of Joy; Life of Peace.*
[3] *The Heart of the Gospel.*
[4] *Life in Christ.*
[5] *From Fear to Faith.* See note 9 below.
[6] *Out of the Depths.*
[7] *Be Still My Soul.*
[8] *Studies in the Sermon on the Mount.*
[9] *The Assurance of Salvation.*

1953 (Cont.) PSALM 73 (11; IVF, 1965 16).[1]

1954 SPIRITUAL DEPRESSION, various texts (21; Pickering & Inglis, 1965).[2] EPHESIANS . . .
  p.m. Acts 17:1-4 (3). ISAIAH 40 (9; BT, 2005).[3]

1955 EPHESIANS . . .
  p.m. PSALM 107 (8; Bryntirion, 1999).[4] Jeremiah 17:5-15 (12).
  GENESIS 3:1-8 (6; Crossway; publication pending 2009).

1956 EPHESIANS . . .
  p.m. Luke 4 (11). Ezekiel 36:16-36 (14). John 1:45-51 (4).
  John 2:23-3:19 (14).

1957 EPHESIANS . . .
  p.m. Numbers 11 (5). PSALM 84:1-7 (2; Crossway, 1991).[5]
  John 1:15–17 (3).

1958 EPHESIANS (interrupted in next year for REVIVAL series)
  p.m. John 5:6-47 (22) Galatians 1 (9).

1959 REVIVAL, various texts (24; Marshall/Pickering, 1986)
  EPHESIANS . . .
  p.m. Matthew 24:1-14 (7). John 7:5-38 (13).
  1 Peter 1:10-21 (7). Luke 1:46-55 (4).

---

[1] *Faith on Trial*. Reprinted, with *From Fear to Faith, Faith Tried and Triumphant* (IVP/Baker, 1988).

[2] *Spiritual Depression: Its Causes and Cure*.

[3] *The All-Sufficient God*.

[4] *Let Everybody Praise the Lord*.

[5] *Seeking the Face of God* (also published in UK by Crossway as *Enjoying the Presence of God*). ML-J preached a series of five sermons on Psalm 84. Two are included in this book, along with seven other texts from the Book of Psalms.

1960 EPHESIANS . . .

p.m. Luke 13 (4). John 8:12-19 (9). Jeremiah 2:13-28 (12).

1961 EPHESIANS . . .

p.m. 2 Corinthians 4:1-7 (7). 2 Corinthians 5:1-17.

1962 EPHESIANS (concluded July 7; 8 vols. BT, 1972-1978).
   HEBREWS 10:19-22.[1] JOHN 1 . . .

p.m. Peter 2:1-10 (10). Philippians 3:3-21 (10).
   Matthew 9:1-18 (5). COLOSSIANS (14; Baker, 1995).[2]

1963 John 1. . . JOHN 1:12–13 (5; Bryntirion, 2000).[3]

p.m. PSALM 1 (4; Bryntirion, 1997).[4] ISAIAH 1:1-18 (9; BT, 1998).[5]
   MARK 1:14-15 (12; Crossway, 1992).[6] GALATIANS 6:7-5 . . .

1964 John 1. . . JOHN 1:26-33 . . .

p.m. GALATIANS 6:7-15 (9; Crossway, 1986).[7]
   ISAIAH 5 (9; Kingsway, 1997).[8]
   2 TIMOTHY 1:12 (11; Hodder/Baker, 1986)[9]

1965 John 1. JOHN 1:26-33 (24; Kingsway/Baker, 1984-1985,

---

[1] First in a series of three (with *Col.* 2:1-3 and *Heb.* 6:11-12) on *Full Assurance*.

[2] *Love So Amazing.*

[3] *Heirs of Salvation: Studies in Assurance* (on Abel, Enoch, Abraham); taken out of his JOHN 1 series).

[4] *True Happiness.*

[5] *God's Way Not Ours.*

[6] *The Kingdom of God.* While Mark 1 is the starting point, this series is made up of various texts.

[7] *The Cross.* While there were fifteen sermons in the original series only nine are here printed. Various reasons exist for such variations, as may be found with other titles.

[8] *A Nation Under Wrath.*

[9] *I Am Not Ashamed: Advice to Timothy.*

1996).[1] JOHN 2:3-25 (12; Kingsway, 1999).[2]
  p.m. ACTS 1-3 (22; BT, 1999).[3] ACTS 4-5 . . .

  1966 John 3:1-30 (26). JOHN 4 . . .
  p.m. ACTS 4-5 (21; BT, 2001) ACTS 5-6 (21; BT, 2003).
    ACTS 7:1-29 . . .

  1967 JOHN 4 . . .
  p.m. ACTS 7:1-29, (20; BT, 2004). ACTS 7:30-60, (18; BT 2006).
    ACTS 8:1-35 . . .

  1968 JOHN 4 (37; Crossway/Kingsway, pub. pending, 2009).[4]
  p.m. ACTS 8:1-35 (18; BT, 2006).

---

[1] Two vols: *Joy Unspeakable; Prove All Things*. In one vol. (1996) as *The Baptism and Gifts of the Holy Spirit*.
  [2] *Spiritual Blessing*.
  [3] *Authentic Christianity;* the other five volumes in this series on Acts proceed under the same title.
  [4] *Living Water*.

12

AN ANALYSIS OF THE SERMONS ON EPHESIANS

As the eight volumes on Ephesians (Banner of Truth, 1972-1982, and tapes from ML-J Recordings Trust) constitute ML-J's greatest Sunday morning series at Westminster Chapel, the following outline of contents may prove helpful. Twenty of the sermons preached were printed in the *Westminster Record* (WR) but were excluded by the preacher on the grounds that they were not so directly connected with the text of Ephesians.

An attempt has been made to give a keyword for each sermon, but this can only be understood in a very approximate sense.

Chapter: Verse	Date (d/m/y)	Book or WR	Tape	Keyword
		Volume 1 – God's Ultimate Purpose		
1:1	3/10/54	Vol 1: p22	4001	Intro
1.1	10/10/54	1:22	4002	Saints
1:2	17/10/54	1:35	4003	Grace
1:3	24/10/54	1:46	4004	Praise
1:3	31/10/54	1:57	4005	Blessings
1:3	7/11/54	1:69	4006	Heavenly
1:4	14/11/54	1:81	4007	Chosen
1:4	21/11/54	1:94	4008	In Love
1:5	28/11/54	1:106	4009	Adoption
1:5-6	5/12/54	1:117	4010	"
1:6	12/12/54	1:128	4011	His Glory
1:6	19/12/54	1:137	4012	In Christ
1:7	9/1/55	1:147	4013	Redemption
1:7	16/1/55	1:160	4014	Blood
1:7	23/1/55	1:171	4015	Liberality
1:8-9	30/1/55	1:184	4016	His Will
1:10	6/2/55	1:196	4017	Reunited
1:11-14	13/2/55	1:208	4018	'We . . . Ye'
1:11-14	20/2/55	1:221	4019	Predestinated
1:11-14	27/2/55	1:232	4020	Experience
1:13	6/3/55	1:243	4021	Sealed
1:13	13/3/55	1:255	4022	"
1:13	20/3/55	1:266		"
1:13	27/3/55	1:279		"
1:13	3/4/55	1:289	4023	"
1:14	24/4/55	1:301	4024	'Earnest'
1:14	1/5/55		4025	His Glory
1:15-16	8/5/55	1:312	4026	Tests
1:17	15/5/55	1:326	4027	Father

Chapter: Verse	Date (d/m/y)	Book or WR	Tape	Keyword
1:17	22/5/55	1:338	4028	Knowledge
1:17	29/5/55	1:350		Enlightenment
1:18	5/6/55	1:364	4029	'The Hope . . .'
1:18	12/6/55	1:378	4030	Inheritance
1:19-20	19/6/55	1:391	4031	Power
1:19-23	26/6/55	1:402	4032	"
1:19	3/7/55	1:412	4033	"
1:20-23	10/7/55	1:423	4034	'His Body'
1:19-23	17/7/55		4035	Consummation

Volume 2 – God's Way of Reconciliation

2:1	2/10/55	Vol 2: p11	4036	Man
2:1-3	9/10/55	2:26	4037	Sin
2:1-3	16/10/55	2:41	4038	Sin
2:1-3	23/10/55	2:54	4039	Godless
2:3	30/10/55	2:69	4040	Wrath
2:4	6/11/55	2:82	4042	'But'
2:4	13/11/55			"
2:4-7	20/11/55	2:96	4043	In Christ
2:4-7	27/11/55	2:111	4044	Risen
2:4-7	4/12/55	2:126	4045	Heavenlies
2:7	11/12/55	2:141	4046	Grace
2:7	18/12/55	2:155	4047	Through Christ
2:8-10	2/1/56	2:168	4048	Through Faith
2:10	15/1/56	2:183	4049	His Workmanship
2:11	22/1/56	2:198	4050	Reunited
2:12	29/1/56	2:212	4051	Christless
2:13	5/2/56	2:226	4052	'Nigh'
2:13	12/2/56	2:239	4053	'Blood'
2:14-16	19/2/56	2:253	4054	Peace

Chapter: Verse	Date (d/m/y)	Book or WR	Tape	Keyword
2:15	26/2/56	2:268	4055	Peace
2:16	4/3/56	2:283	4056	Mediator
2:17	11/3/56	2:295	4057	Peace
2:18	18/3/56	2:310	4058	Access
2:18	25/3/56	2:323	4059	Prayer
2:18	15/4/56	2:337	4060	"
2:18	22/4/56	2:351	4061	Unity
2:19	29/4/56	2:365	4062	Household
2:19	6/5/56	2:380	4063	Citizens
2:19	13/5/56	2:393	4064	"
2:19	27/5/56	2:407	4065	"
2:20-22	3/6/56	2:421	4066	Temple
2:20-22	10/6/56	2:435	4067	Foundation
2:20-22	17/6/56	2:450	4068	Together
2:20-22	24/6/56	2:464	4069	Growth
2:20-22	1/7/56	WR Nov '61	4070	Spirit
2:20-22	8/7/56	WR Dec '61	4071	Being/Doing
2:20-22	15/7/56	WR Jan '62	4072	Activism

Volume 3 – The Unsearchable Riches of Christ

Chapter: Verse	Date (d/m/y)	Book or WR	Tape	Keyword
3:1	14/10/56	Vol 3: p11	4073	Suffering
3:2-7	21/10/56	3:25	4074	'The Mystery'
3:3-6	28/10/56	3:39	4075	"
3:7-8	4/11/56	3:52	4076	Riches
3:9-11	11/11/56	3:67	4077	Planned
3:10	18/11/56	3:80	4078	Manifested
3:12	25/11/56	3:93	4079	Certainty
3:14-15	2/12/56	3:106	4080	Praying
3:16	9/12/56	3:119	4081	Strengthened
3:16	16/12/56	3:130	4082	"

Chapter: Verse	Date (d/m/y)	Book or WR	Tape	Keyword
3:17	13/1/57	3:142	4083	Christ Indwelling
3:17	20/1/57	3:154	4084	"
3:17	27/1/57	3:167	4085	Intimacy
3:17	3/2/57	3:181	4086	'Rooted'
3:17	10/2/57	3:193	4087	'Grounded'
3:18-19	17/2/57	3:205	4088	Love of Christ
3:18-19	24/2/57	3:218	4089	"
3:18-19	3/3/57	3:230	4090	"
3:18-19	10/3/57	3:242	4091	"
3:19	17/3/57	3:254	4092	Seeking Christ
3:19	24/3/57	3:265	4093	"
3:19	31/3/57	3:277	4094	Fullness
3:19	7/4/57	3:289	4095	"
3:20-21	14/4/57	3:302	4096	Doxology

Volume 4 – Christian Unity

4:1	5/5/57	Vol 4: p11	4097	'Therefore'
4:1-3	12/5/57	4:23	4098	Calling
4:2-3	19/5/57	4:34	4099	Unity
4:4-6	26/5/57	4:47	4100	"
4:4-6	2/6/57	4:58	4101	Holy Spirit
4:4-6	9/6/57	4:69	4102	Revival
4:4	16/6/57	4:82	4103	'One . . .'
4:5	23/6/57	4:94	4104	"
4:5	30/6/57	4:107	4105	"
4:5	7/7/57	4:120	4106	"
4:6	14/7/57	4:131	4107	"
4:7-10	6/10/57	4:144	4108	Everyone
4:9-10	13/10/57	4:155	4110	Redeemer
4:7-11	20/10/57	4:168	4109	Gifts

Chapter: Verse	Date (d/m/y)	Book or WR	Tape	Keyword
4:11	27/10/57	4:181		'Apostles . . .'
4:12-16	3/11/57	4:196		Edifying
4:13	10/11/57		4113	Church/World
4:13	17/11/57	4:209	4114	Knowledge
4:14	1/12/57	4:221	4115	Children
4:14	8/12/57	4:231	4116	Craftiness
4:15	15/12/57	4:241	4117	'Speaking . . .'
4:15-16	12/1/58	4:254	4118	Growing
4:16	19/1/58	4:265	4119	Human Energy

Volume 5 – Darkness and Light

Chapter: Verse	Date (d/m/y)	Book or WR	Tape	Keyword
4:17	26/1/58	Vol 5: p11	4120	Doctrine
4:17-19	2/2/58	5:25	4121	Empty Lives
4:17-19	9/2/58	5:38	4124	Darkness
4:18	16/2/58	5:52		Aliens
4:18-19	23/2/58	5:64		Shameless
4:20	2/3/58	5:78		The Contrast
4:20-21	9/3/58	5:91	4125	Learning Christ
4:20-21	16/3/58	5:103	4126	"
4:22-24	23/3/58	5:116	4127	Putting Off . . .
4:22-24	30/3/58	5:127	4128	"
4:22-24	20/4/58	5:140	4129	Mortification
4:23	27/4/58	5:153	4130	Mind
4:24	4/5/58	5:167		New Man
4:24	11/5/58	5:179		Spirituality
4:24	18/5/58	5:189	4133	Doing!
4:25	1/6/58	5:199	4134	Putting On
4:25	8/6/58	5:213	4135	Lying
4:26-27	15/6/58	5:225	4136	Anger
4:28	22/6/58	5:239	4137	Stealing

Chapter: Verse	Date (d/m/y)	Book or WR	Tape	Keyword
4:29	29/6/58	5:253	4138	Speech
4:30	6/7/58	5:264	4139	'Grieve Not . . .'
4:31-32	13/7/58	5:278		Bitterness
5:1-2	5/10/58	5:291	4141	Imitators
5:2	12/10/58	5:300	4142	'An Offering'
5:3-5	19/10/58	5:313	4143	Church/State
5:3-5	26/10/58	5:329	4144	Speech
5:5	2/11/58	5:342	4145	Antinomianism
5:6	9/11/58	5:354	4146	Wrath
5:7-8	16/11/58	5:367	4147	A Christian
5:8-13	23/11/58	5:379	4148	Unfruitfulness
5:9-10	30/11/58	5:390	4149	Fruit
5:9-13	7/12/58	5:401	4150	'Acceptable . . .'
5:7-14	14/12/58	5:412	4151	Light
5:14	4/10/59	WR Feb '68	4152	"
5:15	11/10/59	5:423		Folly/Wisdom
5:15-17	18/10/59	5:436		'Circumspectly'
5:15-17	25/10/59	5:449		Time

Volume 6 – Life in the Spirit

Chapter: Verse	Date (d/m/y)	Book or WR	Tape	Keyword
5:18	1/11/59	Vol 6: p11		Stimulus
5:18	8/11/59	6:26		Power
5:18	15/11/59	6:40		Control
5:19	22/11/59	WR Sep '68	4156	Christian Praise
5:19	29/11/59	WR Oct '68	4157	"
5:19	6/12/59	WR Nov '68	4158	"
5:20	13/12/59	WR Dec '68	4159	Thankfulness
5:21	10/1/60	6:55	4160	Submission
5:21	17/1/60	6:70	4161	For Christ
5:22-23	24/1/60	6:85	4162	Principles

Chapter: Verse	Date (d/m/y)	Book or WR	Tape	Keyword
5:22-24	31/1/60	6:100	4163	Created Order
5:22-24	7/2/60	6:115	4164	Man/Head
5:25	14/2/60	6:130	4165	Love
5:25-27	21/2/60	6:142	4166	'As Christ . . .'
5:25-27	28/2/60	6:155	4167	Sanctification
5:25	6/3/60	6:170		For Glory
5:25	13/3/60	6:183		One Flesh
5:25	20/3/60	6:195	4170	Bride
5:25	27/3/60	6:208	4171	Husband
5:25	3/4/60	6:222		Marriage Unity
6:1	1/5/60	6:237	4175	Discipline
6:1-4	8/5/60	6:250		Parents
6:4	15/5/60	6:262		Discipline
6:4	22/5/60	6:276	4176	"
6:4	29/5/60	6:289	4177	Upbringing
6:5	12/6/60	6:305	4178	[Summary]
6:5	19/6/60	6:318	4179	Priorities
6:5	26/6/60	6:331		Society
6:5-8	3/7/60	6:343		Serving
6:8-9	10/7/60	6:359	4182	Our Master

Volume 7 – The Christian Warfare

Chapter: Verse	Date (d/m/y)	Book or WR	Tape	Keyword
6:10	2/10/60	Vol 7: p11	4183	Introduction
6:10-13	9/10/60	7:23	4184	Not Morality
6:10-13	16/10/60	7:38	4185	The Enemy
6:10-13	23/10/60	7:53	4186	"
6:10-13	30/10/60	7:66	4187	"
6:10-13	6/11/60	7:79	4188	Wiles
6:10-13	13/11/60	WR Aug '62	4189	War
6:10-13	20/11/60	WR Sep '62	4190	Demonology

Chapter: Verse	Date (d/m/y)	Book or WR	Tape	Keyword
6:10-13	27/11/60	WR Oct '62	4191	Spiritism
6:10-13	4/12/60	WR Nov '62	4192	Devil Possession
6:10-13	11/12/60	WR Dec '62	4193	Grace
6:10-13	18/12/60	WR Jan '63	4194	Christ Conqueror
6:10-13	8/1/61	WR Feb '63	4195	Vantage Ground
6:10-13	15/1/61	7:94		A Subtle Foe
6:10-13	22/1/61	7:108		Heresies
6:10-13	29/1/61	WR May '63		R. Catholicism
6:10-13	5/2/61	WR Jun '63	4196	Schism
6:10-13	12/2/61	WR Jul '63		Divisions
6:10-13	19/2/61	7:121	4199	Cults
6:10-13	26/2/61	7:133	4200	Counterfeits
6:10-13	5/3/61	7:148	4201	Watchfulness
6:10-13	12/3/61	7:162	4202	'Philosophy . . .'
6:10-13	19/3/61	7:177	4203	Pride
6:10-13	26/3/61	WR Jan '65	4204	Deity of Christ
6:10-13	2/4/61	WR Feb '64		Resurrection
6:10-13	16/4/61	7:191	4205	Faith/Experience
6:10-13	23/4/61	7:206	4206	Physical, etc.
6:10-13	30/4/61	7:221	4207	Assurance
6:10-13	7/5/61	7:235	4208	"
6:10-13	14/5/61	7:249	4209	"
6:10-13	21/5/61	7:263	4210	Quenching
6:10-13	28/5/61	7:276	4211	"
6:10-13	4/6/61	7:289	4212	Temptation
6:10-13	11/6/61	7:303	4213	Discouragement
6:10-13	18/6/61	7:317	4214	Worry
6:10-13	25/6/61	7:332	4215	Self
6:10-13	2/7/61	7:346	4216	Zeal
6:10-13	9/7/61	7:360	4217	Worldliness

Chapter: Verse	Date (d/m/y)	Book or WR	Tape	Keyword
		Volume 8 – The Christian Soldier		
6:10-13	8/10/61	Vol 8: p11	4218	Strength
6:10-13	15/10/61	8:26	4219	His Battle
6:10-13	22/10/61	8:40	4220	And Ours
6:10-13	29/10/61	8:54	4221	Morale
6:10-13	5/11/61	8:69	4222	Food
6:10-13	12/11/61	8:84	4223	Exercise
6:10-13	19/11/61	8:95	4224	Discipline
6:10-13	26/11/61	8:111	4225	Promises
6:10-13	3/12/61	8:126	4226	Trust
6:10-13	10/12/61	8:140	4227	Avoid
6:10-13	17/12/61	8:155	4228	Stand!
6:14	14/1/62	8:170	4229	Armour
6:14	21/1/62	8:182	4230	Truth
6:14	28/1/62	8:194	4231	Authority
6:14	4/2/62	8:207	4232	Scripture
6:14	11/2/62		4233	God's Truth
6:14	18/2/62		4234	"
6:14	25/2/62		4235	"
6:14	4/3/62		4236	"
6:14	11/3/62	8:221	4236	Breastplate
6:14	18/3/62	8:234	4238	'Feelings'
6:14b	25/3/62	8:247	4239	'Put On'
6:14b	1/4/62		4240	"
6:14b	8/4/62		4241	"
6:14b	15/4/62		4242	"
6:14b	6/5/62		4243	
6:14b	13/5/62	8:258	4244	Pilgrims
6:15	20/5/62	8:270	4245	Feet
6:15	27/5/62	8:283	4246	Mobility

Chapter: Verse	Date (d/m/y)	Book or WR	Tape	Keyword
6:16	3/6/62	8:296	4247	Faith
6:17	17/6/62	8:309	4248	Helmet
6:17b	24/6/62	8:323	4249	Sword
6:18	1/7/62	8:337	4250	Praying
6:18-20	8/7/62	8:350	4252	"

My contention is that the increase in Roman Catholicism is due to one thing only, and that is a weak and flabby Protestantism that does not know what it believes. There is only one thing that can counter it, and that is a biblical and doctrinal Christianity. A Christianity that just preaches 'Come to Christ' or 'Come to Jesus' cannot stand before Rome for a second. Probably what that will do ultimately will be to add to the numbers belonging to Rome. People who hold evangelistic campaigns and say, 'Ah, you Roman Catholics, go back to your church', are denying New Testament teaching. We must warn them. There are innocent people who are being deluded.

ML-J, PREACHING ON 'THE WILES OF THE DEVIL', JANUARY 29, 1961.

13

IS THE REFORMATION OVER?
A REVIEW

In view of its relevance to an understanding of Dr Lloyd-Jones's
position, I include my review of the recent book, Mark A. Noll,
Carolyn Nystrom, *Is the Reformation Over? An Evangelical Assessment of Contemporary Roman Catholicism* (Grand Rapids: Baker/
Paternoster, 2005).

Is the Reformation Over? 'The answer is both yes and no.
Largely, it is yes' (p. 140). These words of the authors, in discussing a parallel question, may be taken as a summary of their
case. They believe that a change 'unimaginable forty years ago'
has taken place between evangelicalism (or at least 'most' of it) and
Roman Catholicism. That a change has taken place in these years
is well documented; we are assured that instead of the evangelical
opposition of former times, there is a new openness, and any con-
tinuing 'outcry' is left to 'a few' (p. 160), who include the 'para-
noid or ignorant'. But except for this one lapse, Noll and Nystrom
eschew name-calling. We do not disagree with their repudiation
of the ugly language which has sometimes marred the divide. It is
a parody of Christianity which allows anyone to suspend love for
one's neighbour if that neighbour is a theological opponent. This
is not the same, however, as accepting that Roman Catholicism as

an institution warrants more respect than was given to it in former centuries.

The main issue the book raises is whether the Roman Church as an institution has so improved that evangelical Christians ought now to abandon the position of the older Protestantism. The authors believe that the change in Rome is so significant that 'evangelicals can embrace at least two-thirds of the *Catechism*' (p. 119). 'The Catholic *Catechism* also announces loud and clear many, perhaps most, of the theological concepts dear to the hearts of evangelical Protestants. They are basic beliefs of these two branches of the Christian faith' (p. 122).[1] These statements are a little surprising given that remaining differences are acknowledged, but the authors insist that on the fundamental matter of salvation, and what constitutes a Christian, a new unanimity has been reached. On justification only details of disagreement remain: the main truth is agreed: 'If it is true, as once was repeated by Martin Luther or John Calvin that *iustificatio articulus stantis vel cadentis ecclesiae* (justification is the article on which the church stands or falls), then the Reformation is over' (p. 232). 'In its official teachings which are found most recently in the documents of the Second Vatican Council and the Catholic *Catechism*, the Roman Catholic Church now articulates positions on salvation – even on justification by faith – that are closer to the main teachings of many Protestants' (p. 180). Thus, as far as basic Christianity is concerned, evangelicals and Catholics can now embrace one another as fellow believers. The divide that remains has to do, not with salvation, but with the doctrine of the church. This is called 'the key difference' and

---

[1] The reference is to the *Catechism of the Catholic Church*, UK edition (London: Geoffrey Chapman, 1994). These confident statements are hardly in harmony with a later sentence, 'a great deal of teaching is found in this official document that evangelicals will not accept' (p. 130). To judge this discussion the reader needs to obtain the *Catechism*. These issues are far too important to be taken second-hand.

'the central difference' (pp. 236-237). 'Ecclesiology represents the crucial difference between evangelicals and Catholics'
(p. 147).

Before proceeding I will make a few brief comments on aspects
of the authors' procedure. In several places the same ground is
gone over a number of times – partly, no doubt the effect of dual
authorship. The repetition is unnecessary.

At no point is there any interaction with Scripture. We are
told the 'differences . . . are deeply rooted in history, culture, and
habits' (p. 249). Ought not Scripture to have had a place in the
list? The Catholic claim that the mass is 'anchored in Scripture',
with the proof text given as John 6:53, is quoted as though the
reference alleged was legitimate (p. 231). While Roman Catholicism is compared with less commendable features of contemporary American evangelicalism, there is no attempt to compare it
with Scripture. Instead, beliefs which evangelicals once believed
had the authority of Scripture are only cautiously stated.

Although the authors write as 'we evangelicals', they want to
preserve a measure of what might be called neutrality or objectivity. No connection between former evangelical beliefs and Scripture is asserted; rather we read such sentences as, 'Hodge regularly chastised Catholicism for what *he thought* were its manifest
theological errors' (p. 44, italics added). Yet they are prepared
to express certainty at other points. For example, we are told that
the change in evangelical opinion with respect to Catholicism 'must
be that God willed the changes to take place' (p. 59); again, 'the
new charismatic movement blurred the barriers of Protestant-
Catholic demarcation as participants together followed the wind
of the Spirit' (p. 65).

There is also a lapse in objectivity in the way the distinctives
of Roman Catholic belief are allowed to claim the support of the
early church Fathers; we are told that evangelical readers of the

Catholic *Catechism* will 'discover a better connection with early fathers and mothers of the faith, a clearer picture of their brothers and sisters from the other side of the Reformation' (p. 150). There is not so much as a hint that the appeal to the church fathers has been effectively challenged by many Protestant authors in the past.[1]

THE REAL 'KEY DIFFERENCE'

I turn now to the claim that the key remaining difference with Rome has to do with the nature of the church. I believe the statement is misleading. The Roman doctrine of the church – that she possesses infallibility and is the sole representative of Christ – is derived from another more fundamental belief, namely, that Scripture alone is *not* the rule for the Christian's faith and practice. Of course, papal infallibility cannot be found in the New Testament; nor the intercessory role attributed to Mary and to 'saints'; nor purgatory and indulgences;[2] nor a sacrificing priesthood; nor baptismal regeneration and a raft of other beliefs and practices which have the official endorsement of the Roman Church. Yet this, it is replied by spokesmen for Rome, need not disturb anyone, for the Holy Spirit has inspired the 'tradition' of the Church, as he

---

[1] The Tractarian movement in England was built around the claim that it marked a return to the church of the first centuries. One of the refutations of that falsehood was the massive two-volume work of William Goode, *The Divine Rule of Faith and Practice* (London: Hatchard, 1842).

[2] Far from being an obsolete Reformation issue, the 1998 Papal Bull, *Incarnationis Mysterium*, states in detail how by obtaining an indulgence the pains of purgatory may be reduced for oneself or for the dead. One current way to obtain a 'full indulgence of sins' is to climb the now restored *Sancta Scala*, or Holy Stairs, in Rome. The twenty-eight steps, said to have been brought from Pilate's Palace to Rome, and stained with Christ's blood, are so 'holy' that they must only be climbed on one's knees. Benedict XVI has promised further indulgences for the year 2008.

has inspired Scripture; we may therefore trust the Church's teaching as much as we may trust Scripture. Indeed we may trust the Church *more*, because we cannot depend on our own understanding of Scripture: *'The task of interpreting the Word of God authentically has been entrusted solely to the Magisterium of the Church, that is, to the Pope and of the bishops in communion with him.'*[1] The words (and the italics) come, not from the sixteenth century, but from the official Vatican teaching of 1994. The convert to Rome today is required to believe 'what the Church believes'.

The issue of authority is indeed the key to the Roman/Protestant division. Far from being an isolated belief it underpins everything that stands against evangelical Christianity. Let Rome's claim to share in the rule of faith with Scripture be taken away, and her claim to mediate salvation through priest and sacrament must fall. It is irresponsible for Noll and Nystrom to write as though the nature of the church is an issue separable from the way of salvation, especially as they know that Rome claims their Church to be 'an integral part of the Gospel'.[2] On this point the Roman *Catechism* which, they say, evangelicals should find it 'a treat' to read (p. 116), is also explicit: 'They could not be saved who, knowing that the Catholic Church [i.e. Rome] was founded as necessary by God through Christ, would refuse either to enter it, or to remain in it.'[3] Hence the anathemas pronounced by the Council of Trent in the sixteenth century on those who left 'the

---

[1] *Catechism of the Catholic Church*, p. 28. The charge made by John Owen long ago remains true: 'The church of Rome lays claim to the very same authority over and conduct of the consciences of men in religion as were committed unto Jesus Christ and his apostles.' *Works*, vol. 14, p. 499. The whole of that Owen volume deals with the controversy with Rome and remains very relevant reading.

[2] *Evangelicals and Catholics Together: Toward a Common Mission* , Charles Colson and John Richard Neuhaus, eds., (Dallas: Word, 1995). Dr Noll was one of the contributors to this volume.

[3] *Catechism of the Catholic Church*, pp. 196-197.

Church' to uphold evangelical belief.[1]

On the primary issue nothing has changed. What has changed is presentation or what Pope John XXIII called the Papacy's 'manner'. This is notable in the Evangelicals and Catholics Together (ECT) movement in which the chief promoter on the Catholic side is the irenical John Richard Neuhaus. But when a reviewer of ECT denied that the Roman Catholic Church is 'an acceptable Christian communion', Neuhaus dropped the ecumenical spirit when he replied:

> I take note also of your opinion that the Church sanctified by the martyr blood of the Apostles Peter and Paul, the Church in continuity with the Petrine ministry established by Christ, the Church that has sustained the Scriptural, patristic, conciliar, and the theological traditions that define Christian orthodoxy (also for Protestants), the Church that has claimed the allegiance of the great majority of Christians over two millennia is not 'an acceptable Christian communion.' Really.[2]

This is nothing more than the old claim that the Roman church of the apostolic age is the same Church of Rome today – the true Church as compared with the communities that only began with Martin Luther and are not to be called 'churches'. So without any window-dressing Pope Benedict XVI, in his decree of July 10, 2007, answered the question why the Second Vatican

---

[1] Noll and Nystrom tell us that these anathemas are now removed (p. 111), but they are only removed for those ready to blur the evangelical beliefs recovered at the Reformation. How can a person be an evangelical and acquiesce to such official statements of Roman belief as, 'Justification is conferred in Baptism, the sacrament of faith . . . It is the sanctifying or deifying grace received in Baptism.' *Catechism of the Catholic Church*, pp.433-434.

[2] Letter from Neuhaus to Michael S. Horton, July 7, 1994, quoted by Noll and Nystrom, p. 157. That Protestants are dependent on the Roman Church for the first formulations of Christian doctrine is false. None of the early creeds (Apostles', Nicene, Athanasian) was drawn up by Rome and all say nothing of papal authority.

Council did not use the word 'church' when speaking of the congregations of the Reformation: 'According to Catholic doctrine,
these Communities do not enjoy apostolic succession in the Sacrament of Orders and are, therefore, deprived of a constitutive element of the Church.'

James I. Packer

With regret, I have to take up another feature of this book, namely,
the extent to which the authors rely on, and quote extensively from,
Dr J. I. Packer. The opening page of the book bears the dedica-
tion, 'To J. I. Packer, discerning pioneer.' I say 'with regret' for
numbers of us regard Jim Packer as a friend, and the evangelical
world is indebted to him for valuable books. But the truth is that
the thinking behind *Is the Reformation Over?* is virtually Packer's
thinking. The book stands on his opinion that 'Catholics and Protestants fighting together for the basics of the creed is nowadays
more important [than discussion on individual doctrines] (p. 249).[1]
The 'basics' include the way of salvation, so the two sides should
now evangelise together as he argued with others in *Evangelicals and
Catholics Together.*[2] That serious differences remain is not denied,
but they are not such as to warrant any questioning of Roman
Catholics as fellow believers.

Noll and Nystrom speak of the 'distance' Packer has moved
since his earlier years (p. 34), and Packer himself wishes that
to be known. In explaining recently how he has outgrown 'sectarianism', he wrote, 'Christian conservatives who love Jesus my

---

[1] The quotation is from Packer's Foreword to George Carey's book on unity
with Roman Catholicism, *A Tale of Two Churches: Can Protestants and Catholics Get
Together?*

[2] *Evangelicals and Catholics Together: Toward a Common Mission*, C. Colson, J. R.
Neuhaus, eds. (Dallas: Word, 1995).

Lord – Pentecostal, Roman Catholic, Anglo-Catholic, and Orthodox for starters – are my fellow believers, sometimes despite their official doctrine.'[1] Packer is right that 'sectarianism' is unworthy of Christians, but it does not follow that we are obliged to see all who adhere to Roman Catholicism as 'fellow Christians', as he encourages us to do.[2] Certainly, where there are basic gospel truths, Christians may be found. That such basic truth survives within the formularies of the Roman Church is not denied, nor has such a denial ever been part of the Protestant case against Rome. The issue is whether the system of teaching and practice with which Rome indoctrinates her people is consistent with those basic truths. The Reformers judged that system from Scripture and showed the fundamental contradiction. Instead of upholding the New Testament gospel, the Roman system is calculated to lead away from faith in Christ to faith in the Church and faith in the priest; from faith in gospel promises to faith in sacraments and 'good works'; from faith in the Bible to believing 'what the church believes'. Let the reader take up the Roman *Catechism* and judge whether this is true or a caricature.

It is affirmed and repeated by the upholders of Evangelicals and Catholics Together that the justification of sinners 'is not earned by any good works or merits of our own'. But this is a specious use of words. The Roman Church has always claimed that 'the good works' necessary for justification are performed in

[1] Scott Larsen, ed., *Indelible Ink: 22 International Christian Writers Discuss the Books that Shape their Faith* (Farnham, Surrey: CWR, 2005), p. 103.

[2] That same encouragement is in the Nottingham Congress Statement of 1977 (the follow-up to Keele 1967), and it is inherent in the ECT documents. Integral to Packer's thinking is the need for 'conservatives' (i.e. those upholding the supernatural) to stand together against a liberal pluralism. So Roman Catholicism is to be regarded as an ally. But the warning of Bishop Hall (on the lying prophet in 1 Kings 13) remains true: 'There is no temptation so dangerous, as that which comes shrouded under a veil of holiness, and pretends authority from God himself.'

cooperation with Christ. Thus Cannon XXXII of Trent teaches that good works performed through the grace of God and the merit of Christ 'truly merit eternal life'.[1] No matter what is credited to Christ, works remain a necessary part of justification, and because no-one can know if his works are of sufficient quality Rome denies the possibility of assurance, and teaches the necessity of sacraments and of purgatory for most 'Christians'.

One does not deny a Roman Catholic *may* be a Christian; but where that is the case it is in spite of the system that keeps so many in darkness.[2] The reformers left the See of Rome because she misled the world on the way of salvation. In Calvin's words:

> The schools of the Sophists have taught with remarkable agreement that the sacraments of the new law (those now used in the Christian church) justify and confer grace, provided we do not set up a barrier of mortal sin. How deadly and pestilential this notion is cannot be expressed – and the more so because for

---

[1] 'Canons and Decrees of the Council of Trent,' P. Schaff, ed., *Creeds of the Greek and Latin Churches*, (London: Hodder and Stoughton, 1877), p. 117. 'If any one saith, that by faith alone the impious is justified, in such wise as to mean, that nothing else is required to co-operate in order to the obtaining of the grace of justification . . . let him be anathema.' (Canon IX). See also *Catechism of the Catholic Church*, p. 438. As Calvin says (on *John* 15:5), 'The doctrine invented by the papists is, that we can do nothing without Christ, but that, aided by him, we have something of ourselves in addition to his grace.' Contrary to Rome, the Reformers held that justification is not a process but an act of God, accounting the work of Christ to the sinner who receives him. It is a once-for-all event, of which good works are not a part but a consequence.

[2] That Roman Catholicism gives small, if any, place to preaching is the direct result of her teaching that 'what the Church believes' is enough for her adherents. So the Pope, visiting foreign lands, will customarily be found not preaching but celebrating mass. A Roman opponent of John Owen claimed: 'Nowhere was ever sermon made to formal Christians, either by St Peter or Paul, or any other, as the work of their religion that they came together for; nor did the Christians ever dream of serving God after their conversion by any such means, but only by the eucharist or liturgy.' Owen, *Works*, vol. 14, pp. 412-413. See in that volume, *The Church of Rome No Safe Guide: or, reasons to prove that no rational man, who takes due care of his own eternal salvation, can give himself up unto the conduct of that Church in matters of religion.*

many centuries it has been a current claim in a good part of the world, to the great loss of the church. Of a certainty it is diabolical. For in promising a righteousness apart from faith, it hurls souls headlong to destruction.[1]

Although the statements do not appear in the book I am here reviewing, Packer is on record as saying that he could not belong to the Church of Rome. But the concessions he has made, and which are repeated in this book, could be enough to encourage others to take that step. Inducements from the Catholic side are not lacking. In the present fragmented state of Christianity, and threatened by rampant secularism and materialism, why should evangelicals remain apart from the 'greater unity' which Rome professes to offer? If evangelicals have discovered that the differences do not concern the essentials of the gospel, and there is now agreement 'on the basics', why should there not be reunion? This is the very question that Neuhaus, one of the chief promoters of ECT, has asked evangelicals to face. Adding his own emphasis, he wrote: *'If at the end of the twentieth century, separation for the sake of the gospel is not necessary, it is not justified.'*[2]

On this question neither Packer nor the authors of *Is the Reformation Over?* appear to have anything to say. The only effective answer to Neuhaus is the one given at the time of the Reformation. Whether that answer has the authority of God and of Scripture is one of the most crucial issues now facing evangelical Christianity.

All the Roman doctrines, contested in the sixteenth century, remain unchanged. It is by Scripture that the decision must be reached whether a Reformer such as John Hooper was mistaken in being 'willing to give up his life rather than consent to the wicked papistical religion of the Bishop of Rome'. When urged to recant

---

[1] John Calvin, *Institutes of the Christian Religion*, Book IV, chapter 14.
[2] *Evangelicals and Catholics Together*, p. 199. I have discussed this more fully in *Evangelicalism Divided*.

with the words, 'Consider that life is sweet, and death is bitter', the one-time Bishop of Gloucester replied: 'The life to come is more sweet, and the death to come is more bitter.' While we do not appeal to history to settle this issue, let it be remembered that the Reformers were men who both knew Scripture and the religion they had themselves once thought to be Christian. Unless there is a renewal of what made Protestantism, the uncertainties which this book promotes can only influence larger numbers.

AUTHORS & SOURCES CITED

Alexander, A. *The Log College*, 40

Alexander, J. W. *Thoughts on Preaching*, 42

Alderson, Richard, *No Holiness, No Heaven!* 160

Allan, Tom, *Evening Citizen* (Glasgow), 30

Allis, O. T., 'Old Testament Emphases and Modern Thought', 67-68, 79

Anon, *Spurgeon, By One Who Knew Him Well*, 110, 118, 121

Arthur, W. *Tongue of Fire*, 39

Barclay, Oliver, *Evangelicalism in Britain 1935-1995*, 179, 182-183, 197

    'Where is Academic Theology Heading?', 197

Bonar, A., *Gospel Truths*, 153

Bonar, H., *Life of John Milne*, 150

Bray, Gerald, 'Review of McGrath on Packer', 189

Breed, D. R. *Preparing to Preach*, 46

Brencher, John, *ML-J and Twentieth-Century Evangelicalism*, 169-170, 172, 177, 185, 190, 196

Brown, John, *John Bunyan*, 46

Bruce, F. F., Review of *Fight of Faith*, 199-200

Bull, Josiah, *Letters of John Newton*, 157-158

Bunyan, John, *Works*, 46, 71, 112

Calvin, John, *Gospel of John*, 187, 258, 265
    Institutes of the Christian Religion, 265-266
Carey, George, *A Tale of Two Churches*, 186, 263
Catechism of the Catholic Church, 183, 258-265
Catherwood, Elizabeth, 'ML-J: the Man and his Books', 43
Catherwood, C., ed., *Five Evangelical Leaders*, 196
    ML-J: Chosen by God, 168, 181, 207
    ML-J: A Family Portrait, 188
Charles, Thomas, *Spiritual Counsels*, 153
Colquhoun, John, *Treatise on Spiritual Comfort*, 152
Colson, C. (with R. J. Neuhaus), *Evangelicals and Catholics Together*, 261, 263, 266
Cook, T., *Days of God's Right Hand*, 54
CRN Journal, 161
Crowe, P., *Keele '67*, 179-180
Cuyler, T., *The Young Preacher*, 60
    Thoughts on Heart and Life, 46
    Recollections of a Long Life, 115
Dallimore, Arnold, *Life of Edward Irving*, 157
Davies, A. M., *Life and Letters of Henry Rees*, 115
Davies, Gaius, *Genius, Grief and Grace*, 169, 198
Douglas, J. D., *Evangelicals and Unity*, 181
Edwards, Jonathan, *Works*, 157, 162
Evangelical Quarterly, 200
Evangelicals Now, 197-198
Fant, C. E. (with W. M. Pinson), *Twenty Centuries of Great Preaching*, 33
Fairbairn, P., *Pastoral Theology*, 39
    on 1 Timothy 4:14, 136
Flavel, John, *Works*, 132, 157-160, 162
Fullerton, W. Y., *C. H. Spurgeon, A Biography*, 111
Guthrie, Wm., *Christian's Great Interest*, 151

Hodge, A. A., *Evangelical Theology*, 176
Hopkins, Mark, *Nonconformity's Romantic Generation*, 116
Howe, John, *Works*, 192-193
Jenkins, D. E., *Life of Thomas Charles*, 82
Johnson, T. C., *Life and Letters of B. M. Palmer*, 17
Johnson, D., *Contending for the Faith*, 197
Jones, Owen, *Some of the Great Preachers of Wales*, 49
Kendall, R. T., *In Pursuit of His Glory*, 159-161
Ker, John, *History of Preaching*, 40
Kidder, D. P., *Treatise on Homiletics*, 32, 34
King, J. C., *The Evangelicals*, 179
Larsen, Scott, ed., *Indelible Ink*, 264
Leith, J. H., *From Generation to Generation*, 82-83
Lloyd-Jones, Bethan (Mrs) *Memories of Sandfields*, 17
Lloyd-Jones, Elizabeth (see Catherwood)
Lloyd-Jones D. Martyn,
    Authentic Christianity, 148, 244
    Authority, 27
    Basis of Christian Unity, 174-175
    Christian in an Age of Terror, 8, 129, 234, 241
    EPHESIANS
        God's Ultimate Purpose, 12, 14, 16, 128, 139-141,
            144-145, 156, 246
        God's Way of Reconciliation, 11, 45, 48, 51, 247
        Unsearchable Riches of Christ, 13, 248
        Christian Unity, 7, 12, 174-175, 249
        Christian Warfare, 13, 16, 131, 146, 161, 252
        Christian Soldier, 87, 196, 254
    'Evangelical Unity: An Appeal,' 175, 184
    FIRST JOHN *Love of God*, 51, 53
    God's Way Not Ours, 74, 243
    Great Doctrines of the Bible, 140, 144

MacPherson, J., *Life of Duncan Matheson*, 52

Macleod, Donald A., *C. Stacey Woods and the Evangelical Rediscovery of the University*, 19

Merle d'Aubigné, J. H., *Germany, England and Scotland*, 16

Miller, C. John, *Outgrowing the Ingrown Church*, 49

Morrison, G. H., *Flood-Tide*, 66

Murray, Iain H.,

'Evangelical Reaction to the Ecumenical Movement', 166

Forgotten Spurgeon, 116

Jonathan Edwards: A New Biography, 157-158

ML-J: First Forty Years, 16-17

ML-J: Fight of Faith, 14, 21, 61, 64, 134, 171-172, 200

A Scottish Christian Heritage, 63

Nevins, Wm., *Select Remains*, 153

Noble, T. A., *Tyndale House and Fellowship*, 194, 197

Noll, M. A. (with Carolyn Nystrom), *Is the Reformation Over?* 186, 257-267

Owen, John, *Works*, 47, 142, 176, 261, 265

Packer, J. I.,

(with R. R.Beckwith & G. E. Duffield), *Across the Divide*, 185-186

'A Kind of Puritan', 168

Evangelical Anglican Identity Problem, 187-188

(With C. O. Buchanan, E.L.Mascall, and G. D. Leonard) *Growing into Union*, 184-187, 205-206

Palmer, B. M., *Threefold Fellowship and Assurance*, 152

Payne, D. J., *Theology of Christian Life in J. I. Packer's Thought*, 187

Phelps, A., *The Theory of Preaching*, 42

Porter, Ebenezer, *Lectures on Homiletics*, 50

Ryle, J. C., *Holiness*, 152

Upper Room, 93

Schaff, P., ed., *Creeds of the Greek and Latin Churches*, 265

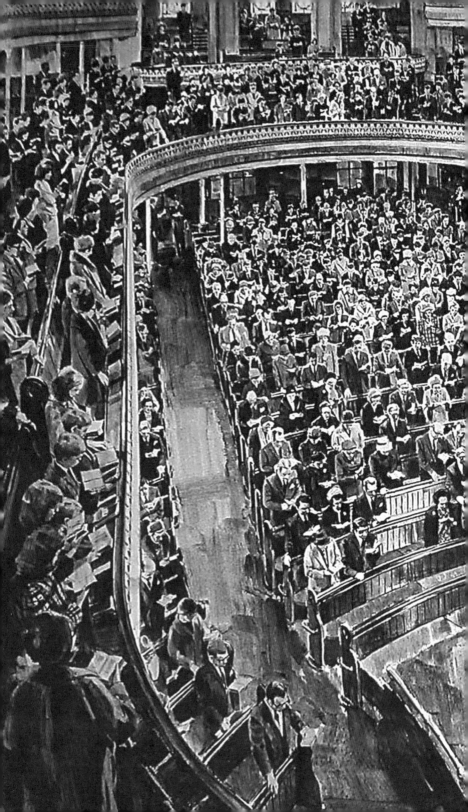